HOW TO
GET A JOB
IN THE
MUSIC
INDUSTRY

by Keith Hatschek
with Breanne Beseda

3rd Edition Includes
New Career Tool Kit &
Social Media Strategy

Berklee Press

Editor in Chief: Jonathan Feist
Vice President of Online Learning and Continuing Education: Debbie Cavalier
Assistant Vice President of Operations for Berklee Media: Robert F. Green
Assistant Vice President of Marketing and Recruitment for Berklee Media: Mike King
Dean of Continuing Education: Carin Nuernberg
Editorial Assistants: Matthew Dunkle, Reilly Garrett, Emily Jones, Zoë Lustri
Cover Design: Robert Heath

ISBN: 978-0-87639-153-2

1140 Boylston Street
Boston, MA 02215-3693 USA
(617) 747-2146
Visit Berklee Press Online at
www.berkleepress.com

Study with
■ **BERKLEE ONLINE**

online.berklee.edu

DISTRIBUTED BY

HAL•LEONARD®
CORPORATION
7777 W. BLUEMOUND RD. P.O. BOX 13819
MILWAUKEE, WISCONSIN 53213
Visit Hal Leonard Online at
www.halleonard.com

Berklee Press, a publishing activity of Berklee College of Music, is a not-for-profit educational publisher.
Available proceeds from the sales of our products are contributed to the scholarship funds of the college.

Contents

Foreword

**By Tony Brown,
Record Producer**

*Record producer Tony Brown has left an indelible mark on
the modern country sound that is known around the world as
one of America's signature cultural treasures. He is a respected
musician, producer, former record label president, and mentor to
countless emerging artists. In this foreword, he shares his career
path, and gives some insights into why and how many of the
people he has mentored over the years have found success in the
music industry.*

When I started playing piano professionally, many years ago
with the Stamps Quartet, if a person had come up to me after a
performance and predicted that I'd be the president of a record
company one day, I would have replied, "Not in a million years!"

At the age of thirteen, I got my first glimpse of the life I wanted
when gospel groups like the Statesmen Quartet and the
Blackwood Brothers mesmerized me. The performers wore flashy
clothes and drew huge audiences that they left cheering for more
at the end of the night. To me, they were just like movie stars. It
was then that I decided that I wanted a career in entertainment.

I started to play piano with a number of local gospel groups and
began meeting the people who have helped me build my career.
Meeting J.D. Sumner of the Blackwood Brothers forged one of
the first links in my "chain" of the people and the relationships
that have opened doors for me. J.D. introduced me to a number of
important people and eventually helped me land a gig as a piano
player for Elvis Presley in 1974.

As I worked with Elvis, that relationship led me from playing
gospel music to country music. When Elvis died three years later,
his previous piano player was leaving Emmylou Harris's band
and recommended me as his replacement. Soon my chain grew to
include Emmylou, Ricky Skaggs, Vince Gill, Rodney Crowell, and
Rosanne Cash, each of whom influenced my career tremendously.
Constantly striving to meet and work with people more talented
than me helped me learn and grow. I believe that I learned
so much because my eyes and ears were wide open, and I was
soaking up every bit of knowledge I could.

However, today, I've noticed that many young people aspiring to a career in the music business tend to remain in small circles of friends, and as a result, their world becomes very limited. From my point of view, the only way to succeed and enjoy this business is to enjoy all of it. You've got to constantly work to expand your universe.

Another important attribute to develop is self-assurance: learn to trust your vision and instincts. When Jimmy Bowen invited me to join him at MCA in 1984, he asked me if I had a vision that I wanted to achieve. I told him that, yes, I wanted to bring the amazing talent of instrumentalists like Mark O'Connor, Edgar Meyer, and John Jarvis to the public. These were session players I hung out with and played with every day, but they were completely unknown outside of Nashville.

I put a proposal together, and soon, MCA's Master Series was born. The Master Series allowed me the opportunity to collaborate with a tremendous range of jazz, classical, and pop artists with whom I might have never worked. And it proved so successful that eventually MCA merged it with a larger jazz label, GRP. The impact of the Master Series on the artists involved has been long lasting. I was thrilled when Edgar Meyer performed for an audience of millions with cellist Yo-Yo Ma on the 2000 GRAMMY® telecast.

To bring the Master Series from a dream to a reality, I had to trust myself to know the difference between something that's really good versus something that's mediocre. There were times when I felt that I was in way over my head, but I realized I just had to keep my ears open and keep asking questions.

As I've made transitions from musician to producer to record company executive, a number of other skills have helped me to succeed. Being aware of what's happening around you, always remembering to follow up, developing the skill to really listen to people, and working to keep up with the trends and technologies shaping the music business are all critical skills that have to be practiced constantly.

You should take advantage of the people around you who can teach and help you expand your world. Keep your vision focused on what you want to do and make the most of every opportunity. Take the information in this book and combine it with your own creative abilities, and you've got the makings for a great career in the music business.

Tony Brown
Nashville, Tennessee

TONY BROWN'S CAREER PATH

Throughout his career, Tony Brown has worked with an incredible range of performers, including Emmylou Harris, Vince Gill, Jimmy Buffet, Elvis Presley, Wynonna Judd, Lyle Lovett, George Strait, Alabama, Brooks and Dunn, Shirley Caesar, Rosanne Cash, Rodney Crowell, the Mavericks, Reba McEntire, and Trisha Yearwood. He joined MCA Records in 1984, and guided the company to its position as the number one label in Nashville in the 1990s. In 2002, eager for a new challenge, he founded Universal South in partnership with former Arista Nashville head, Tim DuBois. In 2007, Tony decided to leave the executive boardroom and return to his first love, stating, "I realized what I really wanted to do most was produce, and I really didn't want to be a label executive anymore, but just a producer and get in there and make some smash records." Back in the studio, six projects he produced for artists including Reba McEntire, George Strait, and Brooks and Dunn all debuted at number one on the Billboard charts.

Tony Brown has been awarded *Billboard* magazine's coveted Top Country Producer honor seven times, while album projects he has produced have exceeded one hundred million units in sales. His track record with singles is equally impressive, garnering more than a hundred number one singles. Add to that more than a dozen GRAMMY®, CMA, ACM, and American Music Awards his records have won. Through it all, he has retained his reverence for great performers, a wonder for the "magic" in melody, and the simple joy of making music.

Acknowledgments

FROM KEITH HATSCHEK

The impetus to share my ideas on what it takes to launch and manage a successful career in the music industry came more than twenty years ago. When I was working as a manager at the Music Annex, I found myself fielding a regular stream of calls from colleagues and acquaintances asking me to speak with a relative or friend who "wanted to get into the business." A few years later, my friend, entertainment attorney Marc Greenberg, and I were talking about what things we would still like to accomplish in our careers, and I mentioned teaching. Shortly thereafter, he introduced me to Mary Pieratt, the program director of the San Francisco State University Music and Recording Industry program, where I enjoyed lecturing for seven years. My colleagues, Josh Hecht and John Altmann, who teach recording arts, generously answered my numerous questions as I learned to become an effective teacher at SFSU. When I decided to make teaching my first priority in 2001, moving to University of the Pacific, I undertook a substantial challenge: to help students build the necessary portfolio of skills and knowledge to succeed in the music industry. Thirteen years later, I still enjoy getting up for work each day and interacting with tomorrow's industry leaders. My students stimulate and challenge me by asking difficult questions. They continually surprise me with their resourcefulness. At Pacific, I've been surrounded by supportive colleagues including Giulio Ongaro, Maria Pallavicini, David Chase, Robyn Cheshire, Holly Stanco, Steve Anderson, Bill Hipp, David Chase, Dave Duggan, Carolyn Eads, Bob Coburn, Ray Sylvester, Mark Plovnick, Brigid Welch, Margaret Roberts, Elizabeth Griego, Lewis Gale, Tom Brierton, Jeff Crawford, Simon Rowe, Veronica A. Wells, Rhonelle Runner, John Carvana, Glenn Pillsbury, Joanna Royce-Davis, Deb Crane, Chris Haruta, and many other faculty and staff. I would also like to extend my appreciation to colleague, Phil Schroeder, for putting my name forth to take on the program director role at Pacific and for his belief in my ability to transition successfully and make the leap from business to academia.

Since the day in 1965 when my first guitar—a red Orpheus with a chrome pick guard, three pickups, and a whammy bar—captivated me, I've had the good fortune to travel an always-evolving road in the music industry. My journey has been one of enlightenment and friendship shared with so many colleagues that it would be impossible to name each one. But I wish to especially thank David Porter for believing in me early in my career and for teaching me a great deal about what it takes to succeed in any business; Bruce Merley for sharing his balanced outlook on life and business when it has been most needed, and for offering constructive criticism to an early draft of the first edition of this book; Carson Taylor, John Palladino, and Jim Treulich for instilling in me the need to aim high; and Roger Wiersema for helping provide "training wheels" and friendship to a journeyman engineer.

I am indebted to Richard A. Payne and his excellent volume, *How to Get a Better Job Quicker* [Taplinger, 1987]. Mr. Payne's book has provided me with an excellent guide in my own career development. The volume has aged surprisingly well and provides any job seeker with a very complete and highly detailed presentation on successful résumé development, salary negotiations, interviewing, and many other aspects of career development. It represents an excellent investment for any job seeker, regardless of their field of interest, and complements nicely what is presented here.

As my career grew, I was fortunate enough to become acquainted with a number of recording studio sages through the Society of Professional Audio Recording Services (SPARS): Murray Allen, Tom Kobayashi, Chris Stone, Nick Colleran, Guy Costa, and Shirley Kaye. Thank you for sharing so many of your insights regarding business in general and the music industry in particular. This same crew also taught me that when one has friends in the industry, access to a wealth of knowledge and experience capable of solving almost any problem is only a phone call away.

When I shifted gears and launched my music-technology marketing agency in 1995, I was fortunate to tap the wisdom and wit of outstanding mentors Peter Weiglin, Marc Greenberg, and Al Rose. I hope I retain a fraction of the knowledge you have shared with me over our years of friendship.

My fellow educators and friends affiliated with the NAMM Workforce Development Team have been a tremendous resource, assisting me in refining my teaching and curriculum. Likewise, the Music and Entertainment Industry Educators Association (MEIEA) has provided me with access to a diverse group of thinkers and educators with whom I share the common goal of furthering our students' readiness for a successful career in the industry. Both groups of motivated and resourceful educators have inspired me to keep adapting my teaching methods to ensure that today's graduates have every opportunity to be successful. Special thanks to Becky Chappell, Rey Sanchez, Don Gorder, Dave Kopplin, Serona Elton, Cutler Armstrong, Bob Garfrerick, Chris Haseleu, and all of the MEIEA faculty.

Hats off to my publishing team at Berklee Press, headed by editor in chief Jonathan Feist, for this third edition. Jonathan has acted as a faithful and objective sounding board for new ideas, various revisions, and helping us to see ways to continue to improve the usefulness of this book through the second and third editions. His early advice on the book's format and belief in the workshops and other key elements improved this end result. When I first brought the book to Berklee Press, thanks to then-publisher David Kusek who green-lighted it. Thanks to Kristen Schilo and Sue Gedutis-Lindsay for outstanding editing that shaped the words that worked so well in a lecture hall into a cohesive manuscript that formed the first edition. Special thanks to Berklee's Debbie Cavalier for her enthusiasm for this book from the very beginning; you are an inspiration to all of us in the music industry. Debbie's energy, insights, and candor are a wonderful aid to any author or instructor fortunate enough to collaborate with her. Research assistant Jenna Stehney contributed greatly to the second edition, and Patty Ratsamy faithfully transcribed our "Nine under Thirty-Five" interviews, which are new in this edition. Brandon Dill reviewed, updated, and compiled resource lists found in the back materials, and my friend, Steve Sherman from Red Deer College in Alberta, generously helped me to assemble the new list of Canadian music trade associations. Staff at NAMM graciously provided images for the book, and my friend Myrna Vick assisted with some of the graphics.

To the nine very busy professionals who graciously agreed to be interviewed for this book and shared so much of their experience, I salute you. I don't know of a better way to learn practical career advice than to be speaking with and listening to those who have gone before us.

Finally, without the patience, encouragement, and support of my wife Laura, this book would still be just an idea simmering on the back burner of my brain.

FROM BREANNE BESEDA

It was an incredible honor to be asked by Keith to work with him in co-authoring this new edition of his book. I cannot thank him enough for sharing this opportunity with me, for trusting me with such an important part of his work, and for every opportunity he shares with me to impact the future of the music industry through our students. Keith is honestly one of the most kind and generous people I've ever known, and throughout our many years of working together, he has been an amazing mentor and a true friend. He has earned the respect and love of his students, colleagues, and industry partners alike, and I will forever be counted among his biggest fans.

Much of the success I've had in career management is because of Margaret Roberts. She took a chance on me, supported me, and taught me how to be an effective career coach. In the process, she helped me to develop and realize my own career success. She is always willing to share her expertise and energy, and she continually teaches me by example how to be a better professional (and working mom). I consider it a privilege to call her my colleague, partner, and friend.

Throughout my career at Pacific, I've been extremely fortunate to work alongside a family of colleagues and friends who constantly support, challenge, and entertain me. I wish to thank Ray Sylvester, Chris Lozano, Debbi Bell, Lynette Zenor, Myrna Vick, Mary Nevis, Deb Crane, Ron Hoverstad, Cynthia Eakin, Lewis Gale, Giulio Ongaro, and many other staff and faculty for their encouragement, wisdom, humor, and help. I also wish to thank the many students and alumni I've had the pleasure of working with and learning from; they are a constant source of inspiration and motivation.

Thanks to my family—my mom, sisters, brothers-in-law, and the entire Beseda family—for their love, guidance, and support. Thanks especially to my husband Aaron and son Lucas who give me perspective, purpose, pride, and joy beyond measure.

Keith Hatschek and Breanne Beseda
University of the Pacific
Stockton, California
Fall, 2014

Introduction

Two revolutionary events that occurred near the end of the twentieth century irrevocably changed the music industry. One was the 1993 invention of the MP3 algorithm at the Fraunhofer Institute in Germany, which allowed digital audio files to be reduced in size by ninety percent, while still retaining enough of their original character to be recognizable to music consumers. The second was the development of a music-centric peer-to-peer file-sharing network dubbed "Napster" in the dorm room of a nineteen-year-old college student at Boston's Northeastern University. Shawn Fanning's stroke of genius allowed music fans anywhere to share access to their growing digital music libraries, without the need of any money changing hands.

What do these events have to do with this book? In combination, the MP3 and file sharing, coupled with the availability of affordable personal computers and Internet access, created a sea change in how music is discovered, consumed, and promoted. You need only look as far as your favorite artist's promotional methods to see that the primacy of the connection between the artist and his or her audience is what really counts today.

When Keith wrote the first edition of this book in 1998, the previous version of the music industry was still healthy. In fact, the peak years for sales of recorded music immediately followed, 1999 to 2001, which were that market sector's most profitable years. So, the first edition addressed a music industry (of which the record business was the largest engine) that was still structured a lot like the industry had been since the mid twentieth century, with a range of companies that were integrally connected forming the web of products and services to allow artists to build careers. Record labels, concert promoters, ticketing juggernauts, radio syndicates, and music video channels—let's call those companies "middlemen," as they served to identify, groom, and present artists and their music to the world. The middlemen took a share of the earnings. While the twentieth century model of artists, middlemen, and fans still exists today, what might be called the new music industry— one where the role of middlemen is less critical—has emerged. Instead of a record label, an artist may choose to bring her music directly to fans through self-booked live performances, a self-released album, and a self-generated YouTube channel.

(Google "Amanda Palmer" to see an artist succeeding with this model.) If she builds a large enough audience, she has the start of a career, and in time, with adequate growth, may hire a team to help her manage her growing business. That model did not exist fifteen years ago. An artist either was signed to a label and management, or was stuck playing local clubs and coffee houses waiting to get a break.

What this means for getting a job in the music industry is that more of today's jobs have some element of entrepreneurship or DIY (do it yourself) requirement to them. While there are still a number of jobs that are strictly task-driven, more and more firms are seeking what have been termed "self-actualized" workers—people that can take initiative to move a company along a recognized path toward its goals. Today, companies and individuals are increasingly required to "think like a startup" in managing their time and resources, with a greater focus on understanding and aligning the company's efforts with those of the audience that is the target for its product or service, music or otherwise.

In today's music industry, relevant experience is the new measure of one's value. More and more, employers are asking the question, "What can you do for me or my firm on your first day in the office?" This means that part of preparing for your career in the music industry is going to be to seek out and secure internships or apprenticeships, and to also develop your own projects or collaborations that will demonstrate to your future boss the type of impact you are likely to make if they consider hiring you. Understanding the value of initiative and completing tasks you set out to do, employers are using your previous experience and accomplishments to estimate the likelihood of your continuing to complete such tasks as a member of their firm. In short, getting a job in the music industry today means doing relevant work *before* you get your first job. It's not a Catch-22, though, since everyone has access to the tools and opportunities to achieve any number of goals and objectives working right in your hometown and with free tools available online. More on that later in the book.

FIRST STEPS TO BUILD YOUR CAREER

You are likely reading this book to find out what kinds of jobs exist in the music industry. Or you've already made a decision and know that working in one of the fields relating to "the business" is for you. But where do you start to prepare for your career planning and job search?

When discussing music industry careers, students often ask two questions: "Are there jobs in the music industry?" and "How do I go about locating and landing those jobs?" This book will answer those questions and also provide you with an introduction to the career development tools, workshop exercises, and job search strategies that will increase your chances of landing a job in this highly competitive field. You'll also be advised to start to maintain an electronic "career portfolio" to document your learning as you work through this book and afterwards continue to develop your professional career package. Having this career portfolio available online via a free digital storage locker (Dropbox, Google Drive, etc.) is the best way to ensure access from anywhere, anytime.

What kinds of opportunities are out there? What kind of research skills will you need to uncover those opportunities? How important are computer and tech skills in the entertainment world today? And how do you get plugged into specific job opportunities and develop a network where you can find out about job leads as they come up?

In the following chapters, we'll take an in-depth look at the music industry, referring to various market segments to illustrate examples. It's absolutely essential that at the outset of this book, you understand that today's music industry is really a web of interconnected market segments that have mutually beneficial ties. For instance, Internet streaming firms such as Pandora, Beats Music, and Spotify rely on record labels to provide master recordings, music publishers to license the songs, entertainment attorneys to help broker the deals, computer networking and storage firms to help manage their data, and music journalists to help tell their business stories. So, when you listen to a stream of your favorite band, at least six different market sectors collaborated to give you that opportunity. No matter what market segments draw your current interest, certain rules and regulations apply, career-wise, and most apply to other career paths, be they at record labels, management companies, music publishers, Internet music startups, booking agencies, tour companies, or many others. Understanding and becoming a student of this inter-connectedness is a major step toward seeing the varied paths that may be available to lead you to your ultimate music industry career goal.

Workshops throughout the book will help you assemble and organize information related to your current job search and your ongoing career development.

In the chapters and workshops, you'll find out how to do a personal skills inventory and develop a marketable skill set. When you send in a résumé or go for an interview, it's only by identifying what makes you special or valuable to an employer that you will be able to communicate a clear message that positions you to win that job. This process is called "differentiation," and it is essential in the highly competitive music industry.

This book will help teach you to differentiate yourself in the job market so that once you have attained a modest amount of relevant skills or experience, a person hiring will see that you are someone that has something special to offer.

You will learn about internships and come to see the key elements that it takes to conduct a thorough and effective job search. Some of you may be actively looking for a job now. Others may be just beginning to think about what kind of career opportunities exist. Others may be considering a career change or even a so-called "third act" shift to the music business later in life. In each instance, you will have a much better perspective on how to succeed after you read and work through the text, interviews, and workshops in this book.

Discover what kind of tools you need for your job search. If you have access to a telephone and the Internet, you already have access to two of the most important ones. We're going to talk about goal setting for career development. Your goal is to get a job, but that sometimes seems like a distant objective, so you will learn how to break that down into smaller tasks, to make the first milestones on your journey towards finding and securing your dream job attainable. Small steps will lead to your eventual goal, which is landing a great job that you love.

Then we'll tackle the oft-dreaded résumé. This is the task that creates the most hangdog looks from students and career seekers. There's no getting around this key fact: even in the digital age, you must have a strong résumé. We keep our résumés current today and continue to update them to include new accomplishments and skills. The résumé is a critical tool you will need throughout your career, whatever field you're in.

You probably are wondering: how do you get your résumé into the preferred pile of contenders and not the rejection pile? You will learn how to build a résumé that clearly communicates your special skills and worth to future employers, thereby separating yourself from other job seekers.

In addition to a well-crafted résumé, you will need to do some research on the jobs that interest you. How do you get started on your job search? What are the most effective ways to research not only jobs but also potential employers? Have you also established some short-term goals, and are your long-term goals in mind? Publishing and referring to your personal and professional goals is essential to making informed decisions as your career unfolds.

Soon, you will be ready to go out and start working. How do you get there? What's the first step? Do you pick up a phone? Can you find your dream job by surfing the Internet? How can you take best advantage of social media to further your career and maintain a professional image? Do you purchase a subscription to *Billboard* magazine? This book provides a step-by-step approach to succeeding in your job search, and it will increase the odds dramatically of landing the position of your dreams in the music industry. It won't be easy, but by diligently applying the methods we recommend, you will build up career development skills that will be worth their weight in gold throughout your working life.

We will look at many types of careers. A host of opportunities exist in a number of rapidly expanding fields, such as mobile audio, the computer gaming industry, Internet and satellite radio, music blogging, the wide range of new television alternatives (Hulu, YouTube, Netflix, etc.), the music products industry, music licensing, and other affiliated fields where the use of music is becoming increasingly important. Many of these jobs pay significantly higher salaries than an entry-level position in a sound recording studio or at a record label.

To help make the theory "real," we've consulted with a wide variety of working professionals to help ensure that this edition is up to date and relevant to today's music industry. One of the biggest additions to this edition resulted from feedback from readers. It's called "Nine Under Thirty-Five," and features career-oriented interviews and tips from nine young working professionals that have established themselves in various music industry market sectors. They are:

- Blythe Nelson, Artist Manager Assistant, Guerrilla Management

- Candice Choi, Director, Musicians in the Making

- Samantha Juneman, Community Manager, Socialtyze

- David Creel, Agent Assistant, William Morris Endeavor

- Lauren Kasper, Director of Label Business Development, Beats Music

- Dan Radin, Director of Audio Products, SteelSeries, Inc.

- Elisa Asato, Assistant to the President, Rostrum Records

- Ken Shackleford, Senior Manager, Retail Services, INgrooves

- Emma Peterson, CEO and Founder, Tikly

If you can't wait to learn about their career stories, you can jump ahead to part V now, and then come back to start part I after learning about each of our young professionals' career journeys. Read on, and prepare yourself for a career in one of the most exciting industries.

PART I

The Music Business:
An Industry and Career Overview

1

Music Industry Careers: What You Need to Know Before You Pursue One

People looking to get into the music industry share a common buzzword: passion. They talk about their love of music and how much it means to them. However, no matter how great your passion for music, an accurate understanding of the job realities is necessary before you plunge into developing a career in this field. A key part of this process is getting to know yourself and understanding what your strengths and weaknesses may be as a prospective professional preparing to enter this competitive industry. This book includes a number of reflective workshops to help you gain better self-awareness. As you progress through the chapters and workshops, you'll also develop a more complete view of the music industry market sectors that interest you. By studying the people, the companies, the technologies, and the successes and failures in, for instance, the evolving world of online music distribution (or the specific sectors that most interest you), you will become conversant in the names, faces, and trends that are shaping that part of the music industry. This fluency in a select number of music industry market sectors that interest you is another essential marker that will define you as a serious student of the industry.

After applying yourself and the necessary time it takes, you will have adequate self-knowledge and industry knowledge to begin to map out your own career plan. It will address how you will take your growing body of skills, industry knowledge, and passion and move your career forward. Your plan may include formal education, college or vocational study, internship or apprentice experiences, and attending events, concerts, and conferences, plus meeting and speaking in depth with industry professionals. As you gain knowledge and confidence in what you can do, this will lead you to eventually seek a position in a specific industry area. The process is an interactive one, meaning that as you expand your skills and knowledge, you are likely to fine-tune your career goals and direction. And as you develop your strengths and capabilities, you will soon be able to compare your skills inventory with the job openings in your areas of interest to determine how well you fit a particular position. Each of these steps build on your knowledge and is covered in the upcoming chapters and workshops in this book. By following the path we prescribe, you'll soon have the makings of a career plan with goals that are measurable. You'll also be armed with advice and wisdom from a variety of industry professionals, as well as the key career development information you need to help you manage your career successfully no matter where your path may go. A simplified map of this process can be seen in figure 1.1.

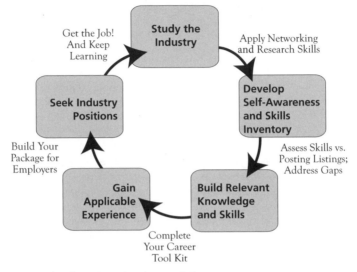

FIG. 1.1. Music Industry Career Development Path

Such processes, often referred to as "virtuous cycles," can then continue as your career grows and you become increasingly successful. Over time, you will come to expand on the skills and knowledge to achieve more significant results from your work in the industry. In essence, the ongoing career engagement and development process (which you will learn by following the guidelines in this book) will form the underpinnings for a lifelong career in the music industry.

As mentioned in the introduction, prospective employers expect you to be able to explain what you have already accomplished that is directly transferable to their company's needs in the music industry. So throughout this book, an emphasis is placed on helping you develop such experience and also how to create a compelling narrative about your experiences that will be attractive to music industry players.

For the vast majority of music industry employers, evidence of your accomplishments is the primary means used to differentiate one qualified job candidate from others competing for the same position. If you have relevant experience for a particular position and another candidate does not, you will likely be the favored candidate. As the pace of change in the music industry has accelerated in recent years, the relevant experience factor has grown in significance, so don't overlook this important aspect of your own career preparation. Remember, too, that experience in a variety of other settings, from that pre-college job selling cappuccinos or working retail, to heading up your club or philanthropy's fundraising campaign, are all excellent ways to develop transferable skills that can nicely support your case as a qualified candidate for the music industry position you are seeking.

The music industry attracts a wide variety of interested career seekers that each has their own goals in mind when they set out on their journey to find a spot in what is one of the most dynamic and exciting career areas. While there are no clearly defined limits on one's age, background, or training to seek a career in music, our years of teaching and coaching music industry hopefuls leads us to identify three broad groupings of aspiring industry players.

- **Fresh Faces.** This group is made up of high school-to college-aged individuals seeking a place in the industry as their first real professional experience. They may choose a path that leads to formal training or simply take the do-it-yourself (DIY) approach that is now feasible in the Information Age. They often make up in enthusiasm what they lack in experience, but they are very computer and tech savvy and quick learners. Many will decide to start their own firm and become successful doing so. They have a lot to offer, and in our experience, are able learners.

- **Career Changers.** Older and more experienced than the Fresh Faces, Career Changers have generally spent a substantial amount of time working in a non-music job. At some point, the siren song of working in a field that they love dearly outweighs the steady paycheck, and they decide to take the plunge and work to change their career path. Fortunately, that life and workplace experience can be a valuable asset in the music industry, especially if skills and achievements can be shown to be directly transferable. Examples of such skills include marketing, customer service, computer programming, social media strategies, finance, logistics, operations, and many others. Note that some Career Changers may already be working in the music business but have decided it's time to move up and to do so likely have to find a new employer. They might more aptly be defined as Job Changers.

- **Golden Years.** A rising group of retirees with both free time and financial independence are looking for pursuits to engage them in retirement. Music and the arts provide an excellent avenue for self-expression, creativity, and for some, a part-time business opportunity. We believe that as the baby-boom generation transitions into retirement, a significant number will reconnect with the positive memories they have of earlier experience in music or the arts and establish or join or found local, regional, or national music-related organizations, non profits, or other arts endeavors. They also have very advanced interpersonal and problem-solving skills that can benefit their own later in life music endeavors. For this group, financial well-being is not the primary motivator. They want to connect with the beauty and power found in participating in the arts. However, they still have the capability of contributing to a vital and important role in their region as an actor in the music industry. As such, they should be welcomed heartily as one more ingredient in our evolving arts milieu.

Throughout the book, a number of workshops will help you to define various aspects of the career development process. These workshops and occasional Action Items will help turn the theoretical into the practical and give you points of traction to use what you have learned about music industry careers and yourself to help move you further along toward achieving your career goals.

Workshop 2 will explain how to build your electronic Career Portfolio, and you can simply move the Workshop 1 results into your Portfolio at that time.

🔲 **WORKSHOP 1.** ESTABLISHING OVER-ARCHING CAREER GOALS

Think about the reasons why a music industry career appeals so strongly to you, and then answer these questions.

1. _____ is my number one long-term career goal.

2. _____ is more important than money.

3. Achieving success in my lifetime means _____.

4. Reflect on your personal motivation for pursuing your intended music industry career path. Describe your ultimate career goals, referring to the following aspects (and ranking the relative importance of each when compared to the rest) in your idealized career vision:

- wealth
- job satisfaction
- opportunity for growth and development
- alignment of personal values with those of the organization
- work/life balance

In your personal reflection, be sure to comment on each of these attributes individually and relative to each other.

FINAL THOUGHTS

It is important to understand that while there are many tremendously successful and wealthy people that work in the music and entertainment industry, overall, they make up just a small percentage of the total industry's workforce. Many more earn a middle-class income with job security and satisfaction. It is great to aim for the stars, but important to be grounded in the reality of this fact. Review what you wrote, add it to your Career Portfolio, and refer back to it as you reach decision points throughout your music industry career.

2 Today's Job Market: The Big Picture

JOB SUPPLY AND DEMAND

Like all industries, the music industry adheres to the law of job supply and demand—a basic rule of all economic systems. When it comes to jobs and opportunities, the supply of industry jobs falls well below the demand of those wishing to enter the industry. This makes every job precious—even those internships that don't pay one cent. It also means that in order to better your chances for success, you have to take advantage of every single ethical opportunity to better your skills and status in the industry.

One of the music industry managers we spoke with reports that she receives an average of four to five unsolicited résumés a week. Some of those job seekers follow up with a phone call and express their willingness to work for free, often as an intern or assistant. This is a time-honored tradition in the music and entertainment field, a form of "paying one's dues" to build knowledge and gain connections to working professionals that can help advance a fledgling career.

When there are more people willing to work for no pay, it makes it harder to get paid. That's the first reality you'll discover about entry-level positions in the industry. There are very many people doing some portion of entry-level jobs as interns or unpaid assistants.

The second reality is that when it comes to succeeding as a performing and/or recording artist, what now constitutes "success" is vastly different than what it was fifteen years ago. Today, fewer and fewer artists reach the threshold of platinum album sales—that is, selling one million albums. Artists have been signing so-called "360 deals," which allow record labels to share in all the artist's various revenue streams: records, concerts, publishing, merchandise (aka "merch"), and more. Album sales have declined more than 50 percent since the rise of file sharing. While it's not time to write the obituary of the record business, new, artist-centric labels are challenging the monopoly held by the major labels for nearly one hundred years. More importantly, artists and savvy music managers are no longer looking to large industry behemoths, such as major labels or large management firms, to shape their careers. Artists and managers realize that maintaining control and ownership of their careers and music can allow for a very profitable, yet smaller scale business model. It is just these types of artists and managers that are seeking the next generation of DIY-capable team members.

In the first edition of this book, we cited that the vast majority of recordings failed to break even for their record label. Depending on what the overall budget was to make and promote a new album, back in the day, an artist needed to sell 250,000 to 400,000 copies of their album to pay off the investment made in getting the album out to the public. While superstar acts such as Beyoncé, Radiohead, Taylor Swift, or Enrique Iglesias may still sell hundreds of thousands of albums, today's industry is realigning to a much more modest model of what "success" means. Younger artists, well schooled in the realities of earlier contracts that made profitability a long shot, are not rushing to sign record deals. Furthermore, the album is no longer seen as the be-all, end-all of the artist's career. It's just one more way to present the artist to their fans and for emerging artists—maybe even a "freemium" item, made available for free to fans in exchange for an email address or signing up for a newsletter. From the perspective of a job seeker, this new music industry offers a nearly limitless range of possibilities, especially for those that are prepared to develop and demonstrate your own flexibility, ingenuity, and creativity.

By applying the techniques found in this book, you will greatly enhance your opportunities to be part of this new music industry. That's why we encourage you to look at careers not only as a recording artist or record producer, but at the cornucopia of other jobs in the music industry. Don't lock yourself into one career trajectory too early in the game. The very same skills and passion you've developed for your music can be a tremendous asset in the business side of the industry.

SKILLS NOT JOBS

The new music industry is changing fast. In fact, one of the only constants that can be counted on is that the rate of change is likely to keep up for the foreseeable future. To succeed in such a rapidly evolving environment, one must look at the types of skills that are valued in what is largely transforming itself into a stream of the Information Economy alongside video gaming, film and television, etc. Job-hunting is still a part of your activities, but before you start researching openings, it's essential to understand that today's music industry employers are seeking candidates with a range of skills that allow their employees to continually adapt to the changing industry. In 2013, we took a survey of music industry employers and asked them what skills, knowledge, and attributes were most critical when they were evaluating potential new hires for their companies. We've broken the highest ranking results from that survey down into four broad areas that will allow you to see what will help you be well prepared for a long and successful music industry career.

1. Communication, Interpersonal, and Problem Solving Skills

- Written, oral, and presentation skills at a "professional" level (networking skills)
- Persuasion skills (aka sales)
- Problem-solving and conflict-resolution skills
- Listening, following instructions, and effective at collaboration

2. Computer and Media Skills

- Basic Web creation and editing skills
- Proficient with MS Office Suite programs
- Basic media (audio and video) capture, editing, and distribution (e.g., YouTube, SoundCloud, ReverbNation, etc.)
- Content creation and manipulation (Adobe Creative Suite or comparable programs)

3. Professionalism and Integrity

- Respect for self, coworkers, firm, customers, and marketplace
- Self-awareness and sense of purpose in professional endeavors
- Ability to manage self-image (aka personal "brand") and make decisions based on personal integrity and one's core values
- Critical thinking and follow-through

4. Industry-Related Knowledge and Practice

- Structure of music industry and varied relationships in it
- Social media theory and practice
- Entrepreneurial theory and practice
- Marketing for business

Notice that there is no mention of specific skills relating to a particular job. These four broad areas help form the basis of what will make up the underpinnings for your industry-specific career path. The first two areas, communication and computer skills, will generally be evolving over time across your career. The third area, integrity and professionalism, is one that is largely learned by observing those around us. In this regard, lessons learned throughout our lives help to inform what our own code of professional conduct will be. To address this area, one needs to be thoughtful and reflective not only as to your own actions, but also as to the consequences of those actions over time as your career unfolds. The music industry deals with many creative and passionate individuals, and those in it seek out like-minded professionals who share a sense of purpose and values. By identifying and adhering to your own sense of what's right, you will go a long way toward joining the ranks of trusted and steadily employed music industry pros.

PLAYING FOR A TEAM

Talent, perseverance, and people skills are givens to making it in the business. A colleague who worked as a tech manager at George Lucas's renowned Skywalker Sound once said, "Fifty-one percent of my job is getting along with my coworkers, and forty-nine percent of my job is knowing how to keep all of our technology running." Her statement has stuck over the years as one of the most important pieces of information music industry career seekers must understand.

To be successful in a majority of the jobs in the music industry, you've got to be able to work effectively in a group environment. If you feel compelled to work alone, be your own boss, compose on your own, perform on your own, then it will be important to identify roles and functions that can be done in solitude. But for most industry career paths, being an effective team player is essential. Why? Because you've got to be able to get along with people around you. Don't panic now if "people skills" don't appear to be among your strongest talents; you can strengthen them over time, if you focus on that goal. Basically, developing good collaborative skills involves becoming very adept at listening and learning how to think, and acting in the best interests of your working group. Along the way, you will also most likely develop a sense of empathy for your colleagues and the overall mission of the organization.

> *"Fifty-one percent of my job is getting along with my coworkers, and forty-nine percent of my job is knowing how to keep all of our technology running."*

CLIMBING TO THE TOP

Perseverance is obviously a big asset. Depending on the opportunity, there may be from 25 to 2,500 or more people knocking on the door for a single industry job opening. You've got to be willing to persevere. Otherwise, you're going to run out of gas in your quest. A good analogy is to look at your career as a long-distance event such as a twenty-six-mile marathon or a 10K open-water swimming contest. Succeeding at such competitions requires training, mental toughness, and understanding what the critical factors are for any given event. The same applies to your pursuit of a music industry career. Imagine your career as you hope it will unfold, but be realistic about the time, training, skills, experiences, and connections you will need to complete in order to be successful over the long haul.

Just about everybody starts out at the bottom, in this business, even today's top dogs. I encourage you to read one of the books penned by a top record label executive, such as *Follow the Music* by Jac Holzman, the founder of Elektra Records. Another is Ian Copeland's entertaining bio, *Wild Thing*. (All books referenced can be found in "Resources" at the back of this book.) Seeing that just about every top executive started out as a mail clerk, gofer, or assistant will help you strengthen your resolve to climb the mountain ahead with respect to your music industry career.

The benefit of starting out at the bottom of the company's organizational chart is that you meet a lot of people on the way up, you see how a company works, and you learn about every function in an organization. It's very helpful to learn about what parts work efficiently as well as what parts may not run smoothly, and more importantly, the reason why.

Competition is central to a great many roles and functions in the industry. There's always new blood coming in—new bands, new songwriters, new musicians, new app developers, and new artist and repertoire (A&R) staffers. It's the nature of the game. For many jobs in the music industry, it's helpful to have a bit of a competitive nature.

Radio, television, and websites all rely on a formal rating system. That's the way much of the entertainment industry works. The statement that recording artists are "only as good as the sales of their last record" is true, in an economic sense. Competition is always going to be there, so you have to have the drive, an intense desire to be successful, to stick with your dream, and push yourself to make it reality. In fact, if you don't have a burning desire to become a part of the music industry, and perhaps the "cool factor" is your only motivation, now might be a good time to consider alternate career paths. Few things, if any, are likely to come easy to you as you journey along your career path in the industry. You will be earning your stripes every step of the way.

HOBBY OR CAREER?

Are you pursuing a hobby or a career? Why is it important to know the difference? This is an issue that sometimes trips people up, as they look to make a career in the music industry. Many come to the industry because of their love of music. But the reality is, you've got to have bankable skills to deliver, or you're not going to be gainfully employed or grow your career. Many people have sacrificed years of their life because they felt they wanted to be "near the music."

A *hobby* is the pursuit of a field for personal enjoyment. I'm a hobby guitar player today, and I play my guitar once or twice a month. I used to be a professional guitarist, and I was paid well for my skills.

A *career* is your vocation—the daily occupation in which you must excel. Either a hobby or a career can be rewarding; however, you have to decide which one of these roads you're on.

If you plan to make a career in the industry, you've got to be serious about developing your job search strategies, building your skill set, and researching what competition you'll face in specific entry-level job areas. You'll also need to learn to become facile with the range of career development tools we'll cover throughout this book. Take time to also discover what your earning prospects are in various areas of the industry.

It's okay to switch from hobby to career. But make sure you have the required commitment, as the road will be challenging, and you will need to stay focused on achieving your goals.

WORKSHOP 2. CREATE YOUR CAREER PORTFOLIO

We advise you to set up a digital portfolio that you will maintain as your music industry career develops. You can store it on your computer desktop, a flash drive, or use one of the cloud-based services available online. Organize your Music Industry Career Portfolio in sections, as noted below. It's also useful to have access to a future calendar, either online, as an app such as Outlook or iCal, or the old standard, an annual planner notebook available at any office supply store. Use the calendar to mark important events, deadlines, and tasks for which you have set a target completion date. (More details on this will be covered in the upcoming section on Goal Setting.)

Career Portfolio Folders:

- **Jobs.** Compile job descriptions, open job listings, references to specific positions, or internship opportunities. Download a PDF of any interesting job descriptions you see to build a library for study and reference. You can also save screen grabs or scans. Set up a subfolder titled *Job Applications* to keep track of every position for which you apply.

- **Target Companies.** Any time you hear or read about a new company that interests you, start a document in this folder to compile information. Include the company's name, key products or services, spokesperson, and URL in it. Fill in more information as you discover it.

- **Industry Articles.** Every time you come across an article that interests you, especially those that identify specific companies, save it as a document, HTML file, or PDF, and add it your portfolio.

- **Correspondence.** Keep electronic (or "soft") copies of letters to and from the various people and companies you will encounter in your career development.

- **Events.** Record information on industry conferences, conventions, charity events, or any other type of function that may provide you with the chance to meet and learn from others.

- **Reference.** Include notes, handouts, and other classroom/conference handouts or lecture materials that relate to your industry career journey.

- **Résumé.** The evolution of your résumé and your skills at résumé development go in this folder.

- **Journal.** You are embarking on a process of career development that includes a component of self-discovery and personal evaluation. Start a new document titled "Dear Journal." Write a short paragraph reflecting on what you learned about yourself by completing Workshop 1 and any of the questions in it that forced you to think in new ways. Then, continue to use this section of your Career Portfolio for notes to yourself, wish lists, and reflections on key events such as interviews and noting what you learned about yourself in various workshops found throughout the book, identifying and developing mentoring opportunities, going through interviews, and the like. As you expand the "Dear Journal" document, you'll see just how your knowledge and self-awareness is growing, which in turn, will help you achieve a more nuanced perspective of yourself and your motivations, as well as your strengths and weaknesses. You will use this knowledge to help build the most comprehensive career plan possible, customized to suit your needs and goals.

- **Workshops.** Workshop 1, which you should have already completed, can be deposited now into this new "Journal" folder. As you complete the various Workshops, save and drag them into this folder.

As you journey down your own unique career path, feel free to add additional folders to your Career Portfolio as you need them. Perhaps you'll start a section to record details of the job and informational interviews you have and what you learned from them. If you have a device such as a smartphone or tablet, use it to quickly jot down notes or details of a conversation, a reference book, or a company's contact information.

The importance of your Career Portfolio will become clear as the variety and amount of information that you uncover widens. Don't be concerned at first if you only have a few items in each of the sections. By the time you finish reading this book, completing the workshops, expanding your network, and becoming a detective in your industry areas of interest, you will have a rich and bountiful set of resources that will be instrumental in helping you find and land your new position.

Keeping your Career Portfolio up to date gives you instant access to the information you develop. Be sure to back it up to a second source, such as a cloud-based service or USB drive.

USING YOUR CAREER PORTFOLIO

Your Career Portfolio will be a visible investment of your time and brainpower to get your journey started properly. It will help you build a dossier of resource information that you can continually reference. A number of our former students have come back, called, or written—often three or four years after our interaction—and commented, "I'm so glad I kept my Career Portfolio going. I sent that guest lecturer an e-mail, and she sent me back a tip on a company, where I just landed an interview!"

The whole music and entertainment business is interconnected, and it's important to remember where to find things and where to look for people. Your Career Portfolio should have sections on careers that interest you today, clippings on companies that are expanding, notes from meetings, articles on new technology, or online interviews with people in the businesses you admire. If you are interested in a career in digital music distribution, start a list of the music tech companies found in the San Francisco region. Dreaming of a career in the recording field? Build a list of the sound studios in your region, as well as facilities in New York, Los Angeles, and Nashville. Go through their websites, save URLs for key information pages that tell you what kind of work they do, and add those to your Career Portfolio in the proper folder.

A Career Portfolio becomes a reference work to help you determine which career paths interest you, and as you progress through this book, are likely to be the best fit for you. You'll find that over the years, it will become a valued resource—a shortcut to get you closer from where you are today to where you want to be tomorrow. Keep that information at your fingertips.

ACTION ITEM

Decide where your Career Portfolio will be stored: on your computer, a removable USB drive, or in a cloud storage app. Make your first five "deposits," including a "Dear Journal" entry before going to the next section.

VISUALIZATION

Another very important step for your career is to visualize yourself in your target career. For instance, if your career goal is to become an artist manager, you have to cross that bridge and say, "From today onward, I am going to see myself as an artist manager in training. Okay, now that I'm training for my new career, how do I learn to be a better artist manager?" Similarly, if you aspire to develop the next killer music app, you have to follow the same process and visualize and say out loud that you are an app developer. Committing to that career path and stating your intention is a critical step in moving your intended career forward.

Once you see yourself developing along this new career track, it doesn't matter if you're going to work by day as a paralegal, a waitress, a grocery clerk, or a data-entry "droid." In your heart, you know that you are working on developing your career and that you're an artist manager or app developer in training.

MAKING CONNECTIONS TO GROW YOUR CAREER

The music industry is forever evolving, and currently it is morphing itself via the Internet. The means that artists use to connect with fans, promote themselves, to sell records (CDs or downloads), and appear live has been irrevocably changed by the explosion of the information revolution in the fourteen years that have elapsed since this book's first edition. To keep up with the changes, you've got to commit yourself to continuous learning. No matter whether you fit among either the Fresh Faces, the Career Changers, or the Golden Years group, there's a tremendous amount of useful information available online if you know where to look. No matter what age you may be, many of the skills and talents necessary for a successful industry career are the same.

It is vitally important that you become well read on the industry and that you talk to people who are working in the business. If you find ways to meet people that are doing what you want to do and ask them intelligent questions, you will most likely discover your path to get into the business. That is the surest way to be aware of the changing trends that affect our business.

As an example, in the Northern California region, there's a songwriting organization—West Coast Songwriters, with 1,200 active members—that hosts fifteen to twenty events each month. They host an outstanding annual fall symposium. You should attend the symposium if you live in the region and want to make it as a songwriter. You should be networking with other songwriters. You've got to be talking to those publishers who are in attendance at the NCSA fall symposium. That's your Super

Bowl. You have to be there. You've got to commit yourself to lifelong learning and getting involved with others doing what you aspire to do.

> *"If you find ways to meet people that are doing what you want to do and ask them intelligent questions, you will most likely discover your path to get into the business. That is the surest way to be aware of the changing trends that affect our business."*

For aspiring record producers, there's the Audio Engineering Society (AES) convention in the fall, and the National Association of Music Merchants (NAMM) conventions in winter and summer. There are producers' forums that are open to the public (for a small admission fee) co-hosted by the Recording Academy, where you can listen to some of the most successful producers in the business talk about what it takes to make it as a producer. Top producers talk for two hours about what they do, how they got their breaks, and what they recommend for up-and-coming producers of the future. How can you miss that if you want to be the next Bruno Mars, Max Martin, Kanye West, or Tony Brown? You've got to find opportunities to learn and network.

If you can't get to an event, find out whether it was broadcast or archived on the Internet. This information is out there. The people who have presented and appeared at the event are usually happy to talk to you in the right setting, and share the information, ideas, and experience that they have. You've always got to be looking for opportunities to soak up more information. Become an information sponge. Fill your Career Portfolio with links to interviews, articles, your own notes, and information on careers and companies that pique your interest and spark your imagination. As your Career Portfolio grows, so will your ability to speak knowledgably about the areas of the industry that most interest you.

Obviously, you've got to learn and practice your craft too. You've got to keep engineering or writing songs, you've got to keep booking bands, using social media to promote your favorite undiscovered local act—whatever avocation you aspire to. But focus part of your energy on getting near people that are doing what you want to do at the highest level possible. That's the fastest way to learn about the dos and don'ts and the ins and outs of our business. There is no substitute for exposure to working professionals.

CHAPTER **3** | # Does Geography Matter?

This is your music industry geography lesson. On the map below are important cities in the United States for the combined music and entertainment industries: New York, Nashville, and Los Angeles, plus a fourth important region, San Francisco/ Silicon Valley.

The Four Entertainment Capitals

FIG. 3.1. Entertainment Capitals

Certainly, for the record business in North America, these cities represent the most significant concentrations of music industry companies. If you aspire to make it to the top, at some point, you're probably going to do business in one of these cities. That's where it largely happens for the record business. If you're a recording engineer, if you're a songwriter, if you're an engineer/ producer, or if you're going to work with a label, sooner or later, you will become familiar with these three regions—though you might not necessarily actually have to live there. The addition of Silicon Valley as a fourth entertainment capital is warranted by the inexorable shift of the discovery, distribution, and filtering of music by consumers using the Internet. There are few, if any, sectors of the music industry that have not been affected by these changes in how people find and enjoy music of all genres. A wide range of digital music companies including Pandora, INgrooves,

Amazon MP3, iTunes, Rhapsody, Google Play, and many others all have offices to draw on the talented programmers and music managers in the region.

Don't despair if you aren't living now in one of the major cities. If you live in or near Seattle, Chicago, Atlanta, Miami, Boston, Austin, St. Louis, Denver, Memphis, Houston, New Orleans, Philadelphia, or another good-sized metropolitan area, you can develop an excellent skill set and put it to use in the regional music industry. For instance, you might work at an indie label, or with a radio station, or learn how to make a great-sounding recording at a studio, using such experiences to build up your skills without having to be in such a big shark tank where there is such intense competition that you need a fully developed skill set along with buckets of ambition and drive to succeed.

> *"Rather than jumping feetfirst into one of the top music markets, it's an excellent strategy to work in a smaller market to really learn the basics of how the industry works."*

Rather than jumping feetfirst into one of the top music markets, it's an excellent strategy to work in a smaller market to really learn the basics of how the industry works. It may be helpful to work with a concert promoter, a booking agency, or other related firm in your area of interest. One day, you will feel that you may have outgrown your situation and that you're ready to take the next step in your career development.

METRO-PHOBIA?

Do you really have to move to L.A. to have a career in the music industry? No, migrating to one of the entertainment capitals is not the only path, anymore. It's essential to note that the proliferation of new tools, techniques, and business models to create value and awareness for music and music-related products or services is allowing startups to grow and prosper outside the major entertainment capitals. If your product or service is truly game-changing, you can live and work just about anywhere. Two DIY music companies, Saddle Creek (located in Omaha, Nebraska) and Righteous Babe (based in Buffalo, New York) are shining examples of this new paradigm that can work for entrepreneurially minded individuals who have no desire to sit in traffic in one of the major markets.

When recent graduates believe they are ready to make their move to the big markets, we suggest they visit first. We encourage them to take two weeks off from their current job, travel to one of the major markets, and rent a room or stay with a friend to do some networking and some informational interviewing (covered later in this book). You need to make sure that you're ready to go on to the next level. Moving to one of the top markets is expensive due to the higher cost of living, and it's emotionally intense. Check it out before you pull up your stakes and jump in. You have to have your eyes open before you take the plunge. Prepare yourself to succeed when you make your move to one of these four regions. Those are the practicalities of music industry geography.

WORKSHOP 3. LANDING IN AN ENTERTAINMENT CAPITAL

Pick one of the four major entertainment capitals, and research the following information.

1. Identify three firms in your chosen region that have business operations in the area of the industry that most interests you. For instance, if you are planning to work in entertainment marketing, you might identify the marketing department at a record label, a concert promoter, an industry PR firm, and a radio or television network.

2. Using a localized resource such as Craigslist, look up the cost to rent an apartment or a room in a house or apartment.

3. Make a short list of your current living expenses. Replace your current rent or housing costs with what you've researched on the major market.

4. Finally, think about who you currently know that might provide an introduction to a working professional in the city you've chosen to research. Finding a "local expert" is an important step toward learning about the actual working situation, job market, and cost of living in one of the major markets.

 ACTION ITEM

Add your results from this workshop to your Career Portfolio.

4

What Kinds of Jobs Are Out There?

In career development classes for the music industry, students often ask, "What jobs are there, in addition to obvious ones such as recording artist, songwriter, musician, or talent manager?" Look carefully anywhere that music or sound is heard, and you'll discover dozens of jobs to investigate. Any list that was developed would be out of date within a few months, since there are so many new opportunities developing each year as the music and entertainment industry continue to shift to the Information Age model.

However, before we discuss a few of the jobs and market sectors that exist, let's look at the roles that people play in the music industry via broad function and let you consider which one of these areas you may fit in most comfortably. We've broken down the music business into three broad areas:

1. **Creators.** These are the artists, arrangers, lyricists, directors, producers, instrument builders, and entrepreneurs who take a tiny idea or inspiration and create a story, a new music-related company, product, or a song, then mold it into something that can be shared, valued, and monetized.

2. **Technologists.** These are the hardware and software developers, network techs, sound and video technicians, encoders, compressionists, riggers, social media experts, concert sound crew, instrument techs, who build, expand, and maintain the tools, pipelines, and channel paths to allow music and entertainment to get out to audiences around the world.

3. **Managers.** These are the dealmakers, connectors, and gatekeepers to the final work that the Creators and Technologists have partnered with to complete. Managers, agents, publicists, entertainment attorneys, music publishers, tax specialists, performing rights organizations, and concert promoters all play a vital role in ensuring that not only will there be an audience for new music, but also that anyone who is owed compensation is treated fairly as prescribed by law and convention. No managers—no payday. And yes, a few creators and technologists are also able to self-manage their businesses, especially at the early stages of their careers.

WORKSHOP 4.1. ARE YOU A CONTENT CREATOR, TECHNOLOGIST, OR MANAGER?

Rate yourself using the following questions. Go with your gut instinct on each.

Part 1	YES	NO
1. I am comfortable learning and using new technologies such as computer programs.	☐	☐
2. I read about and investigate the latest music and entertainment technologies.	☐	☐
3. My friends often ask me to help them install or use new audio or video software, gadgets, or apps.	☐	☐
4. I'm interested in how music-making devices and software actually work "under the hood."	☐	☐
5. I enjoy experimenting and pushing the envelope with the music technologies that I use.	☐	☐

Part 2

6. I am able to function in situations where I meet and talk with new people.	☐	☐
7. If a conflict arises, I am able to maintain composure and work to settle the conflict.	☐	☐
8. I have succeeded in situations where I helped lead a team of my peers.	☐	☐
9. I have a genuine interest in listening to and learning from many different people.	☐	☐
10. I have the ability to communicate well with people who others say are difficult.	☐	☐

Part 3

11. I am someone that enjoys any hands-on creative outlet, such as drawing, poetry, dance, acting, mime, rapping, or songwriting.	☐	☐

	YES	NO
12. I enjoy new books, movies, and music and then sometimes think about what I might have done differently or better than the original author.	☐	☐
13. I have consistently exhibited the ability and self-discipline to work for extended periods of time to improve my own performance or output.	☐	☐
14. I am comfortable working on my own for long periods of time.	☐	☐
15. I have demonstrated the ability to follow through on what I needed to do to achieve my goals and vision for the future.	☐	☐

Score your test. If you answered yes to four or more questions in part 1, chances are you are well on your way to a career in which you will develop or use new musical technology. Alternately, if you answered yes to four or more questions in part 2, you may find the greatest career success by participating in the business end of the industry as some type of Manager. If you scored four or more in part 3, you may have the makings of a Content Creator and should look at the next steps available in your area if you plan to pursue that path to continue to grow your skills.

If you scored high in two or more areas, surprise! You may be headed for an executive position, as many top performers have the ability to work in multiple modes.

Don't overthink the results of this workshop, as many persons can thrive in more than one of these broad categories. In fact, quite a few Managers have been known to get involved creatively with artists (think of a producer that handles both the creative and business aspects of record making), and many Technologists have gone on to become past masters at deal making as their careers have unfolded. Not surprisingly, musicians are leading the charge when it comes to evolving careers that allow them to become entrepreneurs and leaders in multiple roles. Such "multi-preneurs" would be embodied in the careers of Amanda Palmer, Puff Daddy, Janelle Monae, or Russell Simmons, to name just a few.

The purpose of this workshop is to start you down the path of self-reflection to determine which of these broad areas are of greatest interest to you. Knowing this as you design your own career plan will help you weed out career areas that require different skills or traits than those you have developed or are willing to learn. That's why it's important to know which areas you prefer. Today's music industry requires some basic level of technology facility, and an increasing value is being placed on what are sometimes termed "soft skills," that is, active and careful listening, the ability to follow and give direction clearly, and the ability to prioritize and stay on top of assignments. Don't fall into the trap of believing that your strong technology skills will be enough to make it in the industry or conversely, that your amazing gift of gab and people skills will eliminate the need for you to know office productivity programs inside and out. They won't! And while anyone can be trained if they have the desire to broaden their functional knowledge and skills, past experience has shown that many people gravitate to one of these categories a bit more than the others. Note where your preferences lie and refer back to that information as you move ahead and work through the upcoming sections of this book.

 ## ACTION ITEM

Post a reflection on the results of this workshop in your Career Portfolio's "Dear Journal."

MUSIC INDUSTRY JOB SAFARI

Let's dive a bit deeper and go on a safari to learn a bit about a host of music-related job categories, which include vitally important roles for talented individuals that fit the three functional areas mentioned above: Creators, Technologists, and Managers. In an upcoming chapter, we'll look at examples from three different music industry areas and map out the path from entry level to manager in greater detail for those specific areas.

Affiliated music and sound careers abound in the film, computer, mobile, theater, and educational arenas. Education is an often-overlooked career path, but it's essential, because if no one is learning how to make or appreciate music, there won't be any music—and certainly, many less savvy music consumers.

Television and radio, Internet and mobile, computer hardware and software, video game music and sound, and theme parks. At Disney, rather than calling their audio staff "engineers," they call them "imagineers." Think of all the sounds there are at a theme park such as a Disney or Universal Studios location. Imagineers not only create the sounds, but they also design the playback systems and keep the sound running properly around the clock. Mobile companies such as Verizon and AT&T recognize music as one of the key deliverables to their users and often enter into agreements with artists or labels to provide access to music. Close your eyes and listen to the virtual world created in any of the most popular video games. It takes a team of sound designers and editors to conceive, create, edit, and mix those sounds that vary throughout your game play.

Music instruments and products, recording equipment, builders of the latest concert sound equipment, sound recording programs, compressors, reverbs, amplifiers, mixing boards, headphones, microphones. Someone has to imagine, design, and build them all. This is the gear that musicians use to create the music we enjoy. As technology improves and the world shrinks, there are new and more opportunities for innovative business people to partner with the technologists who make, refine, and market the tens of thousands of instruments, equipment, and software devices used to make today's music.

Feature film music and sound personnel including composer, music editor, sound editor, ADR recordist, music supervisor, dialog or sound effects editor, boom operator. There are dozens of sound personnel working for weeks or months on nearly every major motion picture. Smaller budget independent films have a proportionally smaller sound and music staff, but still employ a range of professionals.

Singer, songwriter, studio musician, arranger, sound engineer, music producer. These are the creatives who take ideas, emotions, and feelings, and turn them into songs and records. Like most creative fields, it takes a certain level of proficiency to be noticed, but developing that proficiency is something that can be learned if one has the requisite drive, inspiration, and instruction.

Artist manager, publicist, music video director, record producer, label staffer, music publisher, entertainment attorney, music journalist, business manager, music supervisor, video game project manager. These folks take care of business on behalf of artists, musicians, music companies, and music users. Watch your favorite weekly television series with a pencil and paper at hand and make a dot each time any music is heard. Each one of those music snippets, called "cues," required permission and license payments before it could be included in that episode. Managers were required to secure all those permissions.

Music educator, music librarian, orchestrator, copyist. These people educate, disseminate, curate, evaluate, and help ensure that music can be recreated in a wide range of different settings.

THE 50-TO-1 RULE

Newcomers to the music industry have often been attracted to the field by the glamour of a particular job or artistic pursuit. We like to point out that the less glamorous "off stage" roles for music industry pros abound in far greater numbers than roles for divas. Hence, our "50-to-1 Rule." For each of the thousands of successful recording artists worldwide, there are as many as fifty support people behind each one, many in good-paying, exciting, and stable careers. They may not share the spotlight, but they have very rewarding careers in the music industry.

Take for instance U2's 2009 to 2011 *U2 360°* tour, which according to *Billboard*, employed 137 crew that traveled around the world with the band and 120 local techs that were hired in each city the tour visited. Importantly, music managers' careers usually have a much longer time span than the careers of the artists they manage.

> *"For each of the the thousands of successful recording artists worldwide, there are as many as fifty support people behind each one, many in good-paying, exciting, and stable careers."*

The Resource section of the book lists two other books and a website that provide snapshots of many different jobs that relate to our industry: *Career Opportunities in the Music Industry (6th Edition)* by Shelly Field; *100 Careers in the Music Industry* by Tanja L. Crouch, and the music resource website, www.artistshousemusic.com. Field's book details roughly eighty job descriptions, salary ranges, and necessary skills. Crouch's book is much more intimate, using first-person interviews with a range of leading professionals to profile exactly what they do in their work and how they got their start in the industry. These two books complement one another. Artists House Music is a different type of resource in that it features a few thousand video interviews with working music business professionals and as such, gives a wonderful range of searchable resources to learn more about what an artist manager, booking agent, recording engineer, or music editor does. If you would like to expand your own knowledge about the wide range of industry jobs, start by looking through the video interviews on the website and then consider locating a copy of the two books. Doing so will help you really see the substantial number and range of music industry jobs. Also, if you are enrolled in a college or vocational program, your school may have a career day where local professionals visit and talk about what they do every day in their jobs.

Getting to know about the variety of jobs and what kinds of skills and aptitude are required for each is one of the most important activities you can undertake. How can you find out if you are well suited for a job if you don't know what it takes to do it well?

> *"How can you find out if you are well suited for a job if you don't know what it takes to do it well?"*

ACTION ITEM

After reviewing some of the jobs we learned about in our Music Industry Job Safari, start your own list of the jobs that most intrigue you. Keep your list handy in the Jobs section of your Career Portfolio. (You *have* started your Career Portfolio, haven't you?)

 # WORKSHOP 4.2. MAGIC LAMP

Imagine you've just found the proverbial "magic lamp" in the attic of your family home. You have three wishes, but a note attached to the handle says that the wishes can only be used to discover the perfect career for you.

Although such a lamp didn't come with this book, this workshop will allow you to identify the three jobs that most interest you. What jobs do you wish for?

1. _____

2. _____

3. _____

Now, via an Internet search, find an interview with a working professional for each of the three dream jobs you've identified. Bookmark the articles, and after reading them over carefully, ask yourself if your interest remains high for each job. What is it about that person's job or career that excites you? Do they mention how they got to where they are in the industry today? Will you be willing to go through a similar learning process (often referred to as "paying your dues") to reach a similar position?

Write down the answers to these or any other questions or observations that come to mind after reading the articles and post your thoughts in your journal.

ACTION ITEM

Finally, add links to these articles to your Career Portfolio Industry Articles section. If you are using this book for a class, pick the best article and share it with a classmate.

These are only a handful of the music-related fields that need talented newcomers to jump in and help make a difference. In fact, as the baby boomers (who in large part operate the entertainment industry today) come to grips with the impact of the Internet and other new technologies such as mobile content delivery, they will only continue to be successful by utilizing the skills, talents, and adaptability that today's younger generation has with regard to such technology. By the time you are reading this, there will be many new job titles created as our industry continues to evolve and change in the face of new technologies.

Don't limit your view to one or two career paths. Do some serious investigation before you settle on any one route. We'll look next at some significant trends that are having outsized impact on the overall entertainment marketplace, which is becoming increasingly globalized—and in fact, where a number of music-related market sectors are converging. As you consider the rich diversity of music industry jobs and market sectors, here are a few more areas to help you further your views to the range of music industry career possibilities.

HOW INFORMATION AND ENTERTAINMENT ARE THE NEW "GOLD STANDARD"

In the late 1990s, young Wall Street investment counselor David Pullman began an investment fund that allowed the public to purchase shares of future earnings (appropriately called "futures") on the songs written by David Bowie, which resulted in $55 million being raised on behalf of Bowie. In exchange, Bowie would receive no royalties for the next ten years, the income instead paying off the investors.

Initially, this was viewed as an anomaly, but as time marched on, the Pullman Group signed on more and more artists anxious to take the investment funding against their future royalty stream. Artists such as James Brown, the Isley Brothers, Ashford and Simpson, the estate of Marvin Gaye, and Holland-Dozier-Holland joined forces with Mr. Pullman. Looking back on those deals today, although they have fallen out of favor (in large part due to the decline in recorded music sales), they highlight the concept that songs or other forms of intellectual property can be monetized in new and different ways to provide access to music. While the Bowie Bonds sizzled in the last days of the 20th century, in the 21st century, it's clear that today's new entertainment currency is the control and monetization of information and entertainment. In fact, a recent study by the International Intellectual Property Alliance cited a $1.01 trillion valuation for value-added services to the 2012 U.S. Gross Domestic Product, up dramatically from $885 billion in 2009. The same study found that U.S. copyright-related industries employed a total of 5.4 million people and grew at more than twice the rate of the annual economy from 2009 to 2012.

> *"While the Bowie Bonds sizzled in the last days of the 20th century, in the 21st century, it's clear that today's new entertainment currency is the control and monetization of information and entertainment."*

One more notable example would be the hit television series, *Glee*, which has not only generated hundreds of millions in advertising income for its producers, but its episodes have also been sold successfully online. *Glee* soundtrack recordings have gone on to generate tens of millions of downloads of mostly cover tunes performed by the show's cast. So even though the old model of selling CDs is fading, new opportunities to make and share music and entertainment continue to be invented. There is no end to the ways creative industry folk are developing myriad means to continue to profit even as album sales continue to fade. Music today can be found in more places and used in more ways than in any previous generation. Long live music!

THINK GLOBALLY

Roughly 42 percent of the world's population resides in four growing countries: China, India, Indonesia, and Brazil. By 2025, GeoHive projects that Asia's overall population of 4.77 billion people will represent 60 percent of the world population. In comparison, by that date, North America will account for just less than 5 percent of the world population. For anyone preparing for a high level career in the music world, addressing these populations of potential music consumers must receive consideration.

Most people in Asia do not speak English. However, they do listen to western music. They do play western video games. They do enjoy western movies. *The Wall Street Journal* recently reported that 68 percent of revenue for the $32 billion film industry comes from overseas markets. To prove this point, the action blockbuster *Iron Man 3* opened a week earlier in overseas markets than it did in the U.S. Two weeks after its release, it had broken the $1 billion box office plateau with $776 million in overseas ticket sales and $337 million here at home, neatly matching the 68/32 (foreign/domestic) split cited earlier. U.S. movies also rank number one in box office revenues in Japan and Western Europe. Entertainment today is a rapidly expanding global industry that transcends language barriers. And the growth only seems to be accelerating as *The Wall Street Journal* also reported that the fall 2013 foreign premier of *Thor: The Dark World* racked up $268 million in just twelve days of exhibition. A senior Disney executive acknowledged the shift stating, "The international landscape is growing at an extraordinary clip."

> *"Info-tainment has become the new gold standard."*

Tracking entertainment companies such as Fox, Electronic Arts, or Sony on a global basis leads one to a conclusion that I share with many future-oriented business leaders: Info-tainment has become the new gold standard.

INTERNET MEDIA AND VIDEO GAMES

The same skills that apply to a career path in the music industry will apply to electronic media and information-age careers. Loosely described as convergence, new media and gaming marks the intersection of information, entertainment, and business. It is where the latest technologies for the Internet, computers, cable or satellite television, broadband delivery, movies, and music converge. Job opportunities are exploding just as fast as new companies are born and bought, as the industry races to develop and deliver the most compelling content to a worldwide audience hungry for information and entertainment. Consider how much time you spent today enjoying some form of entertainment, whether it was listening to the radio or music, watching television, going to movies, reading magazines, viewing videos, surfing the 'Net, or playing some type of game. Chances are, it was more than a few hours in total.

Another form of convergence that has dramatically changed the rules in the entertainment industry is the rise of content channels such as YouTube. By allowing musicians, managers, and fans equal access to new and/or remixed content, music can be shared globally using desktop media production tools. One need only look at the success of groups such as Karmin, Pomplamoose, or OK Go, to realize that a new model exists for artists and savvy managers that understand Internet media to build a fan base at a fraction of the cost it would take without such platforms.

Another example of the opportunities rapidly emerging in new media is the explosion of sites such as ReverbNation, BandPage, TuneCore, CD Baby, and DIY blog sites such as Tumblr, that provide the interactive tools for artists to expand and monetize their audience.

When it comes to the world of video gaming, in 2012, research firm NPD Group cited 211 million video game players in the U.S. The Entertainment Software Association reported that the average U.S. household had at least one video game console and that Americans spent more than $24 billion on games, consoles, accessories, downloads, and upgrades. Overseas, the Interactive Software Federation of Europe reports that more than 81 percent of the region's 95 million game players enjoy interactive video games online with one or more friends. As a result, there are thousands of companies involved in the production of video games, all of which incorporate music and sound, and as the market has grown, so have production standards, which necessitates more people involved in making the game content. Furthermore, the market has expanded exponentially with at least five different sectors including consoles, computer, tablet, mobile, and portable game devices each having its own audience.

Let's check in on one such job in the video gaming field: that of a music composer. Today's games offer well-crafted musical scores that can rival that of a feature film in sophistication, orchestration, and playback fidelity.

Globally, the overall video game market is expected to remain substantial. For example, *Call of Duty: Black Ops 2* grossed more than $1 billion during its first fifteen days on the market in late 2012. The *Just Dance* series of home dancing video games has sold more than 25 million copies, and the ever-popular Sims series in all its permutations has sold more than 125 million copies, demonstrating that action/warfare video games are not the only category to do well.

Is composing for the game industry right for everyone? Hardly. But if you are a talented composer who is comfortable working with computer audio and MIDI programs, you should investigate your opportunities. Long hours and critical deadlines can lead to some all-nighters for those in this field, but the financial rewards can be quite lucrative.

Staff positions as a music composer at the larger software developers pay in the $45,000 to $70,000 range with benefits, paid holidays, and profit-sharing programs. Freelancers working for game developers can also do well on a project-by-project basis, but without medical benefits.

And not just composers are needed. Any skill or craft that goes into the making of a feature film is likely to be required when a new game is on the drawing board: session musicians, recording engineers, dialog editors, voice talent, computer graphics designers, sound effects editors, production assistants, continuity, video editors, localization experts, and on and on.

Other areas that are growing exponentially include the mobile music and legal online digital music market. Cricket Wireless is currently one of the first mobile phone services to allow unlimited music access from its catalog of millions of songs for a flat monthly fee. It's likely this model will expand if enough consumers come to appreciate taking music with them anywhere they go. Meanwhile, Apple's successful iTunes music store recently surpassed the 25 Billion Songs Sold mark, which if annualized over its nearly ten years of availability means that music consumers downloaded and paid for more than seven million songs *each day*. The end of year 2012 statistics provided by the RIAA show a recorded music industry whose revenue now comes from 60 percent digital sources including downloads and streaming services. As physical CD sales continue to fade, it's inevitable that more new music distribution platforms will be developed. The so-called "access" model used by Spotify, Rhapsody, Rdio, and others now represents 15 percent, or more than $1 billion of the overall $7 billion U.S. recorded music industry. (Source: 2012 RIAA Music Industry Shipment and Revenue Statistics.)

And don't overlook what is projected to be a $435 billion worldwide market for television programming services including the major networks, cable, satellite, streaming (Netflix, Hulu Plus, Amazon Prime, etc.), on demand, and pay-per-view. The expanding universe of content requires new talent to help create and produce programming for the hundreds of channels available.

Consider any media that utilizes audio, music recording, and sound editing. You'll see that literally dozens of new opportunities are being developed each week—for instance, the emerging market for new video programming now being funded by Amazon, Netflix, Amazon, YouTube, and other alternatives to the major television networks and film studios. Dive in and start exploring the possibilities offered by new media.

Another very hot area is the administration and protection of intellectual property as an entertainment attorney, paralegal, or copyright administrator. Look for careers in this area to continue to grow at a steady pace as newer, faster, and more secure technologies emerge. Another growth area will be international relations and distribution deals in a global marketplace where borders and laws are difficult to enforce due to the continued expansion of Internet access, especially via mobile phones in emerging regions.

Companies are working harder than ever before to maximize the earning potential of each new entertainment vehicle. Movie tie-ins, tour sponsorships, sheet music folios, soundtrack albums such as *Les Misérables*, the 2012 hit movie *Pitch Perfect*, and Adele's theme song for the James Bond film *Skyfall*; television series such as the aforementioned *Glee*, that spawn soundtrack albums, as well as biopics on the lives of recording artists such as *Ray*, *Cadillac Records*, *Dreamgirls*, or even the recent Broadway show *Motown: the Musical*, all bring new and potentially lucrative earning opportunities for a wide range of creative and business personnel who are mining the power of music to tell stories in a way that few other media can do. In many cases, it's an example of savvy music business pros putting "old wine in new bottles" to attract an increasingly younger and more diverse audience willing to spend money on music-related entertainment. Remember the 50-to-1 rule; you can be one of those savvy music managers.

To really prepare for a career today, force yourself to think outside the box. There's a great big beautiful world in the entertainment industry for those who are motivated to make their mark. Push yourself to look beyond the record company or recording studio and at least explore the potential for what creative and financial opportunities may exist in these exciting new media market segments.

MUSIC PRODUCTS CAREERS: ENABLING MUSIC MAKERS

Another form of entertainment is making music, not only for the professional musician, but for the growing demographic of Americans with leisure time and disposable income looking for a hobby or interest that is fulfilling, not fattening, and enriching. Enter the music products industry. Young music career seekers often overlook the global music products industry, yet it provides many opportunities for all types of music-related careers.

What are music products? A music product is any instrument, device, object, book, or accessory that someone might need to make, teach, study, create, or share music. Everything from musical instruments such as guitars, trumpets, harmonicas, synthesizers, and grand pianos, to sheet music, recording equipment, karaoke systems, music education software, and loudspeakers, to name just a few of the products encompassed by this market segment. Additionally, the millions of Americans that are involved in studying music in schools or in private lessons are also all customers for the music products industry. In the U.S. alone, the music products industry is a $6.6 billion a year business, so it is large enough to offer a wide range of career opportunities for those passionate about music.

One of the greatest attractions to a career in the range of market segments within the music products industry is that those working in it are surrounded by peers who make and love fostering the growth of music making. And the mission of every company in the industry (be it manufacturer, distributor, retailer, online merchant, or vintage dealer) is to help others learn to enjoy making music.

Twice each year, the NAMM convention occurs, in winter (Anaheim) and summer (Nashville). If you are fortunate enough to secure show credentials, no matter where you look, you will see people who are sharing their passion and doing what they love to do as their so-called day gig. Those who are successful in this segment spend the bulk of their time either making or helping others make music, or they provide music making opportunities through distributors, retailers, or other business partners. Simply put, there's a lot of genuine love and enthusiasm present in this market sector and ample room for new professionals to join the industry and make an impact.

FIG. 4.1. The NAMM Show. The semi-annual NAMM Conference provides an outstanding networking opportunity for music industry job seekers. New companies and musical products are launched continuously, providing numerous opportunities for making the all-important connections vital to early career growth." (Photos by David Livingston, Getty Images for NAMM)

Another observation about the music products industry is that unlike some other industry segments, there are a great many owner-operated firms—some that have been managed successfully by the same family for more than a hundred years. As a result, new employees who are passionate about music and dedicated to helping others learn about and make music are valued assets. Unlike some of the recent record company layoffs due to the continual rounds of label consolidation, the music products industry is actually anxious to find talented new employees to continue to grow the pool of professional and recreational music makers in America. Starting salaries in the music products field are generally higher and offer better benefits than the record industry, too. While the severity of the early 2000s recession certainly affected the music products industry, it has come back convincingly and continues to offer a number of stable career options for music-oriented individuals.

For those who may have been attracted to a music industry career because of their own creative aspirations or an interest in working closely with high profile recording artists, jobs within the music products industry offer these opportunities and more. For instance, every major manufacturer of music products has an artist relations department that provides support for the artists using their products. For those who prefer to make music, a position as a clinician or product specialist gives you the opportunity to travel around the country teaching others how to use your company's instruments or products.

The National Association of Music Merchants is the trade association that hosts the semi-annual NAMM conferences where nearly 100,000 music makers and music products professionals convene to share information, do business, and enjoy the world of music products. With nearly 8,000 member companies spanning the globe, this trade association provides a window through which the diversity of companies and career opportunities can be viewed. The NAMM show itself is not open to the public, but one of the easiest ways to identify companies in this industry is to visit the association's website (www.namm.org) and download the exhibitor list from the most recent NAMM show. You may be surprised to see there are quite a few in your geographic proximity.

WORKSHOP 4.3. INTERNET MEDIA AND MUSIC PRODUCTS OPPORTUNITIES

List three companies of interest to you that compete online in the Internet media, such as music apps, music delivery, or music/concert review sectors.

1. Find an article written in the last twelve months reporting on each of the Internet media companies and its latest product or services written in a newspaper, magazine, or influential online source that is *not* affiliated with the company itself. Bookmark the article and add it to your Career Portfolio under Target Companies.

2. Visit each company's website. Go to the Careers section, and see what, if any, types of job openings exist that may interest you.

Start the process over with some research to develop a list of three music products companies that interest you. They may make or sell instruments, software, sound or recording gear, accessories, or published music.

1. Find an article written in the last twelve months reporting on each of the music products companies and its latest product or services written in a newspaper, magazine, or influential online source that is *not* affiliated with the company itself.

2. Visit each company's website. Go to the Careers section, and see what, if any, types of job openings exist that may interest you. Bookmark them for later use in an upcoming workshop.

ACTION ITEM

Bookmark all six articles and the respective Jobs/Careers pages for these firms and add them to your Career Portfolio. Report any new career tracks that you discovered for further research in your Journal.

EQUAL OPPORTUNITY FOR ALL?

Males have traditionally dominated the non-performance jobs found in the music industry. (Women performers have nearly always had plentiful work options, although their treatment was often not equitable.) Historically, at least 90 percent of the people working in recording studios, concert production, and many technical roles were male, and few women were found behind the sound board or boom microphone. That has been changing over the last twenty-five years. In terms of the recording industry, there are now more opportunities for women to work as engineers, producers, A&R execs, technicians, label presidents, and any position that men have traditionally held. Although the number of women working at record labels has been high historically, it's only recently that women are common in the top ranks. In Hollywood, women head up some of the largest film and recording studios.

A lot of ancillary fields, such as live sound, concert production, staging, cartage, and rigging, are still dominated by men. A woman aspiring to a career in the music industry must be aware that there are numbers of people who have been in the industry for many years who possess extremely chauvinistic attitudes. A woman should be mentally prepared for that. She has to have faith in herself, and know what strengths she has and how she can utilize them. She has to conscientiously work to say and act upon what she believes in. The solution is to have the skills and ambition to do the job well, and you will move ahead on your career path. Women artist-entrepreneurs such as Madonna, Amanda Palmer, Sarah McLachlan, Janelle Monáe, Dolly Parton, Queen Latifah, Reba McEntire, Beyoncé, Alanis Morissette, Ani DiFranco, and many others have influenced or are influencing our industry, and you can do it too. Remember when you are in a position to hire a person to help your company prosper, don't ignore the benefits of fostering a gender-diverse workforce. The Society of Human Resource Management reported that [similar sized] companies with high levels of gender diversity averaged nearly $600 million more in revenue than companies with low gender diversity. It's just such gender diversity that is a key factor in sustaining a dynamic and future-oriented organization.

5 | Why Understanding Career Ladders Is Essential

How do you advance from an entry level to executive or leadership position in a particular market segment? And what are the intermediate steps along the way? To determine this, you need to research and discover the career ladder for your music industry areas of interest. One of the best ways to be able to fill in the various career ladders you are investigating is to speak with working professionals to learn the steps on the career ladder and as much detail as you can about the duties, responsibilities, and salary levels in that field. This will allow you to gain insight into what happens in any segment of the industry, what promotions occur as you build a career, and what type of earning potential there is at each step of the way. Without this depth of knowledge, you will likely be groping in the dark to find out what is involved in any music industry career. Let's now look in depth at three market sectors and their respective career ladders.

MUSIC PUBLISHING AND LICENSING

First, we'll explore the field of music publishing and its affiliated field, music licensing. A music publisher controls and administers the copyright for an original musical work. Music licensing professionals then work to help anyone who wishes to use a song for any purpose, negotiating the fees that will be required to do so. For instance, EMI Music Publishing publishes Kanye West's original songs. So, if a filmmaker wished to use one of his songs in a new motion picture, she would contact EMI Music Publishing with her request. Speaking with someone in the EMI Music Publishing's licensing department, they would negotiate a fee for such use.

The basic steps on the career ladder in this field start out with an entry-level position, which is often called a coordinator, copyright analyst, associate, or administrative assistant. It's important to understand that the position title may vary from firm to firm, but the responsibilities will be similar at each one. At a larger music-publishing firm (EMI Music Publishing controls more than one million song copyrights), the entry-level hire may be assigned to either publishing or licensing administration, whereas at a smaller publisher, they may assist in both areas. Here is a table showing the career ladder at a mid-sized U.S. music publisher.

Music Publishing Career Ladder

Vice President of Music Publishing or Licensing

Director of Music Publishing or Licensing

Department Manager

Publishing, Licensing, or Copyright Specialist

Music Publishing Coordinator

FIG. 5.1. Music Publishing Career Ladder

N.B. There may also be "senior" level positions with added responsibilities at the VP, director, and manager levels, e.g., senior vice president of licensing.

This ladder will vary based on the size of the publishing firm and the number of song copyrights that are under its control. In essence, the larger the catalog, the more different job positions there are likely to be. Thus, the largest music publishing firms such as Universal Music Publishing Group, Warner/Chappell Publishing, and Sony/ATV/EMI Music Publishing will have the largest staffs and the most levels using their own proprietary ladder of job titles.

A mid-sized music publisher will have fewer positions than the major publishers, but all the basic functions will still be fulfilled. The smallest music publishers, of which there are thousands, are boutique or vest-pocket music publishers that may have one to three employees and may choose to rely on outside parties to help with some of the functions, such as foreign subpublishing, license administration, litigation, etc.

What differentiates the positions on the music publishing career ladder? In part, experience is the greatest differentiator; however, the tasks and roles change as one moves up the ladder. For example, a coordinator will be filing copyright registrations, processing royalty statements, creating invoices, doing songwriter and rights holder research, and handling mechanical license requests. As one moves up to specialist and manager, added duties may include handling counter claims, assisting with audits, preparing reports, and helping to resolve disputes that may arise. Mentoring junior staff will also become part of your role. At the senior levels of director or vice president, relationship building takes on a greater role, as well as doing data analysis, income and royalty liability projections, and tracking the performance of various copyrights under the control of your firm. You will also likely be involved in attending conferences, seminars, annual meetings of trade associations, and possibly travel to meet and collaborate with overseas partner firms or sister companies.

At the time of this writing, the *Nashville Business Journal* had just announced that one of the three major publishers was expanding its administration staff by 40 percent, to keep up with the demand for its songs. Similarly, another of the major publishers was advertising four open positions in their Southern California offices. This is evidence that the music publishing and licensing arena is one area of the music industry that is likely to remain robust for those job seekers that have the right mix of skills and experience. As to salary data, our source stated, "When I started out in music publishing fifteen years ago, entry level salaries were roughly $25,000 per year. Today, a full time position should pay in the range of $33–40,000." However, if the position is located in the New York or Los Angeles area, one should try to negotiate a starting salary near the top of that range due to the higher cost of living.

DIGITAL MUSIC DISTRIBUTION

We interviewed a range of managers at some of the most successful digital-music distribution companies to learn about the career ladder in digital music distribution. Furthermore, students of ours have been interning with some of these companies since 2004, so we have nearly a decade of experience watching these companies evolve and managers help grow these businesses. The managers we spoke with reiterated that there is a dues-paying period required to establish oneself in digital music. Another factor that differentiates digital music distribution from other fields is that the market sector is still very new. It's a bit like the American West in the 1870s to 1880s; changes are occurring at lightning speed. Many of the firms that are operating in the digital-music distribution space also are struggling to earn a profit. A number of the business models follow the Internet 1.0 "build it, and they will come" mantra: paying customer acquisition and income generation are often an afterthought to the founders, who focus on building scale and user population, in the belief that once those are attained, some form of monetization will be achieved.

Another important characteristic of the digital music distribution sector is that this area does not employ scores of people, as more of the content management processes become highly automated. As a result, it's idea-driven with fewer people, each doing more work. Accordingly, job opportunities are not as plentiful as they are in some other music industry sectors, and since there is a high residual demand for jobs in digital music distribution, those wishing to make their mark will have to work very hard. One manager commented, "Don't aim for a career in this field with rose-colored glasses on. You're going to have to work your ass off, so it better be something you really believe in." These trends and factors impact the career ladder and salary ranges found in the digital music distribution market sector.

Here is the career ladder at one Silicon Valley digital music distribution firm.

Digital Music Distribution Career Ladder

Vice President of Client Relations, or other areas such as Marketing, Business Development, etc.

Client Relations Director

Client Relations Manager

Production Manager

Production Coordinator

Content Ingestion, Data Input (paid)

Unpaid Internship: Content Ingestion, Data Input

FIG. 5.2. Digital Music Distribution Career Ladder

While the salaries found at the vice president level are comparable to those found in other areas of the music industry, entry-level jobs (even coordinator and manager) pay very little, compared to other professional industries. Nearly all internships in digital music distribution begin unpaid and require a real dedication and commitment to doing an exceptional job to stand out among the crop of other interns. A typical summer-long internship of ninety days may lead to an offer to continue doing content ingestion and data input, but then, being paid for your work.

However, remembering the information about "build it, and they will come" thinking, the pay will likely be the prevailing minimum wage. At the time of this writing, in California, the minimum wage is $8.00 per hour (although in San Francisco city proper, it is $10.55), which translates to monthly pay of $1,387 ($1,688 for a month of 40-hour weeks in San Francisco) and an annual salary of $16,640. And that's before any payroll deductions such as taxes or unemployment are taken out. As you move up the career ladder, managers will earn in the $40,000 to $50,000 annual range, directors move up to $50,000 to $60,000 region, and vice presidents will be earning $75,000 and above, depending on their areas of responsibility. As many of the leading digital music distribution firms are located in northern California, costs of living in the San Francisco-Silicon Valley area are much higher than the national norm. As a result, if this is your intended career path, you should consult with various cost-of-living websites that analyze and calculate such data to see the difference in the cost of living between your home region and where you hope to work.

Nonetheless, new hires are joining the digital music distribution sector and making their mark. There are those who are rising up the ranks to the better-paying positions. What characterizes them after they prove themselves during their dues-paying period? Unanimously, the managers opined that demonstrating a strong grasp of how content is created and shared through various platforms (YouTube, Twitter, Instagram, Facebook, and whatever new platforms evolve) is an absolute essential set of skills for anyone wishing to build a career in digital music distribution. They also suggested that aspiring candidates start to build those skills with practical experience while you are still in school and before you begin looking for jobs or internships. One offered very specific advice:

> *Start a channel with a band on campus, and work every possible social media. Every digital music distributor wants people that know how to effectively build an audience. By doing this, you can learn how to use the channel to monetize the music, tag, embed, annotate, and get fans coming back or subscribing to your feeds. The goal is to get subscribers, not one-time viewers. Direct people from watching something on YouTube to finding it on Google Play or wherever your songs are available. Doing this will allow you to demonstrate your skills, your passion, your capacity for independent thought and problem-solving, which is what firms are seeking.*

A helpful reference is YouTube's *Creator Playbook*, a free online resource to guide users in building their audiences for their online content. Another manager advised candidates to consider becoming Google AdWords certified, so that they have learned how the basic search engine optimization routines function and are familiar with all the terminology that goes along with search-based marketing and customer acquisition. This advice correlated closely with another digital media manager who advised that in an interview situation, having the data and metrics for project work a candidate has done at one's fingertips will help candidates stand out from other applicants.

Smart companies make decisions "by the numbers," and metrics are the "prove it to me" coinage of the digital music distribution world.

> "Smart companies make decisions 'by the numbers,' and metrics are the 'prove it to me' coinage of the digital music distribution world."

One of the managers we interviewed suggested that a candidate have a project they managed, such as a marketing campaign for a local artist's album release, prepared to present like a case study, with the before and after results and what strategy and methods were employed. Be sure you include the metrics that demonstrate the growth or improvements you helped achieve. It was even suggested that making a two- to three-minute video documentary of the project and its results and saying, "Let me send you what I did," via a link would be very impactful. That level of preparedness is likely to lead the person interviewing you to conclude you are a person that may be a good addition to their team. Based on our conversations with these digital music managers, being able to talk with confidence and in detail about the results of your efforts in music marketing and promotion are absolutely essential to standing out from the crowd of job seekers in this sector.

The other characteristic that can help someone rise up the career ladder in digital music distribution is to be a teacher to the older generation that is still working in and managing the industry. Established managers and executives are looking constantly to younger hires to come up with new ideas—innovative ways to address opportunity and solve problems. If you know more about the social media platforms than the person hiring you, the hiring manager will be intrigued. *The Wall Street Journal* recently reported that many mid-career executives are increasingly tapping new hires to teach them about new technology and its potential impact on their businesses. This is a ready-made opportunity to further distinguish yourself as a job candidate or a new hire. To understand what will be appropriate and relevant, you need to be engaged in the dialog around the workplace and to be an active, full-time listener. Then, when the time is appropriate, see what you might be able to add to the conversation. For instance, thinking about the possible associations between a particular artist and whom they sound like to target a Tweet or blog posting, or doing some targeted advertising that might draw in new subscribers to the band's channels. Or teach your boss a new app that can be linked to some of the content or artists you are promoting to expand the audience. If you are fortunate enough to secure an internship at one of these digital music firms, realize that even if the position is unpaid, you will be closely scrutinized, and that generally after six to nine months, successful interns will often be groomed for a paying position, during which time they will be further mentored. So don't make the mistake of "just phoning it in" for your digital music distribution internship. You'll never be considered for a full time, paid position, if you do. The digital music distribution field is one that holds tremendous promise. Although paid, entry-level positions offer subsistence wages to start, there is a great range of opportunities in the field. For those who are able to identify opportunities and help forge connections between various stakeholders in the marketplace, the future for growth is substantial.

SOUND MIXER FOR TELEVISION

As was mentioned earlier, television production continues to grow as more options for consumers emerge for watching their favorite niche shows. Sound post production for television is a field that offers a range of job options for young professionals, once again, with a dues-paying process up front along with requisite knowledge of sound, audio recording and editing systems, and general practices in the film and television post production industry. My own career included nine years spent helping to launch and manage a successful state-of-the-art audio post-production facility in San Francisco, serving the film, television, and advertising industries. Our clients included MTV, Academy-award winning filmmakers, and many of the top ad agencies in the nation. To ensure that the information about this market sector and career opportunities was up to date, we spoke to a number of sound mixers currently working for cable and broadcast networks in Los Angeles to confirm the career ladder and salary information included in this section.

When one is getting a foothold in the sound for film and television industry, any form of visual media that affords an opportunity to contribute should be taken, no matter if it is a student film, a public service announcement for a nonprofit, or a documentary film project. The key thing is getting real world project-based experience as early and often as possible. There is a clear career ladder in this market sector, which usually includes interns, entry-level positions, then successive promotions until one earns the opportunity to be chosen as a sound mixer for a television series, be it a drama, sitcom, or reality show. (The film sound career ladder is similar, but due to the different production schedules and budgets found in the film industry as opposed to those in television, some of the positions will vary.)

Here is the career ladder in the television sound engineering field.

TV Audio Post Production Engineering Career Ladder

Sound Mixer

Sound Editor (Dialog, Music, or Sound Effects)

Assistant Sound Editor (Dialog, Music, or Sound Effects)

Tape Library/Dubbing

Intern/Runner

FIG. 5.3. TV Audio Post Production Engineering Career Ladder

Depending on the complexity, length, and budget for any given project, there may be as few as one audio engineer to a phalanx of dialog, music, and sound-effects sound crew assigned to a show. Our dialogs with current television audio mixers confirmed that salary range varies greatly, largely based on one's experience and past credits. Nearly all the internship positions are unpaid, with most requiring that the intern be enrolled in some type of program to receive academic credit. If interns distinguish themselves, they may be offered a paid, entry-level position, such as a tape librarian or dubbing technician (audio and video copyist).

Such entry-level positions may pay in the $24,000 to $28,000 range, depending on the facility, the market, and clientele. As one moves up the career ladder, the pay for sound editors may range from $40,000 to $60,000 per year. Once you graduate to being the lead mixer for a television show, depending on the length of the shows and its overall success, annual salaries often exceed $100,000 per year.

Similar to other areas of the music industry, junior sound staff, once they have proven themselves as reliable and capable, are trained and mentored further by senior staff. Through this process, you can work your way up and expand your skill sets. Experience using Pro Tools, the de facto standard for today's audio post production work, is absolutely essential, as are strong aural acuity skills—the ability to hear and listen with great precision. Veteran sound mixers emphasized that once you've developed the technical proficiency, it becomes "all about your ear, which is something that develops over time. The more you learn how to hear and become a very good critical listener, you can decide what is important and what isn't important for a particular scene."

What will help the aspiring audio post newbie stand out among the competition? Similar to the advice offered by the digital music distribution managers we spoke with, having specific projects available for review, and that you can discuss concisely and in detail the problems you addressed and how you solved them is the best way to stand out. Whether it is a student film, a music video for a friend's band, or any well produced short visual media project, this is the most direct way to be evaluated for potential internship or paid position. As one of the veteran mixers stated, "You really, really increase your impact by having an electronic calling card that shows, 'I have done audio-post work, and this is what resulted.'"

One final difference between this career track and the two previous ones, is that a great many audio post-production engineers are making a go of it as independent contractors. Such work, also known as "freelancing," can provide a range of options and a diverse range of clients that call up for repeat work on their successive projects. This allows production companies to flex with need, rather than having too many audio mixers on staff at any given time. It's important to note that before being paid, there is usually a short training period on the production company's equipment (on your own time) until they determine you are up to speed and ready for actual projects. Becoming an established freelance audio mixer can often lead to an offer to take on a staff position, at a production company, television network, or on a sound stage.

So, the road to a stable, good-paying job can start as an intern, working one's way up the career ladder at a single firm, or as a freelance audio post engineer, working at a number of companies, anticipating the day when a full-time salaried position with benefits and other perks may be obtained.

SIMILAR BUSINESS STRUCTURES

Regardless of whether the three industry sectors that were just presented are among your areas of interest, compiling the kind of information just presented on key skills, career ladder, earnings, and advice from professionals working in that sector are absolutely vital to understanding how to position yourself as a viable candidate for that field. Whatever sector of the music or entertainment industry you pursue, you will find very similar ladders of increasing responsibility, challenges, and rewards.

For instance, if you decide that you would like to be head of A&R at a record label or program director at a top radio station, you will need to do the research necessary to map out a career ladder similar to the ones outlined previously. Determine the specific job titles, responsibilities, and earning potential on the career track leading to your eventual goal. Researching and understanding the nitty-gritty details of the career ladder will help you avoid investing in a career path that may never meet your expectations for creative or financial development. Create a chart with the key skills and responsibilities, salaries, titles, and anticipated time frame for promotions before you dive fully into a career path. Doing so will help you to understand what it will take to get to the top in your field of interest.

WORKSHOP 5.1. BUILDING YOUR CAREER LADDER

Pick one of the three "dream jobs" you identified in the Magic Lamp Workshop. Using the blank form below, fill in the various rungs on the career ladder that you think will lead from entry level to the most accomplished level in that field. Add more rungs as needed. If you're not sure of the exact information, start with just the top rung and the bottom rung, and as you learn more about the field, fill in the middle rungs of the career ladder. Don't worry if you haven't yet discovered salary information for your respective career ladders; we'll tackle gathering that info in the next workshop.

What resources can you use to fill in the career ladder with accurate and up-to-date information?

_____ Market Sector

Title	Key Skills and Responsibilities	Salary Range
Intern		
Executive Level		

ACTION ITEM

Make a list of friends, mentors, teachers, and other acquaintances that likely have a link to a working professional in this field. Start a list in your Career Portfolio of connections to your fields of interest.

⑦ **WORKSHOP 5.2.** HOW MUCH WILL YOU EARN?

Now that you are zeroing in on specific jobs and career areas, it's time to develop some specific salary information to plug in to the career ladder you built in the previous workshop. To find out this information, you'll need to invest some time and effort using a variety of these resources to gain access to specific and accurate information.

Researching salary information is one of the most challenging parts of your career planning and preparation. Here's a starting list of resources that you can use now to check on entry-level salaries for your "dream job."

(If your job is extremely specific, for instance, front-of-house mixer for a major touring act, you may find little salary information published online and must rely on networking with current professionals to get a handle on current earning potential.)

Job Category: Production Assistant

Source	Salary Listed	L.A.-Specific	National Average	Comments
Indeed.com	$24,000	Yes		Reported this regional average was 2% above national average and linked to average salary data for fifteen jobs with related titles.
Glassdoor.com	$25,703 $26,395 $36,000 $36,865	Yes Yes Yes	 Yes 	Provided national average, which appears to be high, as well as links to specific job listings in the LA market with salaries posted.
Simplyhired.com	$49,000		Yes	Number is likely greatly inflated due to fact that it was calculated using average salary for all jobs with the term "production assistant" anywhere in job listing
Salary.com	$28,178		Yes	No free regional specific salary data available.
Payscale.com	$31,169	Yes		Stated this was in the "low range" of overall salaries for this position and region.

Online Salary Databases

We looked at five online salary databases that provide free statistics on salaries in hundreds of market sectors. We used the job title of "production assistant" and chose Los Angeles as our geographic point of reference. As you can see in the table on the following page, the results varied greatly. Part of the reason for these variances is that these companies rely on differing data sources including employer-supplied survey data, employee-supplied survey data, or aggregating salary information found on job listings. Glassdoor.com and Payscale.com rely on employees to provide detailed job information and salary data, while Salary.com uses employer survey information to generate its salary projections. The two remaining sites, Simplyhired.com and Indeed.com, build a salary snapshot by scouring job listings found on the Web and analyzing the salary information on those listings to report a salary range.

Taken as a whole, the picture looks a bit murky, especially with the more than 100 percent salary variation. But if we throw out the data found on Simplyhired.com, due to lack of relevance, the seven remaining salary data points yield an average of $29,758 annual salary for an L.A. production assistant position. This is the likely range that an entry level candidate should budget for, if they were seeking to enter entertainment production in the Southern California region. Our advice is to use the salary data websites as rough salary guides after applying some critical analysis to what the resulting data points are, and to be suspicious of any salaries that seem higher than what you anticipated, especially for any entry level positions. Don't stop your salary research with these sites, however. You need to use as many of the following resources as possible to create the most comprehensive salary information you can.

U.S. Bureau of Labor Statistics

A wealth of salary and employment data can be accessed on their website www.bls.gov. It is drawn from their employer surveys. You can search for Wages by Area or Occupation as well as Earnings by Industry. Generally, the site is good to gain a broad overview of a market sector and to see what geographic differences there may be for the same job across the country. It can be especially useful if you are researching a possible career change or relocation to a new city. BLS also provides general trend information that can be useful for understanding how economic factors are affecting the industries it reports on. It does not provide company specific information. The Occupational Outlook Handbook identifies career tracks that may be growing or shrinking and is supplemented every ninety days with an

Occupational Outlook Quarterly Summary. A BLS Occupational Outlook in the Entertainment and Sports area listed that for the designation of "Music Directors and Composers," nationwide jobs will grow to employ 102,800 people in this field by 2020. It also reported that the median annual salary in May 2010 was $45,970. Adjusted for inflation to 2014, this salary would be approximately $49,135. A look at Media and Communication Occupations provides access to a report for broadcast and sound engineering technicians. This reveals that such jobs will also grow to 128,600 by 2020 and that median salary in May 2010 was $39,870, which, adjusted for inflation, should pencil out at $42,615 in 2014. Spend some time looking through a few of the many jobs that are documented on this site, as well as looking over the listings for highest paying, projected fastest growing fields, and what industries will be adding the most new jobs. Again, the salary information should be used as a general guide. The site also allows you to sift jobs by a variety of parameters including the salary range, education required, growth rate, etc. The tabs at the top of each field also provide some basic background information, as well as a final tab that links to trade associations and other information sources for the market area.

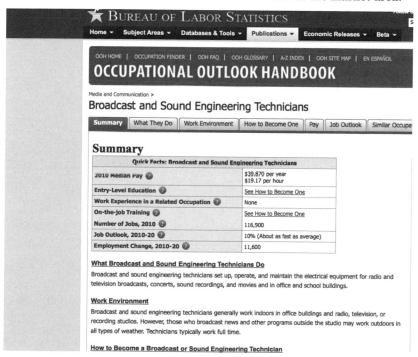

FIG. 5.4. BLS Occupational Outlook. The U.S. Department of Labor's Bureau of Labor Statistics provides annual updates on many music-related careers and job prospects. Here are the *Occupational Outlook Handbook* tabbed pages for "Broadcast and Sound Engineering Technicians," aka sound techs.

Working Professionals

Do you know someone working in the field you hope to enter? If so, they are one of your best sources for entry-level salary information. If you make a point to meet at least one working professional per month in your key areas of interest, you will soon have a network of professional contacts that not only can provide you with up-to-the-minute career and salary information, but who may also tip you off to unadvertised job or internship opportunities as they arise. Remember, instead of asking for very specific salary information, ask your contact for a "salary range" for an entry level position in the field that he or she works in. That's a common request and one they likely have provided earlier to others in your position.

Trade Organizations

Although we'll cover them in more depth in a future chapter, now's a good time to find out if the area of the industry you hope to enter has a trade association, and if so, whether they publish any general or specific salary or wage information. If you can't find such information online, reach out to the relevant organization with a phone call to their head office.

 ACTION ITEM

Add a Salary Information folder into your Career Portfolio, which includes the information you gathered in completing this workshop.

6 Further Expanding Your Career Knowledge Base

After studying the three career ladders in the previous chapter and starting to research salary information in your intended field, you now have the basic idea of how various industry areas are organized with regard to titles, roles, salaries, etc. It's crucial to have a thorough understanding of the skills, responsibilities, hours, pay range, and future prospects for a particular job or field in the music industry, so that you can assess whether or not you have (or can develop) the skills and connections to land that job.

Let's explore various means to research what working professionals actually do. The first step is to identify and keep up regularly with credible published sources including magazines, journals, and websites covering the segment of the industry that you wish to enter while also reading some books that explore various career paths. If you aspire to be a label exec, agent, musician, or producer, then check out a few biographies that chronicle the path that various artists or executives have taken to the top. Record producer Sir George Martin; musician Amir "Questlove" Thompson; label executives Clive Davis, Tommy Mottola, and Jac Holzman; and super agent Ian Copeland each have inked compelling autobiographies that provide the nitty-gritty details of how they became leaders in their fields. Entertainment industry moguls Richard Branson and David Geffen have been profiled in bios, *Losing My Virginity* and *The Operator*, respectively. Apple's Steve Jobs arguably has had as great an impact on the business of selling music and media, so his biography, *Steve Jobs* by Walter Isaacson, makes for insightful reading for anyone wishing to enter the entertainment field. For aspiring record producers, Phil Ramone's autobiography, *Making Records: The Scenes Behind the Music* is essential reading. Richard Buskin's *Inside Tracks*, Howard Massey's *Behind the Glass*, and Maureen Droney's *Mix Masters* provide mini-interviews of many of the most influential record producers of the last fifty years of pop music. *Masters of Music*, by Mark Small and Andrew Taylor, features interviews with a wide range of music industry superstars who reveal how they broke into the big time.

With regard to locating written job descriptions for specific jobs, the Internet is a rich repository of job descriptions in nearly every area of the business. (We'll analyze job descriptions in detail in chapter 8.) Many music industry firms are now posting jobs and internships on one or more of the industry-specific career websites (also detailed in appendix B), as well as on sites such as Craigslist. Additionally, one of the books referenced earlier, *Career Opportunities in the Music Industry*, has useful general descriptions for dozens of music-oriented jobs, while the previously mentioned Artists House Music website, is loaded with interviews with working professionals from nearly every market sector in the music business.

The second means to learn more about the details of a particular career path is to network with professionals working in the business. Depending on what jobs you are aspiring to, most likely, there are working professionals in your area with whom you can make contact. Although this type of research requires more effort on your part, the quality and quantity of information, along with the ability to ask specific questions and the freshness of the information (to complement the information you are learning from print and online sources), make this an essential resource that can provide you with more detailed and nuanced information than you can learn from simply reading.

If you are enrolled in a school program in music business, entertainment management, or recording arts, ask your faculty and fellow students to keep you posted on professionals who may be coming to school to speak or give clinics. Seek out opportunities to be a volunteer at industry events or a conference in exchange for conference access. This is another valuable way to forge insider connections. In the past few years, a number of our students have gained access to a wide range of high profile music industry events by serving as volunteers. Some of these volunteer gigs have led directly to internships or employment with top firms. Lastly, working with your friends and teachers, constantly seek out industry folk who have been helpful in the past in placing students as interns.

WORKSHOP 6. YOUR DREAM SHEET

This workshop is a series of questions to help you do a basic self-assessment of where you hope to go and what you hope to accomplish in the music business. It should be considered a living document, much like your résumé, and kept as part of your Career Portfolio and reviewed every six months.

Answer the questions to complete your Dream Sheet now. When you complete the workshop, add it to your Career Portfolio. Mark your calendar six months ahead that you will read and update your Dream Sheet with the information you have learned in the interim.

Use the "Save As" function to keep the earlier dated copies of your Dream Sheets so you can see how your perspectives evolve over time. A commentary is provided on the pages following the Dream Sheet, but don't look at it until you've completed all the questions in the workshop the first time.

1. What attracts you to a career in the music industry?

2. List, in order of preference, the three jobs you would most like to be doing in the music industry? Although you've been considering your "dream jobs" in earlier workshops, now it's time to focus on the top three and rank them in order of priority.

    A.

    B.

    C.

3. Where do you want to be career-wise in five years? In ten years?

4. Where do you want to be personally and financially (salary range, own home, married/single/family, location) in five years? In ten years?

5. How much money do you think you could earn *in the next one to two years* if you landed a position on the career ladder for any of the three jobs you listed above in question 2?
After doing some basic salary research, list the annual income range for each.

    A.

    B.

    C.

6. Identify and list up to three jobs in which you have felt most fulfilled.

   A.

   B.

   C.

7. For each job listed in (6), identify specifically what made you feel fulfilled.

   A.

   B.

   C.

8. Identify and list up to three jobs in which you have felt the least fulfilled.

   A.

   B.

   C.

9. For each job in (8), identify specifically what made you feel unfulfilled.

   A.

   B.

   C.

10. Pick the number-one company for whom you would like to work today. Imagine you are being considered for a plum internship or position at that company. Assume that hundreds of others will be applying for this same position. Write a paragraph explaining what attributes you believe make you the *best* candidate for the opportunity.

11. State the single, most important thing you hope to gain from a career in the music industry.

7 **DREAM SHEET** COMMENTARY

(Don't read this until you have finished your Dream Sheet!)

In Workshop 1, you identified a few over-arching career goals, which help frame the rest of the work you are doing throughout this book. Understanding your own motivations is essential to develop the resiliency to make it in the music industry. The Dream Sheet workshop bores down deeper into those motivations after you've done more career research and will help you better understand the self-reflection and commitment to ongoing research into your intended field needed to help you position yourself as a viable candidate for the job you aspire to. Career development is purposeful, time-consuming work, but work that pays off handsomely by giving you an edge over many other candidates. The following commentary relates back to the numbered questions in the Dream Sheet on the previous pages.

Question 1: Knowing what attracts you to a career in the music industry will help you prioritize the various options and choices you will be faced with during your career evolution.

Question 2: These are jobs that you need to continue researching in order to determine the skills, job prospects, career ladder, and earning potential for each.

Question 3: Time waits for no one. Setting goals (covered in the next section) on a realistic timeline is an important part of developing your career successfully. You must also confirm that your goals are realistic by discussing them as you meet a wider range of working professionals. Revise your career goals as you uncover the story behind the jobs that interest you most. Doing so will ensure that you keep focused on the next important steps you need to take to realize your dream career.

Question 4: Nearly all music industry career development requires a number of years of dues-paying—working long hours for low wages in often under-appreciated positions. Find out what the people who are doing the jobs you aspire to do are earning as their careers evolve. Ask them how they kept afloat financially during their own dues-paying period.

Question 5: You may be surprised to learn that many low-level positions in the industry pay about the same as working in a restaurant. Many students make the mistake of focusing on the top-tier salaries in a given field and don't adequately consider or prepare for making ends meet on an entry-level paycheck. (Attention aspiring record producers: this is particularly true in your field!) Find out which music career areas offer the best opportunities for advancement and salary growth. The best way to find out is to speak with working professionals. The polite way to ask is to inquire what the "salary range" is for a specific job on the career ladder you are researching.

Questions 6–9: Hopefully, you have had a job that you excelled in—one that made you feel that your contributions were important to the success of the company, regardless of what field it was in. Likewise, you may have also suffered through "the job from hell." Reviewing the high and low points of jobs is another important step in assessing what kinds of tasks and duties you have been successful at. Finding the job you love and can excel in is often the most direct path to career and financial success. There's truth in the old saying, "Do what you really love, and the money will follow." Going through this exercise will also help you identify these points, which are often brought up in job interviews to probe a candidate's suitability for a particular job opening.

Question 10: If you can't articulate your passion for a career in the music industry, you will fail to make a lasting impression on your future boss. Every performer, manager, or producer that we know drives himself or herself relentlessly to be the absolute best. Start practicing now to explain, in specific terms, exactly what you can bring to the employer's firm that will help them be more successful. This so-called "elevator pitch" is an essential tool to have in your career tool kit. We'll look at its role, as well as how to turn it into your own personal YouTube commercial, in chapter 14.

Question 11: Is it money, power, fame, or artistic fulfillment you seek? Knowing this will also help you reach decisions when your career comes to the inevitable fork in the road. It's okay to be attracted by fame and fortune. Just remember that you have to make ends meet on your journey to the top, and the overwhelming majority of folks working in the music business passionately love their job, while earning a middle class salary.

CHAPTER

7 Preparing for Success with Goal-Setting

No matter what you tackle in life, setting and achieving goals is key to becoming successful. And setting goals is really as simple as defining various long-term, mid-term, and short-term goals. A goal must be written down and have a date by which you intend to complete it. For example, applying for ten music industry jobs in your area of interest within the next ninety days is an attainable goal, since you have complete control over whether or not you can achieve this goal. As your career development plans evolve, remember that although we all aim to fulfill our dreams, it's important to focus on the things you can control and that have realistic timelines.

> *"A goal must be written down and have a date by which you intend to complete it."*

As an example, let's say that your eventual goal is to become a successful, full-time songwriter. Right now, you're working at a bank. But your long-term goal (five–ten years) is to write top-10 pop songs. You also need a mid-term goal that's achievable in one and one-half to four years because it's unlikely one can go from being a bank teller to a hit songwriter overnight. So what might be a good mid-term goal? Perhaps a mid-term goal is to be a published songwriter and have two to three songs recorded on an artist's album that's on the charts. Pretty darn good; you got a paycheck. That's a very realistic mid-term goal.

For short term goals (the next twelve to eighteen months), it would be realistic to intensely study and learn the craft of songwriting. For instance, you discover (via detective work) that there will be a songwriting master class going on at Berklee College of Music taught by a well-known songwriter over a three-day weekend. You beg, borrow, and steal the money to go to it. Take time off work. Borrow a car, if yours is a clunker. You get there because you're determined. Other short-term goals may include joining a songwriter's organization, joining a music collaboration website such as Music Gateway, and attending their regular meetings or workshops.

The craft of songwriting requires you to constantly be recording. At one point, you'll be ready to put together a demo. You don't need to hire a symphony orchestra for your demo. If you work with one good musician/arranger, you can do just about anything that's required at this point. This demo may be a short- or mid-term goal, depending on where you start your songwriting odyssey.

How about identifying and subscribing to key trade magazines? That would be a short-term goal. Another is to locate a teacher/ mentor. Say you attended a songwriting workshop given last year, and you began to correspond with one of the teachers via email. Perhaps they would take on a student like yourself because you can learn so much in the right mentor or teacher relationship. Even if they're writing in a different genre than you are, the craft of songwriting is nearly identical across styles and genres. It's learning how to tell a story that connects on a gut level with the listener. And being exposed to those who are further along on your intended career path, no matter what it is, is essential to speeding up your learning process.

This is how developing your own short-, mid-, and long-term goals will help you to chart a path towards your ideal career. Let's say you identify four short-term goals and set a six-month window to complete them. Your mid-term goal mentioned previously—getting songs onto a record—is your one-and-a-half- to four-year window. And your eventual goal of writing a song that goes up the charts is your five- to ten-year goal. Break it down into bite-size chunks, and you will have a clear roadmap to take you to your long-term goals.

Don't just stay up every night biting your fingernails worrying, trying to write that magical hit song. You may nail it, but your odds are so long, it's like playing the lottery. Don't lose sight of your overall goal, intermediate steps, and your timeline. Make your goals concrete with a chart in your composing room. Review the short-term activities in process now that are going to take you to your long-term goals.

Remember, it's human nature to want to avoid setting goals and timelines. However, without using this tool and others like the upcoming marketable skill-set workshop and building relationships to working professionals, careers in the music industry may well seem distant and out of reach. You won't know if your short-term goals are in sync with what's required to make it on a particular career path if you haven't researched your area of interest. Desire alone will not make your dream a reality.

> *"Desire alone will not make your dream a reality."*

If you want to be a music director at an Internet music service such as Spotify or Pandora, you've got to know what it takes to get there. What skills, experience, salary, and geographic moves will be required? All that information must be at your fingertips. Mark down this information gathering as a goal with a realistic time frame to acquire it. When you have that information, it will be crystal clear to you whether or not that is the right career path for you. If you don't do your detective work, you may spend months or years pursuing a career path that really isn't what you want from life. Don't make that mistake.

That's why goal setting is so important in this industry: everybody is following their star and chasing their dream. Almost everyone wants to be in the creative side of the business: to write, record, sing, produce, promote, or engineer that smash hit. But how do you put yourself in the situation where you're actually working with the artist who can write those hit songs? How can you work with a Lil' Wayne, Fall Out Boy, Bruno Mars, or Lady Antebellum?

This is the secret: Define and achieve the little steps (short- and mid-term goals) that will help you eventually achieve your long-term goals. And pat yourself on the back each time another small milestone is achieved.

So to recap, you need to identify attainable goals and set a timeline for accomplishing each one. Review goals as often as possible. Use your calendar planner (MS Outlook, iCal, etc.) and your Career Portfolio to track your progress. If you don't write down due dates and check up on your progress, you won't achieve your goals! Update your goals as you move forward. Some will be completed and you can cross them off. New ones will become clear to you as you continue your career development. Make adjustments as you learn more, meet new mentors, and decide what is most important to your career development.

Finally, remember to be patient. Be sure to keep your career goals visible in whatever way is most present in your daily life; the workshop on the next page will show you a handy format to organize them. Prominently post them near your computer or in your personal rehearsal space, workspace, or other visible spot. Doing so reminds you daily of your goals, nudging you to gauge your progress to achieving them. Share your goals with your significant other or a trusted family member so they can provide encouragement, especially if you hit a rough patch in your journey. Maintain and update those goals, pat yourself on the back when you accomplish each one, and let the goal-setting process work for you. If you are diligent in maintaining your goals, you have a much better chance of achieving long-term professional, financial, and personal success.

GOAL SETTING MODEL: A SONGWRITER'S ROAD TO SUCCESS		
Short-Term Goals **6 – 18 Months**	**Mid-Term Goals** **1½ – 4 Years**	**Long-Term Goals** **5 – 10 Years**
• Subscribe to trade magazines; get RSS feeds of best blogs, tip sheets, and breaking news • Enroll in songwriting classes • Find a teacher/mentor • Join a songwriter's trade association and set up a Music Gateway songwriter account; attend events, conferences • Start to build a professional network in your area of interest	• Publish songs • Begin building relationships with publishers, artists, managers, producers • Two to three songs recorded • Get involved in a performing rights society • Investigate cowriting options • Regularly record demos; write and pitch new material	• Record or write a Top-10 song • Have songs placed in films, TV, or ads • Collaborate with leading artists and lyricists • Win GRAMMY® for Song of the Year!

Fig. 7.1. Goal Setting Model: A Songwriter's Road to Success

WORKSHOP 7. SETTING YOUR GOALS

Identify your ultimate career goal, and list a few of the short-, mid-, and long-term goals that you believe will help you attain your ultimate music industry career goal. Don't ignore personal, life, recreational, and financial goals. They are equally as important as your career goals, as you need to balance work with appropriate play. Successful music industry pros with long careers understand the value of prioritizing both personal and professional career and life objectives. If you plan to have a long and successful career, you will need to also understand how important striving to maintain a work-life balance can be.

List Your Short-Term Goals: 6 to 18 months

_____

_____

_____

_____

_____

_____

List Your Mid-Term Goals: 1½ to 4 years

_____

_____

_____

_____

_____

_____

_____

_____

List Your Long-Term Goals: 5 to 10 or more years

_____

_____

_____

_____

_____

_____

_____

_____

_____

 ACTION ITEM

Save this set of goals to your Career Portfolio, and print out a copy to put on display in your workspace so you see your current goals every day.

A good deal of information has been laid out in part I of the book—essential ideas and information that will allow you to make the most of the upcoming sections. We advise you to review part I after you complete the rest of the book. The ideas and notes about goal-setting bear reconsideration as you explore your career options and build bridges into the communities of professionals whom you hope to join.

With the overview of the music industry and your growing knowledge about the music industry career areas that most interest you, you're ready to embark on the next phase of your music industry career development journey: building your Personal Career Tool Kit!

II

Your Personal Career Tool Kit

In part II, you'll learn the best way to present yourself using a variety of career tools, including a professional résumé, how to leverage social media throughout your professional career, the importance of your personal "brand" to potential employers, understanding job descriptions, how to assemble a "career road map" for the jobs that interest you most, what makes up your marketable skill set, and tips on professional letter writing. When you have completed part II, you will have a Personal Career Tool Kit ready to use in your job search. Let's begin.

8 Analyzing Job Descriptions

There is no better way to gauge your readiness for a particular job than to look over a detailed job description or job profile. Reviewing a comprehensive job description of a role you aspire to will help you to understand typical responsibilities, minimum qualifications, and desired attributes of those in a particular position, and will allow you to take stock of your own experience and skills and how they stack up. Do you have what it takes to not only qualify for the role, but to *compete* for the role? Are there gaps in your skills and experience that you could be addressing now to make you more competitive for such a role in the future? As when we learned to analyze career ladders in chapter 5, we'll now dissect two job descriptions so that you are familiar with the process. Let's start with a job profile for an online media intern, from a San Francisco-based music venue.

JOB OFFERING: ONLINE MEDIA INTERN, LIVE MUSIC VENUE

Job Profile

Duties: Performing tasks in various areas of venue management, including promotions, marketing, ticket sales, and administrative duties under the direction of management.

Key Responsibilities: Marketing and promotion development, social media management, website administration, user engagement and interaction, market research, and ticket sales.

Compensation: $12/hr.; 24 hour per week schedule, rotate between A.M. and P.M. shifts

Prerequisites

Education or Training: Preference given to applicants with college degree in progress or completed in music industry, communication, and marketing.

Experience: Working knowledge of social media tools, Microsoft Office, and Adobe Photoshop and Dreamweaver.

Special Skills and Personality Traits: Strong evidence of excellent written and oral communication skills, ability to work independently, self motivated and driven, organizational and time management skills, eagerness to learn, brightness, aggressiveness, knowledge of music and/or live music business.

Preferred: Own your own smart phone and laptop, extensive knowledge of social media marketing (Facebook/Twitter/Instagram, etc.), experience in similar work.

FIG. 8.1. Job Profile for Online Media Intern

POSITION ANALYSIS

An intern working in the online media support role at a music venue will perform a number of audience related tasks as outlined above. Depending on the size of the venue, the intern may report directly to the house manager, marketing manager, box office manager, or other parallel staff position.

As a venue intern, you will be exposed to all facets of operating a successful live music business. Since the majority of ticket sales are now purchased online, not only are the skills and experiences learned in this position likely to be highly valued by other employers, they will also be transferable to a variety of other fields including sports, theater, and other music venues or tours.

Most internships also involve doing some of the tedious work (mailing list maintenance, data entry, etc.) that is often "saved for later" by regular staff. Such opportunities provide a chance to prove yourself and to learn some of the necessary routines that all successful businesses must complete, no matter how mundane.

Although this internship does offer a wage, most in our industry do not. However, if you are enrolled in a college program, internship credit is often available. Even if you are not getting paid, you still must arrive on time for work every day, maintain a positive attitude at all times, look for ways to assist and support all fellow workers, and contribute constantly to helping the company be more successful. Internships are very often auditions for a paid position at the firm.

Although a position might not open up at the firm where you do your internship, if you have impressed your supervisors and coworkers, they often will know of other opportunities at various firms in the region and may, if asked, recommend you to a manager or human resources staffer at those firms. Once you've proven yourself to be valuable, many savvy managers will try to help you land a position to continue your way into the industry.

Education and Computer Skills

This position gives preference to students studying in a related major. I learned of this position due to a venue knowing that my school has a successful music management program, so use your campus connections to discover similar opportunities in your region. The position is also advertising that some experience in social media is necessary to compete for the position, as well as knowledge of specific computer programs.

Experience/Skills/Personality

For this paid internship, strong interpersonal, communication, and self-management skills are a must. Since the live music industry is a people business, the best candidates will clearly demonstrate a fit with the employer's own sense of purpose, place, and values. Being outgoing will advance one's prospects for this position.

If you're serious about a career in the music industry, you must take apart job listings to really understand the details, specific requirements and salary information. If you haven't done the research and you just blunder along, how do you know you're going to get where you want? How will you know a job has the potential to earn what you want to earn?

Game Music and Sound Designer

Let's examine a different type of job, based on an actual open position listing for a video game developer.

A job description such as this one helps you to lay out a Career Road Map, as it includes the specific skills, talents, and experience needed to obtain this position and prosper in a particular area of the industry. It may also reference salary information. In tandem with an area-specific career ladder, you then have both the general and specific tools to measure your readiness for that position. By developing a Career Road Map, you will be able to know where you're headed and if you have arrived, so don't embark on pursuing a particular career path without one.

With a job description in hand, take an inventory of the skills and knowledge required to fill the position successfully, and determine the areas in which you may be lacking knowledge.

"By developing a Career Road Map, you will be able to know where you're headed and if you have arrived, so don't embark on pursuing a particular career path without one."

JOB OFFERING: VIDEO GAME MUSIC/SOUND DESIGNER

Job Title: Video game music and sound designer; full-time, salaried position

Position Summary: This person will work with software designers and senior sound staff to create music and sounds for the company's latest products. In addition to maintaining the highest possible audio production values, the sound designer will be responsible for adhering to the stylistic approach determined for the specific product. Ability to complete work within an established timeline is required.

Job Responsibilities:

- Edit sound effects and synchronize with animation and other interactive elements of the product.

- Edit dialog.

- Compose music segments, songs, and cues to enhance the product.

- Arrange music for the types of synthesizers utilized in Macintosh and Windows computers, consoles, and mobile devices, as well as general MIDI synthesizers, adhering to the game design specifications published for each project.

- Review sounds and music to be developed with product development team and software engineers to ensure playability.

- Stay current on various developments in MIDI playback systems for gaming applications.

Qualifications:

- Proven ability to compose music in a wide range of musical styles.

- Four-year degree in music or equivalent practical musical knowledge that can be demonstrated through composition and arranging examples.

- Extensive experience arranging music for various types of synthesizers including those commonly used in the general MIDI specification. Thorough knowledge of synthesis techniques, patch editing, and sequencing software.

- Familiarity with digital sound editing tools such as Digital Performer, Pro Tools, Logic, and Sound Forge. Strong understanding of the principles of digital audio and the physical properties of sound. Must know the basic sound properties of the various families of musical instruments (strings, brass, woodwinds, percussion, etc.).

- Experience with Macintosh and Windows computers required. Basic knowledge of computer language such as C++ helpful but not mandatory. Practical experience in a recording studio environment is a plus.

- Ability to communicate effectively with musicians and other sound staff and to work with offsite talent.

FIG. 8.2. Job Description for Video Game Music Developer

POSITION ANALYSIS

This job description is clearly written with lots of specific information as to the skills and experience that the employer is seeking to fill this position. Although it's not specifically spelled out, a qualified candidate should have experience playing video games. Much like film scoring, video game music serves the needs of the game or story line.

The successful candidate for this position will have a good body of experience as a composer, sound designer, and arranger. He or she will have a strong music and composition background and be well versed in MIDI. Note that although composing is generally a solitary pursuit, this position requires frequent interaction with other members of the software development team. Thus, what are often termed "soft skills"—that is, interpersonal communication, empathy, good listening skills, problem-solving ability, and collaborative expertise—will all be integral into being a successful music and sound designer for this gaming company. Soft skills may not always be listed directly on the job description, but in fact, they are usually a key element of what today's employers are seeking, since so much of what is done in our industry is team-based.

In fact, working collaboratively and adhering to deadlines may be as important considerations as innate compositional abilities. Video game creation requires dozens of creative individuals working in various areas (animation, music, programming, etc.) to work as part of a large team to create a successful product.

In addition to composing and sound design, the successful candidate will also be capable of editing dialog and working in a recording studio setting. This job description makes it easy to start making a Career Road Map of the skills that are required and for a candidate to then compare his or her skill set to see if this person is in fact a viable candidate for the position. Note that no salary information was published, so it's up to you to research the salary range for such a position to be fully prepared for potential interviews and offers if you are a finalist candidate.

WORKSHOP 8.1. BREAK DOWN A DETAILED JOB DESCRIPTION

Below, you will find a well-written and detailed job description for a music publishing administration coordinator at a major publishing company (figure 8.3). Use a highlighter to identify the key skills, experience, competencies, and education that the employer is seeking to fill this position. Make notes in the margins and circle the most important characteristics. Are they required or preferred? Are there any particular programs or software that candidates must use or know? How do you think you would stack up as a candidate for this full-time position? Next, draft a Career Road Map using this job position (which at the time of writing, was an open position) to fill in the key information you've identified using the template (figure 8.4) that follows the Publishing Administration Coordinator job description.

XYZ MUSIC PUBLISHING

JOB DESCRIPTION

Job Title: Publishing Administration Coordinator

Department: Business & Legal Affairs/Royalties

Reports To: Director, Publishing Administration

Supported By:

Interfaces With: All Licensing, Business Affairs, and Royalties staff

As Of: August 2014

POSITION PURPOSE:

To provide administrative support and assistance to the publishing/royalties & licensing departments in XYZ's Manhattan office.

CORE RESPONSIBILITIES:

- Provide administrative support to the Director of Publishing Administration and Sr. Director of Music Licensing.
- Oversee data entry for Music Maestro System.
- Work on cleanup projects for publishing and licensing departments.
- Assist in the creation and rendering of songwriter and publishing admin. royalty statements.

OUTLINE OF SPECIFIC FUNCTIONS:

1. Publishing/Royalties Department Duties

   - Assist with the cleanup of Simple Songs Music clients.
   - File BMI & ASCAP registrations.
   - File PA copyrights for new songs.
   - Maintain the official song list.
   - Update and maintain Music Maestro system.
   - Data entry and/or importation of incoming royalty statements from Record Maestro, sub-publishers, and third parties.
   - Assist in the creation and rendering of songwriter royalty statements. Mail out songwriter and publishing administration royalty statements and checks.
   - Code incoming royalty checks and enter into check log.
   - Prepare catch up statements for songwriters who are not current.
   - Provide requested information and statements for internal and external audits.

2. Licensing Department Duties

   - Work with the Royalty Department to facilitate their duties (providing licensing contracts for them to pay artists and writers accordingly, etc.).
   - Work with the Income Tracker and facilitate his ability to follow up on owed income.
   - Responsible for data input into the newly created Contract/Licensing Database with regards to Master and Publishing deals as well as International Approvals.
   - Draft license agreements, generate invoices, and provide payment and wire transfer information to ensure prompt payments.
   - Look at daily Bank Activity to identify any payments received for licensed material. Code payment and assign to appropriate artist/songwriter.
   - Compile and send weekly reports of payments received (Licensing Report) to VP of Licensing and Publishing.

3. General Administrative Duties

   - Sort daily mail and distribute to the department.
   - Mail checks to the lockbox.
   - Mail catalog requests to MedValu.
   - Check messages on Berkeley general phone line.

REQUIREMENTS:

- Qualified candidates for this position must have at least 2 years of experience in a similar capacity. Candidates that have a degree or certificate in Music Business Management or similar field of study can substitute for the 2 years of experience.

- Bachelor's degree preferred.

- Outstanding verbal, communication, and organization skills are required.

- Proficiency with Microsoft programs including Excel and Word (intermediate or above).

- Candidate must be proactive, able to handle confidential materials, and be detail-oriented.

- Must be a multi-tasked individual, work well under pressure, and be patient but diligent in resolving and completing projects.

- Must demonstrate good judgment.

- General agreement and acceptance of the Company's core values (see attached).

FIG. 8.3. Job Description for Publishing Administrator Coordinator

CAREER ROAD MAP FOR PUBLISHING ADMINISTRATOR

Company Name:

Job Title:

Location:

Date Job Listed:

Specific Skills Required:

Experience or Education Needed:

Software or Creative Skills Needed:

Soft Skills Needed:

Career Ladder (Refer to chapter 5 section on music publishing career ladder)

Salary Estimates (Refer to chapter 5 section with music publishing salary info)

List some working professionals you can talk to about this area of the industry:

FIG. 8.4. Career Road Map Template

ACTION ITEM

Sit down with a colleague and review your Career Road Map for this position. Ask them if they see any key information you may have missed. If so, add it to your Career Road Map for this position to ensure it is as complete as possible.

WORKSHOP 8.2. CREATE YOUR OWN CAREER ROAD MAP

Once you're familiar with the process of analyzing a detailed job description, use the Internet to find another job description, this time in one of your primary areas of interest. Save it, and take an inventory of what specific skills, traits, experience, and other qualifications the employer is seeking. The more detailed the job description is, the better, so your career road map can help you see how closely you match the job requirements.

Don't worry if it's not exactly the dream job you hope to land. The purpose of this workshop is to practice analyzing job descriptions and to learn to quickly summarize the key qualifications any employer is seeking. You'll once again use the headings below to start building your next Career Road Map for the job description and market sector that you most hope to work in. If you have difficulty locating a useful job description for this workshop, try some of the entertainment industry career websites referenced in appendix B.

Company Name:

Job Title:

Location:

Date Job Listed:

Specific Skills Required:

Experience or Education Needed:

Software or Creative Skills Needed:

Soft Skills Needed:

Career Ladder (Use information from earlier workshop or research)

Salary Estimates (Use information from earlier workshop or research)

List some working professionals you can talk to about this area of the industry:

ACTION ITEM

Save this Career Road Map in your Career Portfolio, as you'll be using it soon in the next chapter.

9

Your Marketable Skill Set

The career ladders and job descriptions you've reviewed should paint a picture of what is really out there and how qualified you really are to jump into a music industry role. The truth is that in the music industry (and in any industry), you cannot "hope" your way into a wished-for job. You've got to work for it and earn it through relevant experiences and skills, and you have to be able to communicate those experiences and skills clearly to prove to a prospective employer that you have what it takes to be successful in the role. What follows is a Marketable Skill-Set Assessment worksheet—a tool that will help you to achieve your career goals by identifying and clarifying your marketable skills. For instance, if you are fluent in a second language, that linguistic proficiency is a component of your unique marketable skill set.

Marketable Skill Set Worksheets apply to you as a job seeker in the music industry. You have two types of marketable skills. The first type is your foundation skills—the ones you'll need for any job in today's world. Second are job-specific skills that will be required for you to excel in a specific position in the music industry. When you add up your Foundation and relevant Job-Specific Skills, the sum makes up your Marketable Skill Set. If you completed a Career Road Map from the previous workshop based on an actual job listing in your primary area of interest, you've already identified many of the job-specific skills you'll need to move forward through the next sections. If you did not, you may want to go back and complete that workshop first, in order to get the most out of this chapter.

If you are at the beginning of your skill-set development, especially if you are contemplating a career change, don't tackle specifying your marketable skill set just yet. Instead, read over this section and remember to come back to it after you have spent some time in school studying or in an on-the-job-training situation, such as an industry internship. Then, see how your evolving skills stack up against what you have discovered is needed for a particular music industry job. Otherwise, the exercise may prove frustrating to you.

If you have already developed a number of the skills that are key to employment in your field, then jump in and learn how to assess your marketable skill set against the ones required for the positions you are seeking.

> *"When an employer considers whether or not to hire you, they're basically trying to answer one question: What is this person going to bring to the table to make my life easier and the company more successful?"*

To increase your "hire-ability," your marketable skill set should be made up of the skills that a prospective employer would look at and say, "We can use this person's particular set of skills around here." When an employer considers whether or not to hire you, they're basically trying to answer one question: What is this person going to bring to the table to make my life easier and the company more successful?

That's the single most crucial question you must clearly answer when you set out to create a strong résumé or go for a job interview. What are you going to be able to do to make your next boss's life better and easier, and make the company more efficient and profitable? Your marketable skill set lays out what you're able to do to help your prospective employer.

WORKSHOP 9.1. FOUNDATION SKILLS ASSESSMENT

Taking an inventory of your own marketable skills is a key step in your career development. In today's fast-paced entertainment world, foundation skills are a prerequisite to being considered for most jobs. Foundation skills include professional communications (reading, writing, speaking/presenting), computer applications (word processing, database, Internet), and interpersonal skills (leadership, teamwork, motivation, collaboration). Most employers in any industry will set a minimum threshold for qualification in these areas.

Rate your foundation skills below:

	Strong	Moderate	Needs Work
Reading and writing	☐	☐	☐
Verbal communication	☐	☐	☐
Listening	☐	☐	☐
Understanding and following instructions	☐	☐	☐
Observing and assessing situations and problems	☐	☐	☐
Decision-making	☐	☐	☐
Leadership ability	☐	☐	☐
Teamwork/collaboration	☐	☐	☐
Motivation and work ethic	☐	☐	☐
Computer word processing	☐	☐	☐
Computer database ability	☐	☐	☐
Computer spreadsheet ability	☐	☐	☐
Internet navigation and research	☐	☐	☐
Basic HTML skills	☐	☐	☐

ACTION ITEM

Which areas need improvement? Decide now on a timeline and a means to improve those areas that will strengthen your foundation skills. Write them down in your Career Portfolio as short-term goals, and assign a due date on your calendar for each skill you need to strengthen.

The first nine skills are interpersonal skills that most people will have developed some proficiency in through school, social, and business situations. The last five relate specifically to computers and the Internet. Today's job seeker must have a basic knowledge of those functions in order to be a productive member of any music or entertainment industry company.

If you believe you could benefit from strengthening your interpersonal skills, you should see a counselor at your school or local community college and investigate what type of class will help you develop your skills in this area. Speech, language, and writing classes are a few that can help. Getting involved in a campus or community organization can also help you strengthen those skills. For computer skills and applications, community colleges or online schools offer a low-cost means to develop satisfactory basic skills in each of the five crucial computing areas mentioned in the list.

ANALYZING A SAMPLE MARKETABLE SKILL SET

As an example, let's look at the marketable skill set for an aspiring audio engineer. Remember, this example is illustrative of the level of detail you should strive to assemble for your own music business career path, regardless of what area of the industry you hope to work in.

MARKETABLE SKILL SET FOR AUDIO ENGINEER

Foundation Skills

- Reading/writing/following instructions
- Having the ability to communicate clearly
- Ability to stay calm and cool
- Intermediate to advanced computer skills

Job-Specific Skills

- Critical listening skills
- Audio engineering expertise
- Professionalism, with a good "bedside manner" in the studio

Here's a breakdown of the critical skills that today's recording engineer must possess or develop.

Foundation Skills

1. **You have to be able to read, write, and (yes,) follow instructions.**

    Why is this critical in a recording studio to follow instructions? Well, you could damage the equipment. You will likely be working with people's master recordings that are the result of thousands of hours and perhaps hundreds of thousands of dollars' investment. More importantly, following instructions means that the studio, the first engineer, or the head tech can say, "Tim, go take care of this for me." That person is not always going to have the time to sit and coach Tim through that activity. So they must be confident that Tim is going to be able to listen, integrate what the request is, and get it properly accomplished. If that's the case, then Tim is a person a studio will want to employ. Because they can teach, mentor, and coach him, they can move him ahead on the career track. They can develop a valuable employee for the firm. Following instructions is critical to learning how to work successfully in any type of a studio or production environment.

2. **The ability to communicate clearly.**

    In the recording environment, the client will often say that what they are hearing, "just isn't right," although they may not have the lingo to express exactly what is not working. Recording exposes one to a varying and always interesting cast of characters, each with different backgrounds, goals, and expectations for what they hope to get out of their time in the studio. Sound techs often spend hours trying to find out what it takes to "get it right." Or you may find yourself working with musicians from another culture or a totally new genre of music. You have to be able to communicate clearly in order to be as efficient as possible in the recording studio. Many of the delays and problems encountered in the studio are the result of poor or a complete lack of communication skills.

    Knowing *when* to communicate is also crucial. We mentioned earlier the psychology skills an engineer must develop. With practice, you'll learn when to tell an artist, "This isn't working, what if we tried something like...." You also must know when it's more appropriate to remain quiet and allow the producer or recording artist to solve that problem for themselves.

3. **The ability to stay calm and cool.**

Artists and other creative types get emotional in the studio. They're pouring out their whole persona into their performance for everyone to hear. So, they do get emotional. A capable engineer must know how to stay cool when an artist vents their frustration. Tempers can flare and criticism can be taken to heart very easily. When that happens, it's rarely conducive to the creative process. As a sound engineer, you have to stay cool, and you have to remember your job is to keep the project on track.

4. **Intermediate to advanced computer skills.**

How much computer knowledge do you need to make it as a recording engineer today? A lot. Today's records, film soundtracks, video game music, and the millions of songs available online all are recorded, edited, mastered, and stored via a computer. So knowing the hardware, software, networking, backup, file transfer procedures, and compression programs for Internet distribution are just the starting point for anyone wanting to work as a sound engineer today. Many aspiring sound engineers and producers have a good deal of knowledge and experience working on a computer in a sound recording and editing program. That's certainly a plus. The more you know, the more valuable you'll be. But you also need to master the basics such as how to type a letter with word processing software. You must know what a database is and how it works, like the back of your hand. Why? In a support role in the studio, it will be your job to document and keep track of media assets, various tracks, takes and samples, remixes, rough mixes, outtakes, and whatever other data results from the projects you are working on. You must know spreadsheet functions so you can use the computer to add, subtract, multiply, and divide, be it time or charges on a studio work order. You must be comfortable with those three basic applications, in addition to the computer's sound recording platforms.

As mentioned earlier, you can get adequate computer "basic training" at your local community college. A basic computer class covering these applications will teach the fundamentals.

If you walk into your first day as a studio intern, and your boss tells you, "Go log these ten backup hard drives into the media library system using the MS Access software," and he points you to the computer, and you can't figure out the program they are using, you're in trouble.

Should you be proficient on the Macintosh or the Windows platform? Good question. Those using the computer for composing, sequencing, and making music tend to prefer the Mac. The folks who are counting the beans, checking whether the gear has been fixed or not, and managing the business are, for the most part, running Windows. It's essential to know enough about both to use them at work.

As mentioned before, since the majority of people actually listening to the recordings you create will do so over the Internet, you should be very familiar with the most used software programs for converting files to the common playback formats in use, which today include MP3, WMA, AAC, FLAC, and others.

Job-Specific Skills

5. Critical listening skills.

If you have not listened to or experienced music in an acoustic environment, you may not know what you're listening for, and you're going to have problems as an engineer. So, you've got to listen to music. And not just recorded music, because recorded music is an illusion of a performance, even if it is a live performance. Listening purposefully to music, sounds of all types, and nature's own sounds such as birds, waves, wind through the trees, all help to fine tune one's aural acuity to become a better critical listener. How do two instruments or voices sound together? Do they blend or clash? The multi-GRAMMY award-winning engineer and producer Bruce Swedien encourages up-and-coming engineers to get out and experience every type of music there is in a concert setting, from rock to opera to string quartets to jazz, folk, big band, EDM, and blues. Bruce reminds young engineers that records are sonic illusions or sound paintings. In order to become a competent engineer, you have to build up a library in your mind of what instruments sound like naturally—one at a time and in ensembles. According to Bruce, "An individual's knowledge of how music should sound is a big factor in how he perceives music and sound."[1] Truer words were never spoken.

View your time spent developing listening skills just as you would doing homework. Go out once a week or once a month. Listen to classical, listen to jazz. If you want to be a recording engineer, you need to hear it all. Because one day, you're going to be in a session, and somebody is going to come in with an accordion, a didgeridoo, a Sousaphone, a harp, or a banjo. You should know how each instrument should sound naturally.

One day, I was engineering a jingle session, and the producer brought in a gentleman who said, "I'm a whistler." That was one of the hardest things I ever had to record in my engineering career. I had to experiment with a number of different setups to get it right. But I started by just standing in the room with him and moving around to assess how he sounded in different spots in the room as he whistled, before I even plugged in a mic.

---

1. *Make Mine Music,* by Bruce Swedien. Milwaukee: Hal Leonard Corp., 2009

6. **Having audio expertise.**

You have to develop a thorough knowledge of audio, such as signal flow, phase, and microphone selection and placement. Whether you are self-taught or went to a recording school, you have to acquire the basic knowledge of how to make a recording, do overdubs, and handle a mix efficiently.

7. **Professionalism/bedside manner.**

There's a mood or tone that an engineer sets as they work with a client or artist on a session. Why is that important? The most successful studio engineers I know are the ones that create a professional, supportive environment that is conducive to getting creative work done. The finest equipment doesn't mean a thing if the vibe is not good in the studio. Even if you have a $750,000 recording console, what good is it if when the artist walks in, he or she doesn't feel comfortable? If artists are cared for, even pampered, a good engineer will capture their best performance.

So, now you know the marketable skill set required to have a solid career in engineering. The first six points discussed, you can learn in school. The seventh, there's only one way to learn it: experience. You've got to sit down in a session and watch other experienced engineers work, in order to observe and learn what's good about their bedside manners. That's why it's a good idea to start out at an established studio that provides some training or internships. That way, you can learn from pros.

It's also very helpful if you've played music, can read music, or are conversant with the musical language. Know enough about musical structure to understand what forte, ritardando, and the "B" section of a musical chart represent. If you are booked to record a Dixieland band next week, go to a record store or online and find a couple of well-regarded Dixieland records. Spend a couple of hours listening to them to understand how the instruments blend and how the solos sit in the mix.

Then, when that Dixieland band walks in and you meet the musicians, you've already got a point of departure to build a rapport. You can say, "Yeah, I bought a recording by the Jim Cullum Jazz Band, and I was checking out how these guys sounded together." The Dixieland band will think, "Wow! Our engineer took the time to learn something about what we do. All right! Let's make a great recording."

Before we move on, realize that the foregoing discussion of the Job-Specific Skill Set for an audio engineer is quite detailed and that until you find a mentor in your area of interest, you may not have quite as much in-depth information as was just shared. Still, it's good to aim for acquiring this level of information, because the more you know about the job, the work environment, and the field, the more convincing case you will be able to make as a qualified candidate to join the industry sector of your choice. Remember, online resources such as ArtistsHouseMusic.org have hundreds of video interviews available online for you to learn from featuring industry professionals from many segments of the music business.

WORKSHOP 9.2. YOUR FUTURE JOB: ASSESSING YOUR OWN MARKETABLE SKILL SET

Look back at your Career Road Map Workshop from the last chapter for the specific industry job you are aiming to secure.

Since you've already identified the required knowledge and skills needed to be considered for this position, now you can take inventory of yourself and see which ones you have and which ones you need to develop. Don't overlook the Foundation Skills that you have also identified as important for the industry or position you are planning to enter. List both Foundation and Job-Specific Skills in this document.

Marketable Skill Set and Job-Specific Skills Assessment

Job Title:_____

Skill List	Have	Need
_____	☐	☐
_____	☐	☐
_____	☐	☐
_____	☐	☐
_____	☐	☐
_____	☐	☐
_____	☐	☐
_____	☐	☐
_____	☐	☐
_____	☐	☐

Remember to make this sheet a living document in your Career Portfolio. Keep updating it as you speak with working professionals, review job skills, and read or watch interviews with persons doing the job you are researching. In a very short time, you'll have nearly all of the key skills identified.

Next, identify (or confirm) the career ladder in the chosen field you are researching.

Entry-level position: _____ Salary range: _____

Advances to: _____ Salary range: _____

Advances to: _____ Salary range: _____

Advances to: _____ Salary range: _____

Advances to: _____ Salary range: _____

RESEARCHING VARIOUS JOB SKILL SETS

You now have a system to help you throughout your career in whatever industries your career takes you. It is:

1. Research particular jobs via reading, interviews, networking with industry pros, and studying job descriptions for the positions that interest you.

2. Create an up-to-date Marketable Skill Set Worksheet that covers all your relevant skills and knowledge. (Remember to keep this current as you continue to grow.)

3. Develop a Career Road Map for the specific job and field you are aiming for. Match your Marketable Skills with those you've identified on that Career Road Map.

4. Work to fill in any gaps in your knowledge, and begin asking your friends, mentors, teachers, and others who you might meet to help you gain contacts into that market sector.

Using this method will allow you to quickly and realistically assess whether or not you have a good case to be a candidate for any particular job that interests you. The more jobs you check out and complete a Career Road Map for, the more detailed your knowledge of the music industry will be. Don't stop at just one!

Also, don't become alarmed if at first you don't appear to have some of the skills required. Few of us did when we started out, and just identifying the additional marketable skills you will need to develop puts you a step ahead of the wannabes who spend their time dreaming about the industry job they wish they could obtain. You'll be a step ahead, since you will have already identified the skills that you still need to develop to make your own particular music industry career dream a reality.

Follow this two-step process when looking at various career tracks, first doing a Career Road Map, and then matching it up with your most recent Marketable Skill Set Worksheet. Never delete your completed Career Road Maps and other Worksheets. Just add them to your Career Portfolio for future reference.

At the bottom of the Job-Specific Skills Assessment Workshop page is the particular career ladder. While you're completing this part of the workshop, it's also time to continue with basic salary research.

You began researching music industry salaries in part I. Now, it's time to further your knowledge about the earning potential in various jobs. Talk to people in the field, and look at what is available in print. You have to be able to survive while you build your career. If you haven't done your earning homework and

> *"Although you can find a lot of valuable information from books, we strongly encourage you to then review the workshop data with a working professional in that field. It's important to validate your findings not only on salary ranges, but also on key skills and the details on each Career Road Map you develop."*

later find out firsthand that you can't get by on what the lower rungs of your career ladder pays, you may be setting yourself up for early failure.

Your completed marketable skill set workshops will come in handy in the next chapter, as you begin to build your résumé. Knowing what skills are required to be an A&R assistant, a music publicist, or a booking agent will help you craft a résumé and cover letter that demonstrate that you have invested in building the necessary skills to tackle the job duties required for success in that position.

A final point about your research and completion of the marketable skill set workshops. Although you can find a lot of valuable information from books, we strongly encourage you to then review the workshop data with a working professional in that field. It's important to validate your findings not only on salary ranges, but also on key skills and the details on each Career Road Map you develop. Checking and verifying these facts will help you to attain some peace of mind as you begin the career journey ahead.

10 Building a Winning Résumé

THE CHRONOLOGICAL RÉSUMÉ

The most important document you will develop over the course of your career is your résumé. Whether it's a one-pager when you're getting your career started or a two- to three-pager for a grizzled veteran, your written résumé has to effectively communicate everything you can bring to the workplace. It must stand out from a pile of résumés on the desk of a potential employer.

Take a look at the Atcheson résumé in figure 10.1 modeled closely on that of one of our former students who is now working in the live music and festival market sector.

This is a *chronological résumé*. What does that mean? It's laid out in the order of time, from the most recent accomplishments to the older ones. This is also called reverse chronological order. We'll look at another type of résumé shortly.

Remember, your professional résumé is a marketing tool designed to secure the next step in the job acquisition process, usually an interview. It is not your autobiography or your life story, nor must it include every job or volunteer activity you've engaged in. The more directly you can explain to a prospective employer what you are seeking with respect to your career, and make the case for why you are a qualified candidate, the more likely your résumé will result in interviews and job offers.

In both sample résumés in this chapter, job objective is narrowed down to one sentence or statement. The position sought in our sample chronological résumé, working in live music, means they are looking for a specific job in the music industry. It's broad but not *too* broad. They didn't say "Production Manager." As you read further down Robin's résumé, you can see whether or not her *work experience* supports the career path listed in her job objective. In this case, it does. Robin has already taken some important career development steps. She has successfully completed an internship for a major music festival production company. Her résumé points to a likely career path in that field, which is also supported by a good assortment of other experiences, many of which have skills such as customer service that will be important to be successful in the live music industry.

ROBIN E. ATCHESON
123-456-7890   robin.atcheson@yahoo.com   Find me on LinkedIn!

OBJECTIVE:
Secure a position in live music presenting or festival operations and management

EDUCATION:
Five Towns College, Dix Hills, NY   Expected May 2014

Bachelor of Music in Music Business   Dean's List

SPECIAL SKILLS:
- Proficient in: Mac and Windows operating systems, Microsoft Office Suite, and Adobe Photoshop
- Extensive customer service training and experience
- Experience working in a fast-paced and stressful environment
- Fluent in Spanish

RELEVANT EXPERIENCE:
Intern, Superfly Presents, San Francisco, CA   *Summer 2013*
- Managed volunteers at Outside Lands Music and Arts Festival, coordinating and supervising information booth staffing and program distribution, allowing partners more time for high level day-of-show management
- Assisted each member of the office with everything from proofreading festival programs to creating spreadsheets of petty cash spending, thereby increasing efficiency
- Replied promptly to customer email inquiries regarding four different festivals and upcoming events

Intern, SubPop Records, Seattle, WA   *Summer 2012*
- Assembled and mailed packages for national and regional media and tour marketing purposes, while managing the different types of mailings and their appropriate recipient list, as well as multiple daily mailings
- Initiated program to compile digital archive of press clippings for label, manager, and publicist viewing and access through secure FTP site, eliminating need for paper archives
- Supported Marketing, PR, and Distribution Departments as needed to ensure efficient business operations

Sales Associate (seasonal), Dreamcatcher Gallery, Gig Harbor, WA 2011, 2012, 2013
- Managed the register efficiently, providing customers with fast and friendly service during the holiday rush
- Assisted customers with jewelry selection resulting in average per sale transactions of $500
- Reorganized merchandise displays to encourage greater sales and product availability, resulting in 6 percent increase in sales over prior holiday season
- Learned and then taught coworkers how to use inventory item scan system, resulting in 50 percent faster completion of monthly inventory than five other sister stores

ACTIVITIES:
Campus Committee for Sustainability: Co-Founder Fall 2012–Present
- Co-founded student organization to reduce waste and encourage responsible consumption on campus
- Created and led monthly sustainability workshops for students and staff, resulted in 40 percent growth in amount of paper, plastic, and glass that is being recycled on campus

Music Business Student Club Member   *Fall 2012–Present*
- Operations Supervisor for "Band Business Crash Course" seminar
- Sponsorship Chair for the North Shore Battle of the Bands, secured more than $450 in merchandise for band prizes

---

FIG. 10.1. Chronological Résumé

You'll notice that for each experience highlighted, there is a job title, organization name, location, associated dates, and bulleted statements detailing specific accomplishments, transferrable skills, and results of work. The content bullets in the Relevant Experience section should use language found in an employer's job description, whenever possible, to reinforce a candidates' qualifications and marketable skills.

Robin's *education* is listed, stating her degree as briefly as possible, listing the school, the course of study, degree conferred, and date of completion. You need not list anything else. Specifics about coursework completed or your GPA may be shared if they are especially relevant and impressive (or if the employer specifically asks you to include this information), but may otherwise be saved to share during an interview, as appropriate. If you have participated in any specialized training courses or certificate programs (relevant to the job you're applying for), these may also be listed in the Education section. Notice that only college education is included in Robin's résumé.

Special skills are prominently displayed on this résumé since the Career Road Map Robin developed included computer skills, customer service experience, and ability to handle fast-paced, stressful work situations in a number of the job listings reviewed. By putting this type of section near the top of the résumé, a candidate says, "I have the skills you are looking for" right at the top. Spanish language skills are also noted in this section of the résumé.

Two **activities** are noted that further underscore Robin's achievements. Both were campus activities for which she assumed a leadership role. More on why these are useful to include on your résumé, especially at the point in your career where your actual industry experience may be sparse, are discussed later in this chapter. You'll also notice that personal hobbies and interests aren't listed, nor are references (or a line stating that they're available). There is no need to take up valuable résumé space with things that aren't directly relevant to the position you're applying for and that can be shared during an interview or if asked.

The sample résumé's overall presentation is very solid, tight, and has a clean look. Unlike many student résumés, it goes slightly beyond one page, but in this case, the work experiences help provide a more comprehensive picture of Robin's accomplishments, so it is warranted. For most recent college graduates, a single-page résumé should be the goal. It uses white space effectively, thereby avoiding the overly crowded, difficult-to-read document many students develop. An employer or recruiter will likely only spend 10 to 15 seconds with your résumé at first glance, so it is important that it is easy to read and makes clear very quickly that you've got the marketable skills and experience to convince the recruiter to keep reading and consider you for an interview.

THE "OTHER" RÉSUMÉ: A FUNCTIONAL RÉSUMÉ

Another way to present yourself is via a functional résumé. It lists accomplishments in the order you feel best represents your qualifications for a particular career path. In which instance would you consider presenting a functional rather than a chronological résumé? Usually, a functional résumé is most appropriate when you either have gaps in your timeline or if you may be one of the Career Changers or Golden Years persons mentioned in chapter 1.

As a Career Changer, perhaps you've worked as a legal clerk for the last five years. Prior to that, you worked in radio, and you're ready to get back to broadcasting. You don't want the very first thing a screener reads under experience to be your clerking for a large law firm. Because when they get that over at the local FM station, they're going to think, "Hmmm, she's a law clerk wanting to get back into the business." Probable destination for that résumé: shredder pile!

In this scenario, you could use a functional résumé to highlight your skills. You'd lead with your radio experience and accomplishments and list your legal work later in the résumé. That's the difference between chronological and functional. But I would estimate that more than 90 percent of the time, a chronological résumé is the best approach in the early stages of your music industry career.

Figure 10.2 is an example of a functional résumé that would be effective in the scenario just described. Note that the current law job only occupies one line of space on this résumé.

Also note that this functional résumé really drives home the point that this candidate is someone who is well versed in radio station operations and sales, and has a measurable track record of success in the broadcasting industry. It goes a long way toward leading the résumé screener to see her past successes and how the skills and talent is likely to be transferable to a current job in radio. It's ideally presented for a Career Changer.

How should this candidate handle the five years outside radio working in the legal field? The best way will be in person during an interview, and most often, the direct approach is best. State why you changed field, what you hoped to achieve, what changed your mind, and why you believe you are qualified for the current job.

"I was considering going to law school and before making that investment, I thought I'd work in a successful law firm to get a better understanding of how lawyers work. Although I learned a great deal and enjoyed my time in the field, I realize that I'm not well-suited for practicing law, and I realize that my first passion, radio, is what has always been the most exciting to me."

Maryann L. Johnson
422 E. 8th Street, Apt. 4B, Tacoma, WA 98523
mljohnson404@gmail.com • 987-654-3210

JOB OBJECTIVE:
Contribute to the success of a radio station through my skills in sales, marketing, and customer service

QUALIFICATIONS:
- Five years experience in radio station sales and operations including both commercial and college stations
- Outstanding people skills, including conversational Spanish, as well as strong written and oral communication skills
- Comfortable in fast-paced, multitasking environment
- Adept at team-building and problem-solving in a business setting
- Success at regularly meeting and exceeding sales goals as an inside ad sales rep for FM 104.1

PROFESSIONAL SKILLS:
- Proficient in running MS Office, Salesforce management software, MS Access database, Photoshop, Dreamweaver, and MS Publisher
- Operations and on-air experience at college station KPLU radio; Class III broadcasting license
- Supervisory experience co-managing staff of 20 at KPLU

EMPLOYMENT HISTORY:
- Legal and Research Assistant, Baron, Bowles and Smithers, LLC; Seattle, WA: 9/2008 to 6/20013
- Inside Sales Representative, FM 104.1 (Champion Broadcasting), Seattle, WA: 6/2006 to 8/2008
- Assistant Station Manager, KPLU Radio, Pacific Lutheran University, Tacoma, WA: 8/2005 to 5/2006
- Sales Manager, On Air Talent, KPLU Radio, Pacific Lutheran College, Tacoma, WA: 8/2003 to 8/2005

AWARDS AND ACHIEVEMENTS:
- Inside Sales Rep of the Year, FM 104.1, 2007
- Three-time recipient of Tacoma volunteer "Star" award for planning, organizing, and leading three successful holiday canned food drives (2003–2005)

EDUCATION:
B.A. in Humanities (with Honors), Minor in Spanish; Pacific Lutheran University, May 2006

FIG. 10.2. Functional Résumé

Don't copy either of these résumés directly. Rather, look at what is in each, the phrases used, and how it clearly states a case that this person would be a valuable asset to a company in their respective industry. References to these sample résumés will be included over the following chapters, so leave a bookmark near them so you can quickly flip back to them.

MAKING YOUR RÉSUMÉ A "HIT"

There are two sayings about songwriting that apply equally to your résumé development. One states "a song hasn't been written until it's been rewritten." The other is that songwriting is "10 percent inspiration and 90 percent perspiration." Just like a hit song, the best résumés have appeal, hooks, and are very easy to digest. They leave the reader with a memorable impression. They are compact and use the minimum number of words to make the maximum impression. Accomplishing these goals requires a serious investment of time and commitment. In the semester-long classes we teach at Pacific, students spend five weeks writing and rewriting their résumés until they are presentable to an employer. As your résumé evolves, you will continually massage it, trying to figure out a way to boil a paragraph down to ten words. Tighten your career objective from thirty words to twelve words. That's the nature of the task.

A senior human resources executive once shared an interesting fact with me. I had always been under the impression that the people who screen résumés, especially at larger firms, looked for the strongest job histories of those submitted. I was surprised to learn that it's often actually the opposite case.

In many larger companies, a résumé screener's job is to look for mistakes: to take as many résumés as they can and justifiably put them in the shredder. Why? "This one is full of misspellings." (Buzzzzzz... goes the shredder.) "This one says she only will work in A&R." (Buzzzzzzzz.) "This one says he wants to be the president of the label." (Buzzzzzzz.)

In a large organization, the résumé screener's job is not to pick the strongest résumé; it's to leave a pile of résumés acceptable for their supervisor's review. That's why you cannot afford the slightest error or mistake on your résumé. It can quickly eliminate you from consideration.

So, your first task in the résumé quest is to commit yourself to developing a résumé without negatives and errors. You'd be surprised at how many résumés I have seen over the years in which people stated, "I really hated this job, so I quit," or something to that effect, right on their résumé! We've all had a job we didn't like, but please don't put that on your résumé.

It's critically important to make sure that your résumé is read and proofread by other people—ideally an experienced writer who is well versed in proofreading—before you send it to a potential employer. For students, that person might be a campus career counselor. What does it say about you and your attention to the details of life and work if your résumé includes typos, misspellings, or grammatical mistakes?

Your résumé must be compact, concise, well laid out, and clean looking. The one-page rule should hold true until you have somewhere in the range of 10+ years of relevant professional experience. Keeping your résumé to one page will force you to make choices about what to include, keeping it to what is really most important and relevant. It will also keep printed pages from getting separated and important information going missing. With access to a computer, you can generally lay out a résumé on your own. Creating your own document is usually better than using software templates so that you are not limited with spacing and formatting as you continually revise the document. Your résumé should be a tool you continually enhance and improve as your career develops. Keep the various iterations of it in your Career Portfolio.

A well-crafted résumé is a strong statement of why you are a leading candidate for a prospective opening. It is the introduction to your professional "brand," and in many cases, it will be the *only* chance you have to sell yourself to your future boss in the initial efforts by an employer to fill a position.

Let's say there's a job opportunity in a distant city, and you hear about it through your network. What's the first step you take? You should reach out and confirm that the company is looking for someone with some of the same qualifications you possess. They'll say, "Send us your résumé." Well, are you going to fly there to give it to them? Probably not, unless you're heading for a senior level position.

You're most likely going to e-mail them your résumé as an attachment. This piece of paper represents you: your life, your skills, your value, your net worth, and your total marketable skills to date that relate to that job or career path. Will it be the best, strongest, tightest document you can create or a quickie that you copied out of a résumé book you picked up the night before?

In this same scenario, another candidate simply mails in a naked résumé. You send in a résumé and a well-written cover letter. Your cover letter is another opportunity for you to highlight the key points on your résumé, point out things that you have done that have created value in the past, and to show that you have some knowledge of the company and the position the employer is looking to fill. All these things will separate you from the pack, and help you avoid the hungry résumé shredder. So, always make the time to write a solid cover letter. (You'll learn how to craft a knockout cover letter in chapter 12.)

YOUR RECIPE FOR A TOP-NOTCH RÉSUMÉ

It's time to roll up your sleeves and develop a résumé that will set you apart from the competition. As you read the following pages, refer back to our sample résumés frequently to see how they stack up to these criteria. After reading the building blocks of your successful résumé, you'll do a workshop to get you started crafting the first draft of your own hit résumé.

ELEMENTS OF YOUR RÉSUMÉ

Identity

The first thing your résumé must denote is who you are— literally. You have to clearly and boldly state your identity. Your name must be at the top. How big should you make it? It should be bigger than anything else on the page. We recommend 16- to 20-point type if you're using 10- to 12-point in the body of your résumé. Visualize twenty résumés on a table. If your identity is bigger than the rest, but not too big, you've got a little bit of an edge.

Should you use distinctive fonts? No. Often, when it comes to résumés, especially at larger companies like major record labels, your résumé will be scanned. And if you use an unusual or hard-to-read font such as "Antediluvian," your name may appear as a black splotch when opened in a different operating system or when scanned or faxed. So it's good to rely on basic, traditional fonts like Times or Arial. Also, color and complex graphics don't have any place on a professional résumé.

Along with your name, your header should also include a cell phone number and an email address (you may also include a physical address) where the employer can contact you. Be sure the voicemail message on your cell phone is basic and professional (no obscenity-laced ringback tones or the like!) and that your email address is basic as well (usually just first and last name @domain.com, not "surferchick82@yahoo.com" or "tattooluvr@gmail.com"). Even these small details say something about your professional brand.

Objective

The objective statement answers the question, what do you aspire to do? This simple sentence should include the specific position or company whenever possible. This serves two purposes:

1. It makes it clear to the employer what role you are applying for, and

2. It shows a level of attention to detail and genuine interest in the particular position/company.

When the résumé is retrieved from email and printed and placed on a stack on the employer's desk, she will be able to see, quickly and easily, who you are, what you're applying for, and all of the great reasons to hire you. Employers want you to be able to articulate your goals in a clear, concise way that relates to their needs. For instance, if an applicant aspires to become an established songwriter, a good relevant job choice might be at a music publishing or performing rights organization in order to learn more about the business of songwriting. In this case, an effective job objective might be:

To obtain the entry-level administrative position at XYZ music publishing company.

That's a clear objective statement. And you can (and should!) adapt your objective from opportunity to opportunity. That's why you've got your résumé ready to update or customize on a moment's notice.

What if you don't have a specific job objective yet? Then identify a segment of the industry that you have an interest in, such as A&R, concert promotion, or artist management, and start with that. Add a location or anything else that can make your statement specific to what you're after without limiting opportunities.

To secure an entry-level position at an artist management company in the Los Angeles area.

I believe it's essential to list an objective on each résumé draft. Note that a region is also specified on some of these objectives, to provide a bit more focus. If you know you want to be in the recording studio business but you're not sure where, you should say so.

To obtain an entry-level position in an established recording studio in the Nashville region.

Although it's generic, it gives the reader a sense that the candidate has a goal in mind. You'll notice that none of the examples include "fluff" language about soft skills or intended contributions. Not only is it not necessary (and taking up valuable space on your document), it can actually be detrimental. If your objective statement says how much you want to learn and grow and gain experience, some recruiters will take that to mean you are lacking the necessary skills and experience they are looking for in a candidate right now, and your résumé may automatically go in the "no" pile. Your job search tools (and especially your résumé) should communicate what you have to *offer*, not what you hope to gain.

Experience

This part of your résumé gives you the opportunity to detail some of your accomplishments. Many people get intimidated when it comes to listing experience on their résumé. The simple rule of thumb is to emphasize your strongest accomplishments, no matter where you were employed. As your career evolves on the music industry path of your choice, your experience should reflect your career development in your chosen area.

THE SAGA OF THE PIZZA MAN

A former student of mine (Keith's) started working in the eleventh grade for a pizza parlor in San Francisco. He was just finishing up his four-year degree in broadcasting and had been working at the pizza shop for six or seven years. At that time, he was assistant manager with a broad portfolio of responsibilities, including cash management, hiring, and training new staff. He came to me and said, "My goal is to work in a recording studio, so I'm not going to mention this stuff" (i.e., his pizza business experience).

I replied, "You're shortchanging yourself if you omit this valuable experience. Look at all the skills you've developed. You're fiscally responsible, and you hired and managed a staff of ten people. You've developed menus. Those are all important business skills. Put them down on your résumé. You don't have to write volumes, but include what you've accomplished that's noteworthy and that contributed to the success of your employer. Every business owner wants to hire someone who has proven to be a responsible employee."

He did just that and landed that job at a leading post-production studio in Los Angeles shortly thereafter, where his organizational and leadership skills were appreciated.

Never forget to tell your prospective employer what problems you solved or profits you helped create in a previous job. The majority of your competitors will only list the dates and title of the jobs they held. Too bad for them! They miss a tremendous opportunity that you must take advantage of to explain the value you created in your previous and current job.

The Experience section generally includes jobs and internships that you have held but does not include volunteer work. Unpaid internships can be included here. Be sure to reference the following for each organization: name, location (city/state), dates of employment, title, brief description of your work, and bulleted statements that provide examples of the most valued skills in which you demonstrate these skills in action! Go beyond listing tasks. Begin your bullets with action verbs (see examples in chapter 11) and communicate your accomplishments and the *results* of your work, highlighting transferrable skills. Try to include reference points or data (numbers, percentages, budgets, timelines, etc.) whenever possible to reinforce your contributions. The following section on "worth points" will help you to develop effective content bullets.

Never lie or invent any information on your résumé. Chances are, it will come back to haunt you and in some cases may prove to be grounds for dismissal. Recent situations where CEOs of publicly traded companies have had to resign because they provided false information on their résumés point out how important it is never to lie or even "stretch the truth" on your résumé. You don't need to invent or exaggerate experience or skills; you just need to communicate the experience and skills you do have in a relevant and attractive way.

Education

How important is education in the music industry? Increasingly so. There are hundreds of schools and colleges that offer pre-professional training in the music industry. Such training provides future employees with a basic understanding of the industry, how various market segments such as the record industry, artist management, concert promotion, recording arts, not-for-profit arts administration, and the music products market segments operate, to name just a few areas. Studios, labels, management companies, record labels, and other firms that recruit entry-level employees rely on programs such as these to provide candidates with a rudimentary knowledge of the business. Completing a successful internship at a music or entertainment firm is another way to build your skills and knowledge, and enhance one's hireability.

When it comes time to start your job search, your educational background will definitely help you. What if you don't have an education in the music or entertainment industry? It's still important to list your educational qualifications. If you have a high school diploma, list it. If you took college courses but didn't graduate, specify the general area of study and number of years or credits completed successfully.

Prospective employers want to know that you are literate.
Remember that being able to read, write, and follow directions
are important components of your marketable skill set.
Documenting your education and background is important. Some
applicants unfortunately submit a great many résumés that
fail to list any educational accomplishments. That's a mistake.
Today, one must list some type of educational background to be
considered seriously for almost any position.

Other Sections

Depending on your background and experience, your résumé
may include additional sections, such as Professional Affiliations,
Volunteer Work, Leadership, and Extracurricular Activities,
etc. We always recommend including a section for Additional
Skills where you can list the common business applications
you're proficient in using, and industry-specific technology you're
familiar with. If you have expert skills or have used unique tools,
be sure to include these, as they will help you stand out. Are
you multilingual? In today's global economy this is definitely
a marketable skill—don't miss the opportunity to leverage it!
Have you earned any special certifications (outside of your
college education)? Do you have affiliations with professional
organizations related to your career interests? Be sure a recruiter
who reads your résumé sees all of this important information!

Background and Interests

Hobbies and personal interests can help you to build a rapport
with a potential employer, but unless there is a strategic reason
for including them, they really don't belong on a professional
résumé. Rather, these things can be referenced in a cover letter
or shared in an interview conversation. The single purpose of the
résumé is to get you an interview—once you've got the interview,
you can work to develop rapport and convince the employer that
you're the right person for the job, but you've got to convince
them that you can *do* the job first. Don't waste space on your
résumé with anything that doesn't support how you can do the
job you're after!

References

Should you list character references on your résumé? The answer
is no. You don't want anyone else's name on your résumé! And,
there is no need to add a line at the bottom, *references available
upon request*. That is valuable space that could be used to share
relevant skills! If an employer wants references, they will ask
for them (and you will have the opportunity to choose the most
appropriate references and adequately prepare them). At some

point, you're going to need references, so start planning who will provide this important service for you and ask their permission to use them as a reference in your job search. Be sure you provide them with an updated résumé and some information on the job(s) you're applying for. But, don't waste space on your résumé listing other names or letting the reader know they're available.

PROGRESSIVE CAREER GROWTH

As your career and résumé evolve, take the time to clearly delineate the various examples that show your progressive career growth. This is a prime indicator used by prospective employers to measure the development of a job applicant. Simply put, progressive career growth shows how you have advanced in job responsibility and value to your current and previous employers. Ideally, your job titles will have changed to more clearly demonstrate this, but if you have not had a job title change, but your duties and responsibilities have expanded, be sure to specifically cite this progressive career growth. It's also wise to emphasize your progressive career growth in cover letters that accompany any résumé submissions.

PRESENTATION

What about your résumé's presentation? You should make it easy to read, and carefully check and recheck for spelling or grammatical errors. Leave some white space. Do not cram the page so full of information that the reader's eye is overwhelmed; leave it a bit airy. You should also avoid colored paper and nonstandard fonts. If a résumé is so packed with words that the reader doesn't know where to start, you've got a major problem. Job seekers anxious to pack as much information as possible onto their résumés sometimes resort to "tiny type"—fonts of less than 10-point size. Don't do it. If your résumé is running long or looking crammed on a single page, go to another page. Better yet, get a friend, teacher, or mentor to help you edit it down. In the career classes we teach, we often repeat that point, because it is so often ignored, but critically important in aiding your résumé's viewability.

Remember, if you are ready to vie for a position in the music industry, keep the résumé length appropriate to the amount of your relevant professional experience. For recent college graduates, there is rarely a need for your résumé to run any more than a single, well-organized page. For Career Changers, your résumé will likely be longer. If you have a great deal more relevant experience, you can allude to that in your cover letter or mention it during a follow up conversation with a contact or interviewer.

A FINAL THOUGHT ON RÉSUMÉ EDITING

Students often inquire, "Should I revise or edit my résumé for each job opportunity that I uncover as my job search gets into high gear?" The answer is, "No!"

We don't advise overhauling your résumé for every single job opportunity, because you're liable to stray from the carefully crafted document that you spent so much time developing. The basics of your education, your experience, and your talents will not change from opportunity to opportunity. And your basic qualifications and worth points (we'll get to those shortly) shouldn't change either. Over the arc of your career, measured in years, it will change—but not every month.

The one thing that is most likely to change is your job objective. To avoid an overly broad job objective, most candidates customize their job objective to suit each opportunity. You might add a sentence here or there, or you may want to add specific language from the job description it is being used for, but the core of a well-crafted résumé should rarely change, in the short term. A well-crafted résumé is a solid document that clearly states who you are. It unequivocally states what you've done—the scope of your accomplishments and the benefits created by you and enjoyed by your previous and current employers. In your interview and cover letter, you can and should amplify specific skills and key accomplishments that are likely to excite your future boss.

If you're constantly doctoring up the basics of your résumé, you're likely to introduce errors and more formatting problems. Once you have a strong résumé that you are justifiably proud of, think twice before tampering with its basic elements.

7 **WORKSHOP 10.1.** BUILDING YOUR RÉSUMÉ

Review this chapter, and write the initial draft of the ideas and words that will grow into your own "hit" résumé. Once you have some ideas and notes, you'll be ready to start a first draft of your résumé. This will help you avoid that sinking feeling many encounter when tackling the résumé development process. If you already have a résumé, look it over closely and see if you have the requisite sections before you begin revising it. The following instructions are designed for someone drafting a new resume from scratch.

- **Identity:** List your name, mailing address, phone, e-mail address, and other contact information.

- **Objective:** Don't try to write the perfect job objective; instead, simply note a few of the job objectives you aspire to at this time. Most candidates have a number of dream careers they are interested in investigating. List as many as come to mind. Don't agonize over the wordsmithing now, as you will have time to perfect and fine-tune that later.

- **Work Experience:** For now, list it all in reverse chronological order (most recent items go first). Include part-time and unpaid positions. Pay special attention to any jobs for which you received commendations, raises, promotions, or other identifiable accolades. Use "worth points" to expand on content bullets (see next section and workshop).

- **Education:** Keep it short, but don't omit any special training that strengthens your résumé.

- **Other Skills:** Start a list of all the skills you can think of that may be valuable, especially skills such as foreign language proficiency and specific technical skills with computer hardware and software programs. Once you have your list going, poll your close friends and family members to expand your list. Again, in this early phase of résumé development, it's far better to have a wider range of choices and to narrow it down later.

- **Professional Memberships:** If you don't have any professional affiliations yet, perhaps now is the time to do some homework and identify one or two organizations that may interest you. Even if you can't afford the dues, you could become involved as a volunteer.

When you've assembled all the raw materials to complete your first draft, take the time to carefully and purposefully draft a résumé that will help you stand out based on your experience, education, and any relevant training. Save it to your Career Portfolio, and have a colleague or writing pro look it over and offer tips on how it might be improved. Keep the mindset that your résumé can always be improved, especially as you develop new skills.

11

Make Your Résumé Sparkle with Worth Points

> *"Worth points represent the single most effective means to quickly convince your prospective boss that you are a candidate worth serious consideration."*

Once you've got the basic structure of your résumé established, it is time to make the content sparkle! A "worth point" is a well-written, concise statement that will differentiate you from your competition. Worth points demonstrate why you will be valuable to an employer. They clearly state what you accomplished and the results your actions created for your previous employer or agency.

Worth points are worth their weight in gold, so take the time to learn how to incorporate them into your résumé. They make your résumé shine and glisten.

Here's an example of a worth point:

Organized and managed volunteer student committee to raise funds for repair of homeless shelter, resulting in achieving 200 percent of financial goal.

This example incorporates two action verbs in it: organized and managed. It also clearly states that your efforts exceeded the goal or expectation that was established before you tackled the job.

Let's look at the worth point statements in the Atcheson model chronological résumé (see figure 10.1). Here's one of Robin's worth points:

Initiated program to compile digital archive of press clippings for label, manager, and publicist viewing and access through secure FTP site, eliminating need for paper archives.

That's a strong worth point that uses two powerful verbs: compiled and created. The résumé could have simply stated, "compiled and created digital archive of press clippings," and missed a valuable opportunity to make a much stronger, active statement as to the value created for the previous employer.

A worth point is also included under the school activity listed on this sample résumé:

Created and led monthly sustainability workshops for students and staff, resulted in 40 percent growth in amount of paper, plastic, and glass that is being recycled on campus.

The hiring manager who is looking at this résumé carefully is likely to observe, "This person is the type that is willing to tackle new challenges and get things done, exactly the type of person that tends to do well at our live music production company." While not directly in the music industry, this accomplishment helps create a strong positive image of the candidate. It uses "created and led" and also has a data point (40 percent increase) that adds more weight to the accomplishment.

A clearly written, well-stated worth point such as this is very likely to move the sample résumé up near the top of the select pile of "must contact" résumés.

Use this workshop to develop a few of your own worth points.

🔲 **WORKSHOP 11.1.** WORTH POINT DEVELOPMENT

A "worth point" is a well-written, concise way to give yourself an edge when someone is reviewing your résumé. Worth points demonstrate why you will be valuable to a prospective employer.

Review the three sample worth point statements above, and then begin the process of crafting your own.

To develop worth-point "winners," start by listing three accomplishments that you are proud of.

1. _____

2. _____

3. _____

Now, turn them into worth points by using the following formula. A good worth point uses two phrases. The first describes specifically what you did; the second, its results.

Convert your three accomplishments into worth points.

1a. What you did:

_____

1b. What was the result of your action?

_____

2a. What you did:

_____

2b. What was the result of your action?

_____

3a. What you did:

_____

3b. What was the result of your action?

_____

Take your time, and go over your work and volunteer experience. See how many of the job actions you have listed can be "energized" by conversion into a worth point. This is one of the most challenging aspects of crafting a strong résumé that will sell you strongly as a serious contender for your dream job. If you don't have any measurable worth points in your portfolio of accomplishments, consider getting involved with a community organization where you could make a difference and earn a valid worth point to add to your résumé.

The bottom line is that any résumé with well-written worth points jumps out of a stack of competing résumés! Invest the time and effort to see that your résumé has at least one.

WORTH POINT CASE STUDY

Here's another example of success that could become a worth point. During the course of the summer internship at a radio station, "Terry" is asked to reorganize a library of master recordings, which contains previous radio spots, live broadcasts, and other projects. During her three months onsite, she comes up with a comprehensive system to organize the spot library, using an MS Access computer database and tagging all the tapes by sponsor and air date. She put a great deal of effort and some weekend time into the project. In fact, she "went the extra mile" to make the system easy to use and even got input from station vets on how to make it better once it was ready to test. When the system was made available to everyone, it was a huge hit with the traffic department and station management.

Now, it's the fall semester of her senior year of college, and she's drafting her résumé.

Ineffective Worth Point:

> *Internship, Z100 Radio, organized advertising spot library.*

That's a simple statement of an activity. Turning that into a worth point, she energizes it as follows.

Effective Worth Point:

> *Intern at Z100 Radio, developed computer database system for advertising spot library resulting in 50 percent time savings to traffic and production departments.*

See the difference? Terry's résumé will have much more impact because she took the time to develop this worth point. First, it states she developed a functional system using a computer. Second, she had responsibility for an action. And third, Terry's actions led to a clearly stated benefit, saving the station and her employer half of the time it previously took to complete a daily task.

That's how to take an action and turn it into a worth point. If you can do that two or three times in your résumé, and then remind them of those worth points in a targeted cover letter, we promise you, yours will usually be in the top 10 percent of the résumés under review.

People rarely take the time to restate what they've done action-wise with a worth point. Why? It takes time, effort, and extra thought to refine an action into a worth point. But the benefits are huge. If you haven't been in the working world very long, volunteer activities are perfectly acceptable to use as worth points.

ACTION VERB LIST

achieve	document	lecture	reduce
administer	earn	lobby	reference
affect	educate	locate	repair
aid	edit	lower	replace
analyze	establish	maintain	report
apply	evaluate	manage	represent
assemble	execute	measure	research
assist	expedite	mentor	review
attain	facilitate	motivate	rewrite
budget	forecast	negotiate	save
calibrate	fulfill	operate	secure
change	generate	organize	select
check	guide	participate	sell
coach	hire	perform	serve
collect	identify	persuade	set up
communicate	implement	plan	solve
compile	influence	prepare	speak
compose	initiate	present	speed
compute	illustrate	prioritize	streamline
conduct	inspect	produce	strengthen
consolidate	install	program	succeed
coordinate	instruct	promote	supervise
create	integrate	propose	teach
critique	interpret	provide	train
decide	invent	publish	translate
demonstrate	investigate	question	update
determine	judge	raise	upgrade
differentiate	launch	recommend	verify
dispense	lead	record	write

Action verbs sell, in a résumé. They tell your potential employer the things you accomplished and the results that you achieved. The more assertive you are and the more confidently you can state your accomplishments and results, the better your résumé will be viewed. Sales grew, money was saved, accounts were opened, records went up the chart, or hungry people were fed. Each can be represented much more effectively as a worth point. Take a moment to skip back to the sample résumés and see if they incorporate action verbs effectively.

Don't shortchange your résumé. Include worth points whenever you can, and you will be amazed at the difference in the response from prospective employers. You will also find that these worth points will bring you value for a long time as they shine in your résumé and cover letters. They make the case that you are a valuable asset to an employer. Remember to use them in discussions when you move on to interviews. Worth points represent the single, most effective means to quickly convince your prospective boss that you are a candidate worth serious consideration.

 WORKSHOP 11.2. CREATE! PROMOTE! SAVE! COORDINATE! ACTION VERB SCAVENGER HUNT

Review the sample résumé for Kelly Hunter below and circle the action verbs in it. How many did you identify? Does this résumé also contain any worth points? If so, circle those, too. Next, what advice would you offer Kelly to further refine this résumé? If you are part of a class, discuss what modifications might improve this résumé with a colleague.

Kelly M. Hunter

601 Blaine St., Apt. 3, San Francisco, CA 94107 246-801-3579
kellyhunter33@gmail.com

Objective: Seeking an entry level position at a talent or management agency

Work Experience

Intern at Sleepwalker Records, San Jose, CA   *Summer 2012*

- Assisted day-to-day office duties for David Hastings, the VP of A&R
- Prepared and submitted all Grammy Award entries for the label
- Completed royalty rate projections and target market analysis for upcoming albums
- Edited liner notes, reviewed editorial and tech copies for three new album releases

Vice President of A&R at ClickTrack Records, San Francisco, CA   *Spring 2012*

(Student-led label at McKenzie College)

- Maintained clear and open communication between the artists, their management, and the label
- Delegated tasks to three-person A/R staff and held them accountable for their performance
- Coordinated the completion of the editorial and liner notes for the record *Spring Break Mix*
- Established social media presence and marketed release through Twitter
- Organized A&R department's final presentation to industry professionals

McKenzie Student Entertainment Commissioner, San Francisco, CA   2011–2012

- Led team of six programmers for the Arts and Entertainment team, resulting in 135 campus events successfully produced
- Planned and produced a sold out campus concert featuring J Cole (2,400 tickets)
- Maintained and monitored annual budget of $270,000, while providing complete and accurate financial information to student and university administrators
- Revitalized team's marketing strategy to include the marketing manager role and enhanced use of social media including Twitter, Instagram, Facebook, and HootSuite; resulted in increased reach with 25 percent reduction in ad spending
- Developed in-house training for student sound techs to staff weekly open mic, karaoke, and live music nights, resulting in $3,000 annual savings from hiring outside contractors

Education

McKenzie College, San Francisco, CA   *Graduated June 2013*

Bachelor of Science, Music Industry Studies

Collegiate Affiliations

Lambda Kappa Nu Fraternity, Beta Pi Chapter

Magister (Pledge Educator) and Philanthropy Co-Chair

- Created the curriculum for the entire pledge program, supervised pledge orientations
- Developed and managed fund-raising campaign to aid homeless families; raised over $1,000 for cause

Relevant Skills

- MS Office, Adobe Creative Suite, Pro Tools audio editing, Final Cut Pro, and basic HTML skills
- Proven problem-solving, networking, and relationship-building skills

FIG. 11.1. Résumé for Action Verb Scavenger Hunt

12 How to Write Effective Cold and Cover Letters

What's the difference between a cold letter and a cover letter?

A cold letter is one that is submitted, with or without your résumé, in the hopes of securing an interview with a company that interests you. A cold letter is one that you send into the unknown, often blind, as you may not know if the company is looking to hire new staff or not. Simply put, it's a shot in the dark.

A cover letter is written to address an existing opportunity at a company. Let's say you spoke to someone in the human resources department. They said, "Yes, send us a résumé. Here's our address." A well written cover letter starts by referencing that this submission is being sent in response either to a specific job opening or to a company's request to review your résumé and qualifications.

The cover letter accompanying your résumé for a specific opportunity should also state why you believe you are qualified for the position in question. Don't assume that the résumé screener will proceed far enough into your résumé to the location where your carefully crafted worth points reside. Restate two or three key attributes and worth points in your cover letter, and end on a positive and enthusiastic note. Remember that the same care that went into your résumé should be invested in your cover and cold letters. Be sure that there are no typos, use good grammar, leave a little white space, and include your name and contact information on the letter, as it may become separated from your résumé. Keep your letter to a maximum length of one page. And, all of the same rules apply if your cold or cover letter is actually being sent in the form of an email. The content of an email message to which you are attaching your résumé is essentially a cold or cover letter, so please remember to treat it as such with preparation and professionalism!

Figure 12.1 is a sample of a well-written cold letter that Keith received a number of years ago. He took the time to read it and the attached résumé, which looked promising. But this person never secured a phone or in-person interview with him. Why? She never took the next important step: she never made the follow-up call to see if he would give the time for an interview. Her letter said, "I look forward to meeting with you and will be calling you in the next few weeks to arrange a mutually convenient time."

Dear Mr. Hatschek,

Your name came up in my research of the music business in the San Francisco region as someone whose effectiveness and influence on the industry has been exemplary. You are clearly an individual whose knowledge and experience would be invaluable to anyone hoping to enter this highly competitive and relatively closed field.

I am a musically literate, well-spoken, and enthusiastic recent college graduate whose greatest passion in life has always been music. Please be assured that I do not expect you to know of any specific positions in your or other companies. Rather, I would welcome the opportunity to meet with you briefly to discuss the business in general and get the benefit of your comments and advice.

In addition to a lifetime of collecting and listening, I have worked extensively with local acts in both promotion and staging, and am myself a singer and a songwriter. I would be happy to discuss this and other work experience in more depth when we meet.

I look forward to meeting with you and plan to call in the next few weeks to arrange a mutually convenient time.

Sincerely yours,

Jane Doe

FIG. 12.1. Cover Letter

That call never came. It may have been due to the huge number of letters she sent out, or that she landed her dream gig. But if you take the time to write a strong letter and send it out, you should budget adequate time to do at least one follow-up call for each submission.

Although Keith wasn't hiring at the time, he would have given this person time for an informational phone interview based on the quality of the letter and the attached résumé, and that would have been a positive learning (and networking) experience for her.

Remember, often the people who have valuable information may not hire you today, but they could refer you to someone else in the industry that is hiring. So invest the time and effort to make your cold and cover letters strong, concise communicators— especially if they're aimed at what we call "Targets of Opportunity," which we will investigate in a later chapter.

WORKSHOP 12.1. WRITE A COLD LETTER

Identify a local company that interests you as a potential employer in your area of interest. Research to whose attention you should send your inquiry. Keep in mind that small- to medium-sized companies are the best size firms to approach, as large, multinational companies generally will not respond to a cold letter such as this.

Using the following outline, write a cold letter to introduce yourself and request an informational interview. Be sure to mention:

- Who you are and why you are writing. (Do you want a job, an informational interview, or information on the company and its products or services?)

- How you found out about the company.

- What it is about the company or the work it does that interests you.

- How you are preparing to enter the industry. (School, independent study, internship, etc.)

- A restatement of what you are requesting (informational interview, tour of studios, etc.) and how you will follow up (and be prepared to impress the reader by actually following up as promised!).

As always, make sure it's well written and to the point. You'll actually mail or drop off this cold letter along with a copy of your résumé as you wrap up all of the workshops in part II to help you land another informational interview.

 ## Action Item

Have a mentor or colleague proofread your cold letter. What changes, if any, did they suggest? Remember to edit it, and save it to your Career Portfolio.

WORKSHOP 12.2. WRITE A TARGETED COVER LETTER

Choose a job description of a professional role you'd be interested in pursuing and develop a targeted cover letter. Your cover letter should be set up in business-professional format (your contact/address line at top left, double space to date, double space to employer contact/address line, double space to greeting, double space to content), and should have the following:

Opening (1 paragraph)

Introduce yourself, state the job you are applying for, how you heard about or who referred you, and most importantly, concisely state *why you are interested in the particular role and why you would be a good fit*. Opening should only be about two to three sentences.

Body: What You Can Do for the Company (1 to 2 paragraphs)

Explain what you have to offer (*not* what the company can do for you). Use the job description as your guide to highlight your skills/experience. *Don't* rehash your whole résumé; just concentrate on the two or three highlights you really want the recruiter to know about you, your skills/abilities, your interest in the company and what you can contribute in the role.

Closing (1 paragraph)

Summarize why you would make a great addition to the team. Suggest a time/way that you will follow up (for example, "I'll follow up via email next week to make sure you've received all of my application materials and to provide any additional information that may assist in the recruitment process")—and then actually follow up, of course. It will show that you're proactive, have good follow-up and follow-through skills, and it gives you an excuse to contact the employer instead of waiting forever to hear back. Then, be sure to thank the recruiter for their time and consideration, and finish the letter with a professional closing and signature.

A FINAL THOUGHT ON ORIGINALITY AND ACCURACY IN COVER LETTERS

Students often wonder, "Once I have one really good cover letter, can I just use that as a form letter for all the jobs I respond to?" No, you must always customize each cover letter. It doesn't matter if you have thirty jobs you're responding to this week. Break it down into short-term goals for that day. Write a letter. Carefully double-check the accuracy of the spelling and the address. Pay special attention to the name of the person to whom you are sending the letter. If you are unsure of any of the contact information, call the company.

"Hi, I'm sending a letter to Keith Hatschek. I just want to make sure I am spelling his last name right. Is it H-a-t-c-h-e-c-k?"

Receptionist: "No, it's got an 's' in there and no 'c' at the end."

"Oh, thank you, H-a-t-s-c-h-e-k."

You accomplished two things during that phone call. You have gotten your prospective boss's name right, and you made an impression with a person at that firm who is likely to remember that you took the time to call and find out how to spell the boss's name correctly. People remember things like that. So the cover letter originality and accuracy are very important to serious job seekers. You can and should use some of the same sentences and content for similar jobs, but don't fall into the trap of sending out a generic cover letter. You're missing an opportunity to further separate yourself from the pack, if you take that path.

13 | Social Media and Your Online Brand

In today's rapidly changing job market, it is clear that you must be able to leverage technology effectively in order to be successful. Your online brand is a job search and career development tool that is now just as important as your résumé and cover letter. Your online brand is created, in large part, through your social media profiles. There are *many* social media applications out there, but the three that are most used in career development and management are Facebook, Twitter, and the granddaddy of career-focused social media sites, LinkedIn. We'll explore how to best utilize each of these to manage your profiles for career success. The chapter will conclude with a workshop to help you build (or improve) your LinkedIn profile.

WHY SOCIAL MEDIA IN YOUR JOB SEARCH?

A 2013 social media recruiting survey performed by Jobvite (*recruiting.jobvite.com*) revealed the following:

- 94 percent of recruiters use or plan to use social media for recruiting

- 78 percent had successfully hired a candidate through social networking

- Social networks used for recruiting: 94 percent LinkedIn, 65 percent Facebook, 55 percent Twitter

- Hires made through social networks: 92 percent LinkedIn, 26 percent Facebook, 14 percent Twitter

The numbers are impressive; it's clear that social media plays a major part in recruiting today. As a job seeker, it is important that you are aware of where recruiters are looking and what they're looking for so that you can be prepared to use your social media profiles to your advantage.

Social media profiles allow for creativity and flexibility in ways that traditional résumés and cover letters do not. They allow you the space and ability to share your personality and your passion. They also allow for interactive engagement with your network, employers, and the industry at large. Social media tools are powerful, but they must be managed effectively in order to best represent your personal and professional brand. A poor online presence (or absence of one) can be a serious detriment to your success. It is important that you think about and take inventory of your professional brand online. What is the image or impression you want people (namely, potential employers) to associate with you? Your online brand is developed and projected through the way you "act" online, the way (and how often) you "talk" online, and the way you present yourself in photos and videos. Ask yourself, are these impressions consistent with your in-person brand? Are they consistent across social media profiles? Let's go through the different types of social media profiles together and explore how you can make them great and manage them effectively.

FACEBOOK AND TWITTER

If you are between the ages of 13 and 100, it is likely that you have an account and profile on Facebook or Twitter or both. While you may use these tools to follow your favorite celebrities, share pictures of your cat, participate in political debates, or update the world on what you ate for breakfast, these social networking tools can also be leveraged to help you in your job search.

But, before discussing ways the tools can help your career, it is important to note that the tools do have the potential to hurt your job search as well. Inappropriate photos, foul language, and even poor grammar may cost you an interview opportunity. You'll want to take the following steps to make sure that doesn't happen.

Clean Up Your Profiles (and Your Contacts)

Keeping in mind that your profiles represent your personal and professional brand, the images and content that make up the profiles should be brand appropriate. Would you want a potential boss to see your drunken bar photos? Would you want a potential boss to see your political rants, questionable comments, or use of foul language? It's time to take inventory of what is really included in your profiles and clean them up from a professional brand perspective. Review any "about" information you've included (religion, political affiliation, sexual orientation, etc.), and revise (or remove) anything that may be controversial in the eyes of a future employer, not just your zany friend who will try almost anything. Go through photos (your own albums and photos you've been tagged in), and remove any photos or tags that don't support the professional brand you hope to represent. The same goes for status updates you've posted, pages you've "liked" or are a "fan" of, and groups you've joined. A prospective employer can infer a lot about the type of person you are by your "likes" alone! It is also important to really take inventory of the "friends" you're connected to or following. Be sure that anyone who has the ability to tag you or to post or comment on your profile can be trusted to respect your personal and professional branding efforts. Don't be afraid to block or delete the negative and crazy contacts in your network, and be careful about who you choose to connect with going forward. One of the best rules of thumb is if you wouldn't want your grandma or clergyman to see it or read it, hit "Delete."

Pay Attention to Privacy Settings

For Facebook and Twitter (and any other personal social network), you will want to be sure your privacy settings are appropriate. If you don't want prospective bosses (or clients or other professional contacts) to see your personal activity on those profiles, be sure that your profiles (and photos!) are set to be strictly private. We would also recommend utilizing the "Timeline Review" feature in Facebook that requires your review and approval before posting anything (comment, photo, etc.) in which you've been tagged to your profile. If someone tags you in an unflattering photo or includes your name in an inappropriate comment, you will have the ability to "hide" that content before it ever shows up on your profile for others to see. Remember, anything you post or are tagged in (or otherwise put out into the Internet) has the potential to be seen (and judged). Maintaining strict privacy settings can do a lot to help in mitigating that risk.

Now that your profiles are cleaned up and your privacy settings are established, you'll want to start using your Facebook and Twitter accounts to really help you in your career. There are some small steps you can take now that may have a big impact (both immediate and long-term):

Follow Companies of Interest

If you "like" or follow the companies you're interested in, any news posted by the companies will automatically show up in your news feed. This will allow you to easily stay informed about important company decisions and developments, including job announcements! It will also show a specific interest in the company, something that may work in your favor when checked by a recruiter. If I were hiring for my company, I would check to see if the applicants were "followers" or "fans" of the company. It would show me that they were doing their homework. Most importantly, knowing about company decisions and developments will allow you to speak competently and confidently in an interview situation.

Engage Your Connections

In order to make the most of your contacts, you must *actually* contact them! Search your network for anyone who might have any connection to the music industry and make a point to send individual messages to those contacts. Let them know what you're looking for and how they might be able to help you. Be specific! Let your contacts know what information and introductions would be helpful. Make a point to "like" and join music industry groups and to connect with individual group members as well. Appendix C lists an array of industry groups, some of which you may want to follow using social media to enhance your knowledge of particular market sectors.

> *"In order to make the most of your contacts, you must actually contact them!"*

Post Relevant Content

In addition to posting personal status updates and photos, you can build your professional brand by posting content relevant to the music industry. Share your opinions on new music, share music news and articles, share links to your favorite music blogs, or share other content that will make the depth of your interest in the music industry clear to your contacts as well as hiring manager who may be screening you. Commenting, answering questions, and sharing content found on music industry group pages are other great ways to showcase your interest and expertise. When you are working in the music industry it will be essential to stay current and relevant and to provide valuable industry insight to your network, so you might as well start now!

LINKEDIN

LinkedIn is an essential tool and resource for job seekers today. An overwhelming majority of recruiters and hiring managers are using LinkedIn for recruitment and hiring, and as a job seeker, it is important that you are where the recruiters are (and are impressive enough to get their attention). LinkedIn is *the* definitive professional network where you'll want to focus the majority of your social media time and energy to produce the best results for your career launch, future career change, or career growth. There are several aspects of LinkedIn that you'll want to concentrate on.

> *"An overwhelming majority of recruiters and hiring managers are using LinkedIn for recruitment and hiring, and as a job seeker, it is important that you are where the recruiters are (and are impressive enough to get their attention)."*

Your Profile

Your LinkedIn profile is the first thing a recruiter will look for once they get your application or see your résumé (if LinkedIn isn't where/how they found you in the first place). Recruiters want to see that the information you're sharing through your profile is consistent with the résumé and application materials you've submitted, and want to get a better sense of your personality and style. Your LinkedIn profile allows you to introduce yourself and present your professional brand and experience in a way that is much more creative and comprehensive than a traditional one-page, black-and-white text résumé. There are several elements of your profile that are especially important to focus on that we will walk through together in workshop 13, including photo, headline, summary, skills, experience, education, groups, recommendations, and connections. You can make a strong professional impression by completing your profile to "All Star" status (which means filling out all major sections in detail). Once developed, it will be important to maintain your profile and update it often with new experience, skills, projects, photos, etc. Building your profile is important, but being diligent about maintaining and enhancing it is even more important!

Connections, Introductions, and Recommendations

Once you have a profile you're proud of, you'll want to focus on requesting and developing connections with contacts. Try to connect with former colleagues, classmates, managers, clients, and others who can speak to your professional skills and abilities. Do your best to cast a wide net to ensure that your network is comprehensive enough to represent all areas and levels of your experience and broad enough to connect you with a variety of second and third level connections. That said, be cautious about the individuals you choose to connect with, as well. Remember that your network is a large and valuable resource and part of your professional brand. Your professional network on LinkedIn is likely to be quite different from your collection of "friends" on Facebook. Keep in mind that the true value of your network is in its quality, not the quantity of your connections, and it will only grow with time and care.

Some Tips for Requesting Connections, Introductions, and Recommendations

When sending requests, it is always best to include a personal note rather than depending on the automatically generated message. Make requests personal and specific. Do your best to make connection requests as soon as possible after direct interaction so that the contact is clear about who you are and how you're connected. Be warned that requesting connections from those you don't actually know or have a link to may be detrimental. After several people choose to "ignore" or "not accept" your request, LinkedIn will automatically limit the functionality of your account. This is another reason that personalizing your requests is important!

One way to avoid having your connection request ignored is to send it through the Request Introduction function. LinkedIn Introductions give you the opportunity to contact members who you are not directly connected to through connections you have in common. An introduction (and built-in endorsement) from a connection is far more productive than a seemingly random request from a stranger out of the blue. Remember that anything you write in a message to a person already in your LinkedIn network will be seen by the target you hope to make a connection with, so choose your words carefully and maintain a professional tone.

Your request will go to your direct connection, who will then forward your message along with their own additional message of introduction to the target, who then decides whether/how to respond. Explore your second and third level connections. If there is a target contact of interest, see if anyone in your current network is a direct connection who might be able to make an introduction for you. If so, ask for it! The ability to connect directly with those you might not otherwise have access to through "introductions" is a major advantage of LinkedIn, but you must be proactive enough to reach out. With the basic free account, you are given five introduction requests, so you'll want to use them wisely. If you find that you need more, you will have to pay to upgrade your account.

A key request you'll make of your network through LinkedIn will be for recommendations. Request recommendations from those you've worked with and those you've worked for. Try to generate at least one good recommendation for each of the roles you've highlighted on your profile. *Don't* request recommendations from all of your connections. *Do* make your requests personal and specific, and understand that generally accepted LinkedIn etiquette dictates that the favor of writing a recommendation be reciprocated. As such, writing recommendations for others is a great way to prompt them to return the favor!

ACTION ITEM

Send three personal requests for recommendations from contacts from different organizations and experiences. Follow up by taking the initiative to write recommendations for those individuals as well.

Company Profiles, Channels, and Industry Groups

When building your connections, don't forget to think beyond individuals to include connections with company profiles, industry channels, and relevant groups. You'll want to do this for a few reasons. First, just like following and "liking" companies on Facebook and Twitter, connecting with companies and industry groups will show a specific interest and will ensure that all relevant news and announcements show up in your news feed. By making a point to follow industry channels (topical news streams) and share and comment on current industry articles, you are able to take an active role in industry discussion and promotion, alongside the professionals creating the content. Employers want to hire people who are not only passionate and knowledgeable about the industry, but actually *engaged* in the industry.

> *"Employers want to hire people who are not only passionate and knowledge-able about the industry, but actually **engaged** in the industry."*

The primary benefit to joining industry groups: you automatically have access to the profiles of all of the other individuals in that group. Those individuals share a common interest and many of them are working for the companies and in the roles you're pursuing. Take advantage of your access to this treasure chest of information and *use* it! Review and research the professional profiles of those in positions you aspire to. Learn more about them and their specific roles, and pay special attention to their backgrounds. How did they get to where they are now? What education and skills do they have? What companies have they worked for and in what positions, especially in their early careers? What was their career path progression and how long did it take? You can learn *a lot* from the profiles of other individuals about the types of positions that exist and the skills and experience necessary for success, and can more clearly understand the timelines and professional paths to achieving your own career goals. You can search groups by keywords to narrow your field of potential new connections to those who work for that one company you're really interested in or in that particular type of position you're really after. Once you've got some great new targets (and have spent some time reviewing their profiles to learn everything you can about them), it is up to you to take the next step: reach out and make contact! A key benefit of groups is that you can send free private emails (LinkedIn calls them "InMails") to group members who are not (yet) connections. (If you try to send an InMail to someone who is not part of a common group, you will have to pay or upgrade your account to do so.) Another great thing about reaching out to contacts through groups: you already automatically have a common interest as an entry point for an initial conversation. Being proactive about learning and connecting within the music industry will be essential for your career launch (and for your long-term success).

 ACTION ITEM

Find and join at least five new music industry groups on LinkedIn. Budget time each week to check on each group and as soon as you feel comfortable, contribute to the conversation in each one.

 WORKSHOP 13. DEVELOP (OR IMPROVE) YOUR LINKEDIN PROFILE

Establishing a professional online brand for career networking is a critical success factor in any business today. Create or update your LinkedIn profile using the principles discussed in the chapter and the tips provided below.

LinkedIn Elements

Photo: Yes, you should definitely have one. If you don't, it seems like either you're hiding something or just aren't savvy enough to complete your profile, and either perception is not good. People want to see you and when they do, they are more likely to connect with you. Your photo should be of *just* you (headshot preferable) and should look at least somewhat professional. Save the family vacation photos and pictures featuring your date or your dog for Facebook, and stick to something simple, polished, and professional.

Headline: Your headline is your brand statement. It can and should be completely customized. Your headline should communicate more than a job title; it should be a statement about who you are or what you're aspiring to. Be creative and descriptive, keeping in mind that the words used in headlines are indexed in search engines!

Summary: Consider your summary to be your personal introduction; it's your opportunity to share a bit about yourself and your background, and to infuse it with a bit of personality. Use this space to really promote yourself, using relevant keywords whenever possible.

Skills: It is imperative for potential employers to get a clear picture of your skill set (and to see that others are willing to endorse you for those skills). Add both hard skills (software proficiency, foreign language fluency, etc.) and soft skills (communication, leadership, etc.) to your profile, focusing on those that are most relevant for the music industry. If there is lingo specific to the particular area of the industry you are aiming for, be sure to use that lingo in your profile. For example, if you have been a front-of-house mixer for your school's performance series, list that info in appropriate form: FOH Mixer for XYZ Performance Center. Remember, you can list up to fifty skills, and your connections can provide some virtual validation through endorsements.

Experience, Education, and Other Sections: Utilize the experience, education, and other sections (projects, publications, organizations, certifications, volunteer experience, etc.) to organize and share your career path and interest information in a way that goes beyond your résumé. Start with résumé details and highlights, but go a step further to paint a much more broad and comprehensive picture of your true experience and value.

Recommendations: In many cases, LinkedIn recommendations have replaced formal recommendation letters requested by employers. Recruiters may now see your recommendations before they ever contact you directly! Once you've built a strong profile and base of connections, you'll want to aim to obtain recommendations with the goal of at least one good recommendation for each of the roles you've highlighted on your profile. Send requests to your network connections who can share specific positive feedback, and be prepared to return the favor.

Settings: LinkedIn is the network profile you *don't* want to make private! Although it may seem counterintuitive to the plethora of (wise) career advice about utilizing privacy settings in social media, LinkedIn is definitely an exception. You want recruiters to be able to find you and see how valuable you are, right?! Unless you want to remain anonymous and inaccessible (and make it seem as though you have something to hide), be sure your privacy restrictions are turned off and your activity broadcasts are turned on so that others can find you and see what you're sharing. And while we're at it, one thing that might make it easier to be found is a "vanity URL." LinkedIn assigns a long, complicated, default URL to each profile, but you can customize it to be branded with your name. This simple link can now easily be added to your résumé header, your business card, and your email signature line.

Updates: Share connections. Share information. Share value. Let your network know what you're working on and what you're working toward so they can help you! When you post updates or share information, it is seen by your whole network. If your name and face continue to be in front of your network, you have a greater shot at being top-of-mind when a relevant opportunity becomes available.

LinkedIn Premium

To kick the functionality (and hopefully results) of your LinkedIn profile into high gear, consider upgrading to a LinkedIn Premium account. For a monthly fee, you can have access to some additional features and benefits:

- **Better Search.** The "Advanced Search" function is expanded to include more fields by which you can narrow and target your search. You can see more profiles per search, you are able to see more detailed profile information on people showing up in search results, you can save your searches, and you can receive updates when new people qualify for your saved searches.

- **Better Information.** LinkedIn Premium allows you to see everyone who has viewed your profile for the last ninety days, and stats for who has viewed your profile, including the keywords people used to find your profile. This is an incredible resource for potential new connections and invaluable information that can help you to optimize your profile content.

- **Better Contact.** LinkedIn Premium gives you the advantage of InMail, a message you can send directly within LinkedIn to another member you are not already connected with. While any member with a free account has the option to purchase InMails, those with Premium accounts receive a number of free InMails each month (depending on the level of membership you buy). And, LinkedIn guarantees that you will get a response from the other LinkedIn user within seven days or you will get your credit back for the InMail. This feature allows you to communicate directly with hiring managers and decision-makers you wouldn't otherwise be able to connect with.

- **Better Visibility.** If you upgrade to LinkedIn Premium, two new "badges" are attached to your profile that let other users know you're a Premium user, and to show your new "Open Link" designation that allows other users the ability to contact you at no "cost" to them (InMail credits). There are claims that those who display these badges get substantially more profile views and resulting contact.

So, is an upgrade worth the expense? Possibly. A lot can be done with a free account if it is well developed and maintained. Keep in mind that an account upgrade is only valuable if you're willing to invest the time and energy to actively utilize the premium features day in and day out. Whether it is the free version or the premium version, it is still up to you to actually put this tool to work.

Using social media effectively to support your initial job candidacy and continuing as your career unfolds takes a consistent and thoughtful effort. Invest the care in seeing that you present a professional, engaged, and positive image via all your social media platforms. After all, you are the "brand manager" for your image and career. If you don't take the time and care, why would any music industry hiring manager want to meet you?

CHAPTER 14

Schmooze or Lose: Networking Your Way to Your Next Job

> *"Starting today and continuing for your entire career in the entertainment industry, commit yourself to spending a portion of each day building and nurturing your network."*

The most important tactic you can use to develop key industry contacts is networking. Starting today and continuing for your entire career in the entertainment industry, commit yourself to spending a portion of each day building and nurturing your network.

Since most job openings aren't directly advertised, it's only through networking that you uncover "hidden" opportunities. You have to consciously build and work to maintain your network. We recommend that you invest two hours a week on network development. *That's only seventeen minutes each day.* Like other aspects of your career development, networking is work. If you don't hustle and sweat while you are building and maintaining your network, you won't achieve the necessary results to get ahead. The choice is yours. Net-"work" or sit back and hope your dream gig falls in your lap.

How do you manage your network? It's more than sending "friend" requests or making online connections. You actually have to *talk* to people. Network contacts aren't really valuable unless you are actually *contacting* them. You know that smartphone that you use to text and take pictures and play games? It actually does something much more important: it allows you to make calls and talk to people. Use it! Another important step to meeting and talking with people is *showing up*. Attend industry meetings, seminars, trade shows, and events whenever possible to multiply your contact with people in the business. Shake hands. Ask questions. Smile. Listen. Share. Listen some more. Adopt the style and language of the professionals you wish to emulate. Social media can be a good initiator, but live, in-person networking is always the most productive. Whenever you have the chance to meet a new network contact, remember to exchange business cards so that you have the contact information to keep the connection and conversation going! You don't have a business card yet? You can easily order business cards from online printing sites (Vistaprint.com is one commonly used) for very little investment ($5 to $10). Not sure what to include on your business card? Say what you're interested in! "Aspiring Music Marketer" or "Music Technology Enthusiast" might be examples of your "title." Be sure to include your name, phone number, and email address, at minimum. You may also want to include a small headshot so that new contacts can put a face with the name on your card and remember your conversation. Include a URL to your personal website or blog (or a QR code) or LinkedIn profile address for quick access to additional professional information.

POSITIVE FIRST IMPRESSIONS WITH PERSONAL COMMERCIALS

First things first. You must be able to introduce yourself effectively, whether in person or in writing. Prepare and practice your own personal "elevator pitch" or "personal commercial"—a concise, carefully planned, and well-practiced description about who you are and what you are looking for that anyone should be able to understand in about thirty seconds (about the time of an elevator ride). A personal commercial will enable the listeners to gain quick, concise information about the specific, unique, and impressive attributes you have to offer, what you are looking for, and how they can help. It would seem that introducing yourself should be the simplest part of networking, but unless you are truly prepared, there is the possibility that you may get nervous or leave something out or otherwise blow your shot at making a great first impression. In addition to being used for introductions in networking situations, the content of your personal commercial may also be used in a cover letter to highlight your background and key abilities, or in an interview situation in answer to the common question: "Tell me about yourself." Your personal commercial should include the following elements:

- **A "hook."** Get the contact's attention by opening with a statement or question that piques their interest to want to hear more.

- **Passion.** Employers appreciate energy and dedication. Communicate your enthusiasm for the industry and/or role!

- **Memorable language.** Use crisp, concise, and interesting language, avoiding over-detailed and rambling statements. Share descriptive statements of your skills, abilities, accomplishments (remember those worth points?), and experience, with emphasis on your individual strengths, linked to the perceived needs of the contact.

- **A request.** Build in the opportunity for follow-up by asking for something. Do you want their business card, to request an informational interview, or to ask for a referral?

WORKSHOP 14.1. PERSONAL COMMERCIAL DEVELOPMENT

Your personal commercial is a key component in your career management tool kit! It will come in handy in nearly every professional opportunity to meet new contacts and make a strong, positive first impression. Craft it by answering the following key questions in concise one- to two-sentence responses:

1. What are my career goals and accomplishments?

2. What qualities/skills do I possess that enable me to realize these goals?

3. What accomplishment best represents how I have used these qualities/skills to achieve a goal?

4. What am I searching for in a job?

5. How can I immediately benefit the company/market sector/industry?

Refine your statements, and begin practicing reading your commercial. Keep at it until you can do it mostly from memory. Once you feel confident with your personal commercial, start using it! Begin introducing yourself to new network contacts and ask them to share their stories, too. Meet and "interview" others to learn as much as you can about their career paths in the industry as you work to launch your own!

ACTION ITEM

Once you have your personal commercial firmly set and you are happy with it, use a video camera or laptop with camera to record it, and send it to a mentor or professional colleague via a video sharing site (YouTube, Vimeo, etc.) to get their critique. Why? More and more companies are using video interviews as a key part of the hiring process, and becoming comfortable with how you look and sound using video is a skill that will help you greatly as your career progresses. Be sure to store the link, and if you fine-tune it a bit more, be ready to share it with a hiring manager if you feel it helps put your best foot forward as a bright, energetic, and capable candidate for a position at their firm. Be conscious of wearing appropriate attire, the background, and the speed and modulation of your voice. Strive to be yourself, but in a professional manner. Remember to smile at the end of your video.

The Value of Informational Interviews

Informational interviews help you gather information on a company or a position without being in the potentially high stakes situation of an actual hiring interview.

Before we look at how you can secure an informational interview and then craft the questions that will elicit the most useful information, remember that in today's increasingly hectic working world, professionals you will approach may often have difficulty making time for such activities. Don't be dismayed if your requests

> *"By asking your network and mentors for referrals and getting involved in conferences or trade associations, you will quickly find opportunities to land informational interviews."*

for informational interviews occasionally result in turndowns. By asking your network and mentors for referrals and getting involved in conferences or trade associations, you will quickly find opportunities to land informational interviews. Only then will you discover the wealth of information that such an interview can bring to your job search. If you are hidden at home, you can't very well meet people who can help you.

If you will be approaching a company or person "cold" for such an interview, here's the most effective approach.

Introduce yourself via email, phone call, or an old-school letter. If you have just met someone at an industry event, or heard them speak at a panel or workshop, you may also approach them immediately afterwards. Explain briefly who you are and what you are interested in learning about from them. If you are approaching a firm cold, ideally, you will have the name of the person with whom you would like to meet. That person might be the studio manager, head of personnel, tour manager—whoever you feel might be a good information source. Be sure that you are professional and polite. Enlist the help of the person answering the phone in getting an "at bat" to request an informational interview. Do not antagonize the receptionist or assistant, also known as the "screener." If they have to put you on hold, say it's "no problem" for you to wait until they can get back on the line.

If you actually have an existing connection to the person you wish to meet, or their assistant, you must be clear about who you are and why you are calling. Now is the time to clearly state that you are asking for a brief appointment (ten to fifteen minutes is a good length) to find out a bit more about the industry and the company. If they say no, then remember to ask if there is another person in the company who might be able to share a few minutes, either in person or by phone. Another option is that the person to whom you are speaking may know of another working professional they believe may be helpful for you to contact. Always end with a polite thank you for each person's time, no matter what the outcome is.

Once you land an informational interview, brush up on the following workshop, listing some of the basic questions to ask. Be sure to bring a pocket note pad and jot down their key comments. The speed at which valuable information will be coming at you during such an interview will make taking notes very helpful. You won't have the luxury of calling them back to check a fact, name, or phone number. Take your time, and when an important point is made, repeat that point aloud to confirm that you understood exactly what's been said.

ACTION ITEM

Update the cold letter (or email) you wrote earlier in part II, and send it to the firm you identified. Be sure to schedule a follow-up phone call a week or two after sending the cold letter. Make it a goal to arrange for and complete at least one new informational interview each month as you continue to build your knowledge base.

WORKSHOP 14.2. INFORMATIONAL INTERVIEW GUIDELINES

You're in your informational interview… now what? After outlining briefly—in one or two sentences—why you are there and your career goals, use this list of questions as a guide, remembering your host may not have time to answer all of these. Be sure to start the interview by asking how much time your interview subject is able to share with you. Then stick to that timetable.

1. Tell me about your background and your career path.

2. What do you look for when you are hiring a [target job]?

3. Is special training or education required/desired? If so, where is the best place to get such training?

4. Is specific job experience required? If so, what kind? More importantly, how would you recommend getting such experience?

5. Is there any way to break into this field without on-the-job experience?

6. Do you hire people in this capacity often? What's the supply-and-demand situation in terms of job seekers and available jobs in this field?

7. To what level can a person hired at the entry-level advance?

8. What is the usual starting salary range? After two years?

9. Does your company offer internships?

10. Can you suggest other companies or people to contact in your field?

11. What is the most important attribute that someone wishing to enter the field today should possess?

This list will result in a lengthy interview, if all the questions are discussed. If time is tight, you will have to prioritize these questions for each informational interview you secure. Another question that can be illustrative of early-stage careers is to ask how they got their start in the industry.

Your informational interview subjects will pass on a wealth of information in the short time that you are with each of them. Their answers will serve as a guide to further fine-tune your career development and job search plans. Your focused inquiry will say to them you are serious in your approach about entering their field, often impressing them enough to create more opportunities for you.

It's only going to take two or three productive informational interviews to understand exactly which skills are requirements for success for a given job and whether or not you are currently employable in a particular position.

Are such informational interviews easy to obtain? No. Why? Everybody has twelve hours of work to do in nine hours. How are they going to get it done? Many executives and middle managers are just too busy to even consider such interviews. That's why nurturing your network to get an introduction when you are ready for it is so vital to your career development. Don't forget to ask for referrals for prospective informational interview subjects via your social media channels.

If you can't approach a person or a company directly, you may connect with them at a professional meeting, seminar, conference, lecture, or class. In that setting, professionals will often say, "I enjoyed speaking to the class (conference, workshop, etc.) today, so here is my email address if you have any other questions." If you don't write that down and send them an email, you are squandering a prime opportunity. Even better, if you ask for that speaker's business card, you should follow up with a handwritten thank-you note. You'll make a strong positive impression by doing so.

Every time you have an opportunity to network with a working professional, take it, regardless of whether or not that person is directly on the career path you see yourself taking today. You never know when having a wider network may help you. You've got to have access to fresh, reliable industry information to make the most of your career opportunities. In addition to what you will learn from magazines, books, seminars, and classes, networking provides the best source of locally relevant information for someone on a career search.

What else do you bring to your informational interview? Two résumés and some business cards. When you get home from that informational interview, promptly write a thank-you note. Thank them for their time and the information they shared.

Correspondence is an important part of your network maintenance.

Here's a letter Keith received. It's one example of a way to reach out and initiate an informational interview.

Dear Mr. Hatschek,

I read an interesting story about your public relations firm last month in *Billboard*. I am completing my studies in music industry studies at XYZ University and will be visiting San Francisco this summer. I would like to see if I might stop by to introduce myself and ask for a few minutes of your time to discuss my career objectives in the music business.

Sincerely yours,

Jim O'Hara

P.S. I'll call two weeks prior to my trip, to inquire if you will be willing to make an appointment to speak with me.

FIG. 14.1. Informational Interview Request Letter

Letters (or emails) such as the one in figure 14.1 will help you to get your foot in the door. The letter would have been even stronger if there was a referral included, "Joe Jones [someone who knows me professionally] recommended I give you a call while I am San Francisco." If a professional acquaintance is willing to help make an introduction, you have a real leg up over your competition. If you choose to make contact by email, it's wise to put the referral source in the subject line: "Referral from Joe Jones re: music industry careers."

Such a visit will not usually lead to a job offer, but that is not the goal for such interactions. Instead of an offer, you've just widened your network. You've added another professional contact in your database or index file. You've got another person who knows you and you know them. Your range of possibilities just increased. That's how successful networking in the entertainment business is done, day in and day out, by networking gurus. With a steady investment of time, effort, and follow-up, pretty soon you'll be a networking guru too. Only two hours a week.

Another benefit of actively seeking informational interviews is that they help you become more comfortable speaking with working professionals and learning how to compose and control your thoughts and body language in a lower stakes interview environment than a hiring interview. Please don't dispense with doing a round of informational interviews as a warm-up to your job interviews. For students, the informational interviews are often completed as part of one's final semester in school, helping confirm you are prepared for actual job interviews, which will be covered in part III, and widening the network of industry pros that know who you are and something about your career aspirations.

HOW TO USE YOUR NETWORK

Let's say you begin with a network of twenty-five people. That's a good start. Consider them your "team." One day, you make a career decision that you would prefer to work at a record label rather than a concert venue. Each person in your network may know somebody who works at a label.

Successfully working your network means that you send out a message to your network stating, "Hey, I've decided to jump tracks and try to land a gig at a label, ideally one that is into hip-hop music or EDM. Do you know anyone at a label you might be able to introduce me to, to gather more information?"

In this example, if each of the members of your network in turn has their own network of 25 people, you now have a potential 625-person universe (25 x 25 = 625) in the music business to ask questions of. In this scenario, it's likely that you will get one or two positive responses to your inquiry. Your team will ask themselves, "Who do we know in the hip-hop music biz? My friend really wants to learn more about that part of the biz."

Soon, you receive three reply messages, suggesting you check out a certain label, or introducing you to a new contact at a particular company. That's networking, par excellence.

 ACTION ITEM

Network Checkup: What's going on right now in your own career development process? What would provide a boost to your efforts? Use your social media, email, and in-person contacts to ask for some help or advice and to further your use of your growing network. Note what answers you receive in your Career Portfolio.

Giving Back to Your Network

Networking is not a one-way enterprise. To be successful, you've got to "give" when you "get." Reach out and share with your network whenever and however you can. Share articles of interest, share news and events, share job opportunities, share introductions to others in your network, and share your enthusiasm, time, and energy.

For example, if you are living in L.A., there is a celebrity or charity music business event almost every weekend. You may not meet the head of each record label, but you will meet some of the staffers at those labels. One example is the TJ Martell Foundation, which was founded by members of the music industry and has been very active for more than twenty-five years raising funds for leukemia, cancer, and AIDS research. They regularly host charity events in L.A. and New York.

Find out when and where these and other events are being held, and volunteer at a few of them. Two music industry weekly magazines, *Billboard* and *Music Connection*, each have a small column dedicated to reporting good works and charitable projects. They regularly list upcoming charity events such as concerts, celebrity auctions, awards banquets, and tennis or golf tournaments, offering excellent opportunities for savvy network builders to get out and start adding to their network. Nearly every single charitable organization could benefit from your involvement—and you get to meet and learn from working professionals and their peers. Not a bad deal! With the investment of a few minutes' research, a few phone calls, and perhaps a brief personal interview, you can start expanding your network at a whole new level by helping out industry pros on a charitable event.

How do you go "two-ways" and give back real value to your network? Here's how. Let's assume that you work at a hip-hop label in L.A. One day, your boss mentions that the company needs to locate a campus rep in New York City. You mention that you could send out an email to your network (which, by the way, has now grown to fifty people). Soon, a number of résumés are received by fax and e-mail. Just like that, you transitioned from job seeker to a job referral source. That's how a person continues to grow, give back to, and nurture their network.

A well-tended network should grow like a garden. It's unlikely that you will intimately know most of the people in your network. That's not important. What is important is that you manage and grow information and support those with whom you network. Doing so gives you access to an unmatched source of up-to-the-minute inside information.

At the public relations firm Keith Hatschek and Associates, we had more than 1,000 active contacts in our immediate network of associates, editors, vendors, and business acquaintances. Through them, we had the ability to communicate indirectly with another 5,000 or more people involved and interested in the industries we served. That's a potent tool. When someone needed a photographer in Nashville, a staff member simply searched the database for names and numbers of various photographers in Nashville. If a publicist in London was needed to assist a client with a UK project, we'd contact one of our London associates and inquire as to who might be an appropriate referral. It doesn't matter if you have not met any of these referrals personally. So long as they are introduced through a referral by a known colleague, they were every bit a part our company's network. That's how the business of networking in the music industry works. It's powerful, potent, and creates a lifelong web of knowledge and information available at your fingertips.

ONLINE MUSIC COMMUNITIES PROVIDE ENHANCED NETWORKING

In addition to the effective use of social media discussed earlier, a new generation of music collaboration sites are emerging that provide music makers and managers with access to an incredible range of talent around the globe. Three such sites, each with a slightly different focus, provide an introduction to some of the possibilities such networked communities afford. All three of these online music communities were also founded by musicians, highlighting another innovative path to success that some musicians are taking.

- **Music Gateway** is a London-based portal that bills itself as the global platform for the music industry. You register for the free collaboration service and can post projects and invitations to collaborate with other Music Gateway members around the world. It provides the back end to monetize one's creative efforts, and provides a good scouting opportunity to find new talent for music managers.

- **MixMatchMusic** is a Silicon Valley-based firm that fosters a community of musicians and remixers around the world, while also providing a mobile application that any musician or manager can use to share content and build community among music fans.

- New York City-based **Indaba Music** is one of the largest music-related collaboration sites boasting more than 800,000 members using its portal to connect to other musicians and music fans. Members collaborate regularly to build their musical résumés and also receive feedback about their progress.

Networking represents the most surefire method to gather information about a position, industry, or company in which you have an interest. And it's the most effective means to plug into a job that's never going to be advertised. Trade associations, which we'll discuss in an upcoming chapter, offer an additional avenue to keep growing your network.

Remember, there's a big difference between networking and interviewing. Interviews place you in a position to learn directly about a specific company or a specific job opportunity. Networking is the investment you make to meet people and share information about common career interests. Networking is the free exchange of information, usually done informally in conversation over coffee, via email, Skype, social media, or in a phone chat. You must view networking as benefitting you with an ongoing, constant flow of information within your network.

To excel at networking, you have to invest the time and effort to make new and different contacts. Set a goal. "I am going to network with four new people every month…" or whatever you see as being realistic. Don't be afraid to push yourself—to set a goal that is just a little higher than you think you can achieve. Write it as your goal, then work towards it, keeping a scorecard to measure your progress. It is vital to set and achieve short term networking goals, because it is human nature to want to simply maintain the status quo. Though networking can easily become a numbers game, remember to also keep quality in mind. It doesn't matter if you have hundreds of friends and contacts if they are in no way relevant to your area(s) of interest. And, it doesn't matter if you have hundreds of contacts who know you if you are known for your poor work or poor attitude. The goal is to develop a robust network of people who know you and support you and would be willing to introduce or recommend you to others.

Once you get started, you'll find it's not that hard to build up your network. Go to industry events such as seminars, open houses, and workshops that have an informational agenda. Volunteering and involving yourself in trade associations and industry organizations provides the fastest, easiest, least stressful way to expand your network resources. In San Francisco, the local chapter of the Recording Academy stages thirty-five to forty events a year. Volunteer in any capacity, even if you're making nametags and cleaning up after the event.

 ## Action Items

1. Add a daily or weekly quota for networking time to your Short Term Goals you developed in part I. Track your progress to meeting or exceeding that goal each week.

2. Engage and interact with one new network contact each week. Identify something you can do to "give back" to that person in addition to adding them to your network.

If you have any kind of a family or personal connection, now is the time to use it. "My uncle's sister-in-law has a job in finance at Capitol Records. I'm going to see her at a wedding next month." Don't be shy. If you've got your résumé ready to go, pass her a copy of it in an envelope and ask her if you can follow up to see if she might introduce you to someone in personnel. Never waste a family connection, even if you have to gather up your courage to take advantage of it.

> *"Two-thirds of music industry job seekers secure their first industry job through active networking."*

If there's any ethical edge you have to get a foot in the door, use it. Remember, even if that particular person is not able to assist you now, ask them who they may know that might be able to. Just because they may be family, don't expect them to treat you differently. Be professional; tell them what you can bring to the table.

Explain that you are serious about a career in the business. If you are in school, explain that you are studying, learning, and networking, and are dedicated to finding a way into the music business. That's critical.

Two-thirds of music industry job seekers secure their first industry job through active networking.

Never underestimate the power of networking, no matter how far up the career ladder you climb. Even if you aren't the most talented individual that is pursuing your particular career path, if you become a maestro at networking, you're liable to do well.

Performing musicians often have a list of trusted peers that they use for subs—musicians who have filled in for them, or for whom they have filled in. This "call list" is a great place for you to start and practice your networking. If you don't have one, the workshop that follows will help you identify your network constituents.

If at first you are a bit uncomfortable networking, don't worry. Many others have been, too. Remember this principle of networking: If you are giving and getting information, and you are not a pest or a nuisance; you are successfully networking. Start with a simple introduction and alert the other person to what you are interested in. "Hi, I'm Jane, and I'm looking for an internship with a digital music company."

Following is a networking workshop to demonstrate to you that you already have the building blocks of a basic network. Fill it in before finishing this chapter. Another good way to see who is in your "inner orbit" is to analyze your email and text message "Inbox" to see whom you interact with most frequently. Be sure to list them in the workshop, even if you don't think of them top of mind in a professional context. You may be surprised at connections they may afford you.

When you are done with the workshop, pick five members of your network, and ask them to refer you to others who might help you learn more about your current career areas of interest. Keep track of this activity in your Career Portfolio. You may be surprised at how quickly your network starts to expand.

WORKSHOP 14.3. EXPAND YOUR NETWORK

Most people, especially students and working professionals, actually have between 100 and 250 contacts in their extended network, although they may have frequent contact with 25 to 40 persons (the so-called "inner orbit") each week. Identifying and nurturing those "outer orbit" members of your extended network is a great way to start expanding the usefulness of your network.

Family Members

_____

_____

_____

_____

_____

Alumni/Teachers/Mentors

_____

_____

_____

_____

_____

Friends

_____

_____

_____

_____

_____

Business Contacts

_____

_____

_____

_____

_____

Clubs/Organizations

_____

_____

_____

_____

_____

Classmates/Bandmates/Etc.

_____

_____

_____

_____

_____

How can you expand your network? Which areas of new connections are likely to be the most fruitful with regard to industry connections?

As we wrap up the Career Toolkit portion of the book, use this checklist to review and take inventory of the new and improved resources you've got at your disposal and how they can be put to work as you prepare to take your job search to the next level:

	Research	Contacts	Applications	Interviews	Career Development
☐ Job Description Analysis & Career Road Maps	X		X	X	X
☐ Personal Skills Assessment	X		X	X	X
☐ Résumé (Worth Points!)			X	X	X
☐ Cold & Cover Letters		X	X		X
☐ Social Media (LinkedIn Profile)		X	X	X	X
☐ Business Card		X			X
☐ Personal Commercial		X	X	X	X
☐ Informational Interviews	X	X		X	X

FIG. 14.2. Career Toolkit Checklist

Have you put in the time and energy necessary to make sure your toolkit is full and operating at its highest level? Remember, you don't get a second shot at a first impression. Just as a musician must practice and prepare for the audition of a lifetime, you must be sure that you are prepared, professional, and confident as you discover and pursue career opportunities. If you've invested the time and efforts thus far, you should be well prepared to dive into part III, putting your toolkit to work in crafting your own personalized Job Search Action Plan.

III

Putting the Tools to Work
(Your Job Search Action Plan)

Once you've done the necessary preparation to create your own Personal Career Toolkit, it's time to create a Job Search Action Plan that will allow you to maximize the impact of your tools in the hunt for your industry job. This section will conclude with crafting your own Action Plan and then setting it in motion. However, before we do that, there are a few more aspects of career development that we would like to share with you to further enhance your knowledge and skills.

15 Digging in the Dirt

EFFECTIVE CAREER RESEARCH METHODS

Successful job seekers hone their research and detective skills to a fine edge. And never has there been a research tool with the speed, power, and access afforded by the Internet. Using the Internet as a primary research tool, today's job seeker can uncover a wealth of information to aid their career development. However, the Internet also has the potential to lull job seekers into thinking that simply registering with a few job search engines and doing some online research will be all that is needed to help them land their dream job. The truth is quite different, as the Web simply broadens your access to a wider pool of job listing information, but does little to move job seekers closer to landing their next job.

A number of top career consultants advise that no more than 30 percent of your career development time be spent reviewing Internet job sites and applying for positions. Old fashioned networking, informational interviews, visiting with mentors, and reading relevant trade magazines are all equally valuable in identifying job opportunities.

In this chapter, we'll look at a full range of career research methods including libraries, directories, trade magazines, personal contacts, and the Internet. (A separate section listing a host of relevant websites is at the end of this chapter.) Using a broad range of tools and tactics, of which only a portion are Internet based, has proven to be the most effective way to uncover the best job opportunities and put you in a position to compete for them.

WHAT ARE YOU SEEKING?

A wise man once stated, "If you don't have dirt under your fingernails from digging to discover new things, you're never going to uncover the treasure." For job seekers, doing so requires identifying your chosen career path and embarking upon it. As explained in part I, visualizing yourself in the new career and working to self-actualize yourself will speed up your career development and increase your opportunities to find a job. So be cognizant that it's up to you to do the necessary detective work to become well versed in your area of interest. Knowing as much as possible about your career focus is a necessity. Only when you become extremely well versed in this area will you be able to compete effectively, represent yourself as a serious student of that field, and make good career decisions when the time comes to do so.

MAGAZINES AND WEBSITES MIRROR THE INDUSTRIES THEY COVER

Today's music industry trade magazines and market-specific websites offer a fast way to get a glimpse at the companies, trends, and trendsetters that are making news in a particular industry segment. Many of the periodicals listed in "Resources" offer online editions, and a few offer complimentary subscriptions for the print edition upon request. Some are available at larger, well-stocked newsstands. Larger bookstores such as Barnes and Noble carry some music industry trade magazines, too. I would suggest you go and buy a copy, or investigate a good-sized library to get your hands on the ones that cover your area of interest.

Who's hot? What styles of music are on the way up? Which ones are on the way down? Which cities have a thriving live music scene? Which new record labels are coming on strong? Which video game developers are coming up with the most innovative products? Trade magazines and industry-specific websites will answer these questions and many more. They give you the dish on the latest tools, techniques, trends, and success stories. Some of the online editions of these magazines often have extended or exclusive Internet-only content not found in the print editions.

You must invest time on a regular basis to mine this critical information. Set up a regular reading schedule for the industry sources that interest you. For instance, every Saturday morning, you might spend from 9 A.M. until 12 noon reviewing relevant articles and editorials. Whether you are at a library that has a good number of industry trade magazines or prospecting the magazine's online edition, take notes, identify leading personalities and companies, and consider what type of work most interests you. The Clippings section of your Career Portfolio is the best place to build up your library of area-specific resources.

If you are at a library, be sure to sit down and skim through the back issues. You'll likely find a number of articles that interest you. Take notes, and add them to your Career Portfolio. Until you're working in it, reading about the business is the easiest way to continue to learn more about the industry. At the outset of your career development, this is the closest thing you have, unless you have an internship or a mentor, for finding out what's going on in the music industry. If you are interested in a different facet of the business—for instance, touring, artist management, radio programming, or film sound—find out what magazines and industry websites cover those segments and review them religiously.

TRACKING YOUR CAREER INTERESTS

Your career search requires the same kind of planning that a lengthy journey would necessitate. You've got to have resources at your fingertips and know a little bit about the landscape. The other fascinating part of the range of information on the music industry is its global scope.

You may discover a company on the other side of the world that is involved in an area of interest that you share. For instance, Spotify, a leader in digital music streaming and discovery, is based in Stockholm, Sweden. And increasingly, entertainment companies are taking a global view of their business, in part because the Internet has broken down many traditional borders, and also because entertainment programming and products have a much longer product life cycle if they can be marketed around the world, rather than only in the U.S.

If you don't have Internet access at your home or school, call your local public library. Most libraries now offer free or low-cost Internet access.

ADVANCED SLEUTHING

Becoming a detective requires shifting your mind-set. A student once mentioned she had an icon of Sherlock Holmes in his deerstalker hat next to her computer at home to remind her to keep up her industry detective work. It graphically reminded her that one is always digging for information about topics and jobs of interest. Only a dedicated detective will uncover and exploit the best job opportunities.

If you'd like to be promoted from amateur detective to senior sleuth, then begin to read the bible regularly—not the King James version, but whatever "bible" is for the entertainment industry segment that fascinates you. For the record industry, *Billboard* is the weekly bible. For the touring industry, *Pollstar* and the live music reporting in *Billboard* form two of the trusted sources.

Billboard is valuable because it tracks the pulse of the music and entertainment industry. Although it primarily covers the record business, it also covers film soundtracks, home video, intellectual rights and music publishing, mobile/ring tones/video game music, downloads, various musical genres, music distribution and retailing, artist profiles, and it even manages to review new records. *Billboard* gives an excellent snapshot of the industry segments it covers. Another useful news source that covers the record, pop culture, and broadcasting segments, and is available online is www.hitsdailydouble.com. Finally, websites from Rolling Stone, Spin, and Pitchfork Media afford a more consumer-oriented view of the ever-evolving music business.

Well before movie soundtrack albums such as *Les Misérables*; *O Brother, Where Art Thou?*; and *Titanic* had a massive impact on the record industry, *Billboard* had identified and tracked the relationship between hit record albums and other entertainment properties such as movies, television shows, and video games. Television shows such as, *The OC, One Tree Hill, Smallville, Gilmore Girls,* and others, and movies such as the various installments of the *Spiderman* franchise, *Garden State,* and *8 Mile* each provide an example of a primarily visual medium driving hit record sales. Without soundtrack albums, the record business would have suffered even greater setbacks. Soundtrack albums such as those mentioned helped keep some record companies afloat. Those companies and executives who read and absorbed what a source like *Billboard* reports were aware of this trend early, took advantage of it, and surfed the wave as it developed.

So, identify what the bible is for the industry segments that interest you. If you're into recording technology, *Mix, Tape Op, Electronic Musician,* and *Pro Sound News* are some of the bibles for the recording studio segment. For songwriting, *Performing Songwriter* and *American Songwriter* are two of the best magazines. One way to determine your "bible" is to join the right network of people working in that segment. For a songwriter, it could be a regional songwriters group as well as one of the performing rights societies, ASCAP, SESAC, and BMI. The people working in that segment will tell you what they rely on as their bible. Those performing rights organizations also produce very informative magazines, online resources, and in-person conferences and workshops for their members.

Reading your bible regularly provides a senior sleuth with up-to-the-minute information on what's happening in the market segments they are interested in. The magazines also often provide another important insight: what companies are hot and likely to be in growth mode, which often translates to hiring opportunities.

WORKSHOP 15.1. FIND AND USE YOUR INDUSTRY NEWS SOURCES

Identify two print magazines that provide the best glimpse into the industry area that most interests you.

_____

_____

Identify two Web publications that offer up-to-date, insightful news and commentary on the industry area that most interests you. (Note: Don't use the online edition of the magazines already listed; find additional sources.)

_____

_____

ACTION ITEM

Commit to a regular schedule to update yourself on the latest industry news from these four sources.

ASKING THE RIGHT QUESTIONS

Being a detective also means learning to ask the right questions. Asking good questions means you must be knowledgeable before you can know exactly what to inquire about. Prior to joining academia, a few of the people I interviewed for open positions at my PR firm actually asked me, "Mr. Hatschek, can you tell me what your company does?"

Unfortunately, a question like that is the kiss of death for a job seeker. I do everything I can to end that kind of interview in three minutes or less. If someone hasn't taken the time to at least find out what business occurs at the firm they're interviewing at, why should an interviewer have any interest in investing any time in them? Forget it. It's over.

Become a monster detective, if you're serious about wanting to have a career in the music industry. Why? Competition. Other people are doing their detective homework. If you don't do your research and your competition does, they're going to have a big edge when it comes time to interview and impress the future boss with their savvy and intelligence. The person who hasn't done their detective work will often appear to be just another wannabe. Few things impress a prospective employer more than an articulate job candidate who has a basic knowledge of the hiring company's business activities. Having a few well-thought-out questions or observations to bring up in the interview is another way to make a strong positive impression.

An extensive listing of useful research books, directories, industry Websites, and job listing Web resources may be found in the appendices at the end of this book.

WORKSHOP 15.2. CAREER HOMEWORK

Part 1

Visit the nearest library that has a good collection (or online subscription access) of the business and industry directories such as Plunkett's, Hoover's, Ward's, etc. Investigate what information is available on some of the leading companies in your area of interest. Take notes on each company's size, overall revenue, location, key company officers, and other essential data. If you are researching a boutique firm that is not well known, then you may not find much information in some of these directories. But look up a large publicly traded firm such as Apple Computer, Warner Music, or Steinway Music in the directories. You'll see the general information that can be useful to a job seeker.

Next, use one of the online database services that may be available at the library such as Lexis/Nexis or Factiva (aka Dow Jones Information) to investigate any articles that have been written recently about the company and its latest efforts. Also, if the firm you are researching is publicly traded, meaning that anyone can purchase shares in the company, then Google Finance is another good repository of information.

Remember the wealth of detailed company and position research that can be done on LinkedIn, and also, by taking the most direct route—going straight to the company websites. Go beyond the landing pages to really investigate company history, mission and vision, products and services, press releases, earnings reports, and of course, any career information.

Part 2

On the Internet, visit LinkedIn, Vault.com, and RileyGuide.com. All offer a wide range of helpful resources and information. Look over the various topics from interviewing to negotiating salary. RileyGuide.com has an especially useful set of articles and resources pertaining to salary negotiations. Vault.com lists the top ten Media and Entertainment companies to work for, based in part on ratings from their employees. Check out articles and information posted in music industry groups on LinkedIn. After spending at least thirty minutes exploring each website, pick two articles from each website that you find most helpful at the current moment in your career journey and add notes of your findings to your Career Portfolio. Also remember to get in the habit of tapping your own network, as well as online career resources like these two sites when you have a career-related question or job search problem that needs solving.

16

Fast-Track Your Growth with Trade Associations and Mentors

In today's music industry, there's a veritable alphabet soup of trade associations identified by insiders via their range of acronyms: CMJ, NARAS, GMA, GMS, etc. Dozens are involved in the entertainment industry and provide excellent resources to those looking to join the business. (An appendix of some of the leading trade associations for the U.S. and Canada may be found at the back of this book.)

We recommend that you identify, locate, and involve yourself in these organizations on a local, regional, or national level. Most have some type of dues structure. Some offer low-cost student or trial memberships. These organizations produce newsletters, events, trade shows, and seminars, and almost every one of them has a website loaded with inside industry information. Many have paid professional staff who serve the industry and provide outstanding networking hubs for a job seeker.

Some of the most important associations for the music industry are listed in the appendix: the Recording Academy (NARAS), the Audio Engineering Society (AES), the National Association of Music Merchants (NAMM), the National Association of Record Industry Professionals (NARIP), and the Society of Professional Audio Recording Services (SPARS). Check out their websites, and see how you can get involved in their activities and meet their members. You have very little to lose and vital connections and knowledge to gain.

These trade associations provide you with a direct link to working professionals and offer a ready-made pipeline to quickly beef up your network. As an example, in the San Francisco region, there are quite a few active trade organizations: the San Francisco chapter of the Recording Academy and its student wing dubbed "GrammyU," the student section of the Audio Engineering Society at San Francisco State University, Stanford, Ex'Pression Center, as well as the regular AES members' section, the West Coast Songwriter's Association, the Society of Motion Picture and Television Engineers, the American Federation of Musicians (AF of M), the local chapter of AFTRA/SAG (American Federation of Television and Radio Artists/Screen Actors Guild), and others. AF of M, SAG, and AFTRA are unions of working professionals providing additional benefits to their membership. Every one of these organizations presents an opportunity to grow your knowledge and build your network. How many exist in your region? Contact them today, and use the organizations to expand your network.

Most of these trade associations regularly host events and maintain an email list. Get on that list. Attend the events. If you can't afford the admission, see if you can volunteer in exchange for attending. Tapping into trade association resources may be as easy as volunteering. If you volunteer for a trade association, you will immediately gain information and contacts. They may not need a volunteer today, but when they do, you've got to make sure you're at the top of their volunteer list. Offer to volunteer at the office, or their next event. Bring your business cards, get involved, make yourself an asset to the local manager of the trade association, and before you know it, your network will be ten times its current size! But once again, you have to put in the effort to get the reward.

Some also offer job referrals, open position listings, and informal news of positions that become available. Get involved, and see what types of information and resources are accessible. You may be able to take advantage of dozens of potential unadvertised job and internship opportunities.

The sheer number of trade associations can be daunting. After a while, they may begin to blend and look like the aforementioned alphabet soup. Get started by picking one or two that align most closely with your primary area of interest; then, see what develops. Remember, trade associations exist to provide information and resources to their members. Participate in them, and you will move ahead much more quickly than your competitors who choose not to get involved.

 WORKSHOP 16. ATTEND AN INDUSTRY EVENT OR CONFERENCE: A FIELD TRIP

One of the surest means to identify unadvertised industry jobs is meeting and maintaining contact with working industry professionals.

Based on your geographic location and the specific area of interest you are focusing on, research the trade association that serves that market segment. For instance, for record labels, the respective trade associations that intersect the record business include RIAA, NARM, CMJ, A2IM, and to a lesser extent, NARAS. Find out where the nearest upcoming event, conference, meeting, seminar, or other event that you might attend. Then develop a plan to get in contact with that organization, and ask if you can attend one event to check out the association. You might also offer to volunteer to assist at the conference or seminar. The goal of this workshop is to start the process of meeting working professionals in your area of interest. These are the very people who will be capable of tipping you off to unadvertised positions once you have met them and made a positive impression.

ACTION ITEM

Add your list of industry events to your short term goals and calendar program. Make plans for any travel or admission fees you may incur now, and attend the next industry event that will help you to grow your network, meeting the working professionals who can help tip you off to the unlisted opportunities in your area of interest.

MENTORS MAKE A DIFFERENCE

Trade associations also often provide an excellent opportunity to identify and gain the support of mentors: empathetic working professionals who may be willing to educate and coach you in the ways of the business. And there's no way to put a price on the value of that treasure.

The Role of Mentors

A *mentor* is a wise and trusted counselor. Another way to think of a mentor is as a "coach" in a specific area of your career. Close your eyes now, for a moment, and consider, "Who is my music industry mentor?"

Securing a mentor to help guide your own career development is arguably one of the most impactful ways to advance your career. A mentor—someone with extensive industry experience, knowledge, and connections—provides insight that someone new to the industry would take decades to develop on their own. Learning from a mentor is an invaluable aid to fast-tracking your own career knowledge and development.

Where does one find a mentor? Look to teachers, family friends, and the aforementioned industry events, often sponsored by various trade associations. You may also decide to send out an email blast to your network asking if anyone knows of an experienced industry person in a specific area who might be willing to chat with you about careers in their field. You don't have to call them and ask them to become your mentor right out of the box. Instead, simply ask for a few minutes of their time to speak about your career interest and their experience. If the chemistry is right, you may have started a relationship that you can develop over time into that of a trusted mentor to aid you in your career development.

WORKSHOP 16.2. LOCATING A MENTOR

If you don't already have a relationship with an industry mentor, now's the time to approach possible mentors and start a mentor/mentee relationship. Start a list in your Career Portfolio of possible candidates for your mentor, and determine the best way to approach them about sharing some of their experiences.

You probably won't ever have to ask someone if they will be a mentor. Instead, such relationships evolve over time as you engage in a dialog and the professional shares more and more of their knowledge and experience with you. Each of us has to develop an approach to start a new relationship that we feel comfortable with. If asking someone you may barely know to act as a mentor seems daunting, instead, simply call or email, and politely ask if they might have twenty to thirty minutes to meet (or Skype) and chat about the music industry. Based on the chemistry at that meeting, you'll have a good idea if that person might be willing and available to continue meeting or corresponding from time to time. Over time, you should be able to develop a few such relationships so that you have a small group of experts on whom you can rely to help answer your questions as your career journey unfolds.

CHAPTER **17** | # How to Ace Job Interviews

Let's assume you've submitted a résumé for a position that is advertised or that you've learned about through your network, and you've been called in for an interview. How do you maximize this opportunity?

Here is a checklist of what you should do in advance to prepare for the job interview.

PRE-INTERVIEW CHECKLIST:

	Yes	No
1. Your résumé is in tip-top shape.	☐	☐
2. You know something about the company and, if possible, the person with whom you will be meeting.	☐	☐
3. You have a handful of your business cards.	☐	☐
4. You have practiced the interview workshop on the following pages with a friend or family member.	☐	☐
5. Dress neatly, and present yourself professionally.	☐	☐
6. Plan to arrive five to ten minutes early, especially if you are traveling there for the first time.	☐	☐
7. Jot down a few questions about the company, its activities, and the requirements for an employee's success in that company. Make a note to ask these questions when appropriate during your interview.	☐	☐
8. Bring a note pad and pen.	☐	☐
9. Be 100 percent focused on the moment during your interview. This generally means silencing or turning off your cell phone unless there is a compelling reason to use it to enhance the interview.	☐	☐

During the interview itself, just concentrate on being yourself and answering questions as directly and honestly as you can. If you are at the entry-level stage of your career, the person interviewing you doesn't expect you to have all the answers. What they are looking for is intelligence, a positive attitude, examples of your past experience that are relevant to the type of work done by the firm, and whether or not they feel there will be a fit between you and the company.

Take the time to look around the company offices and take a few mental notes. Are the offices neat, bright, and pleasant? Do the people working there smile and address you directly? Is this the kind of place you would like to come to each day? If not, no matter how good an offer, you should consider these factors. Also, if there are pictures of sailboats in the office of your interviewer, and you happen to have a family member who sails, take the initiative to mention that point, and use it to build a rapport.

How should you dress for an interview? Dress appropriately for the company. Determine appropriate dress by doing your homework. If you're going for an interview to a company that does concert production and sound reinforcement, their stock in trade is building, moving, and maintaining big, heavy pieces of equipment. If that's the kind of job you're after, you definitely don't want to be wearing an Armani suit. However, if you're wearing a pair of khaki pants and a neatly pressed shirt with a collar, you will look professional and neat. If you are interviewing for an internship at a well-known Beverly Hills entertainment law firm, you would wear a suit. The impression you make with your dress, your manner, and your questions and comments sets you apart—to your benefit or your detriment. Take the time to rehearse carefully so that you are as comfortable and confident as possible.

The interview drill workshop on the next pages will allow you to build your confidence by practicing aloud the types of questions that you are likely to be asked during an actual job interview. Spend some time thinking about and writing down your answers to these types of questions. Equally important is practicing the interview drills aloud with a friend or family member. Do it over and over until you are very comfortable talking about yourself, your goals, your experiences, your education, and of course every example of value that you created for previous employers. The more familiar you are talking about yourself, your qualifications, and your worth points (how you have created value for your employer in the past), the better the impression. Be prepared to the point that discussing your interests and skills is second nature. Doing so will give you the confidence to present yourself at your best.

⑰ **WORKSHOP 17.** JOB INTERVIEW PRACTICE

You wouldn't show up for a gig with your band without adequate rehearsal, so don't shortchange yourself in an interview. Repeated rehearsal will allow you to be at your best.

Start by looking carefully at the questions below, and write down your answers. Some of these questions will stretch you and may take two or three sessions of thinking and making notes before you can construct a solid response. Interviews can be tense for all parties, and practicing will build your confidence. Once you have answers that you feel comfortable with, enlist the help of a friend or family member to drill you and strengthen your interview skills.

Job Interview Practice Session

Your interviewer is a human resources coordinator for Big Time Records.

QUESTIONS/TOPICS

1. Please tell me a little bit about yourself.

2. What do you feel qualifies you to work at Big Time Records?

3. Could you share a successful project or activity in which you played a key role?

4. Tell me about the most difficult boss you have ever had.

5. Tell me about a time when you failed at something and what you learned from that experience.

6. Where do you see your career taking you over the next two to four years? (A variation on this question is to lengthen the timeline to five to ten years, especially if you are a Career Changer or have significant work experience; use your published goals to help answer this question.)

7. What strategies and tactics do you believe will help a company like Big Time Records remain relevant in the digital age?

8. Are there any other skills or accomplishments that you feel qualify you to work here?

9. Do you have any questions for me before we wrap things up?

Follow-Up Thoughts for this Sample Interview Question Set

• Question 1. Remember your Personal Commercial? Use it as the basis for a proven answer to this question.

• Questions 2. Your work creating Career Road Maps and matching them with your Marketable Skill Set will pay off when you list off the various skills and capabilities that will position you as a prospective valuable addition to the label's staff.

- Questions 3, 4, and 5 are situational questions that ask you to use a narrative response, and showing your own critical thinking to demonstrate your savvy when it comes to the way work and projects actually get done. If you have never practiced answering any of the types of situational questions found in this chapter, these questions will likely throw you for a loop. A sampling of more of these types of questions will be found later in this chapter.

- Question 6 is an opportunity to show that you have well-thought-out goals and that the progression you envision is realistic. If you've been speaking with working professionals and testing your own goals, your career road map information, and have a good understanding of the career ladder in your area of interest, you will be ready to give an engaging and impressive answer to this question or any variation on it.

- Question 7 is a forward-thinking one, and challenges you to demonstrate that you've actually spent some quality time considering what it will take for the firm to stay or become successful. Your answer should address opportunities, threats, as well as the overall environment faced in the market that the firm competes in. So knowledge of the market sector is crucial to answering this question well.

- Question 8 is an opportunity to think about what other skills, talents, or competencies are likely to be highly valued in the firm you are interviewing with. Do you have strong HTML or Web skills? Are you experienced at building audiences using digital media? This question gives you a chance to blow your own horn a little bit and tie in your own measurable successes to the needs of the firm. Remember to quote one of your worth points if you have one, since measurable benefits always make memorable impressions on interviewers.

- Question 9 is not a throw-away question. The interviewer actually wants to measure just how much you've been thinking about their firm, the potential job, and your possible role at the firm. If you make the mistake of answering, "Nope, I'm good," you've just missed the chance to demonstrate that you have given serious thought to your future at this firm. Have at least two questions ready to ask that will demonstrate your level of engagement, in the event your interviewer takes this route.

Remember to thank your interviewer for the time they have spent interviewing you. And when you get home or back to a computer, send an email or handwritten note to thank everyone you met again! Time is the most precious commodity any busy professional can share.

Use this workshop again as a review before you go out on an actual job interview. If you are enrolled in school, visit your school's career center. Ask a career counselor to help you by doing a "mock interview" with you and then give you honest feedback about what you are doing well and what still needs improvement. Go online and research what some other typical interview questions might be and practice those as well.

INTERVIEWING MECHANICS AND OTHER ESSENTIALS

Do your best to answer questions at an even pace, and take a minute to think about your answers. Above all, if you don't know the answer to a specific question on an actual interview (especially if it is a technical question), don't be afraid to answer by saying, "I don't know the answer, but I'm sure I could find out."

How is your body language? Try not to be tense and nervous— easier said than done, we know, but if you're fully prepared, you have no reason to be nervous! It is important to speak clearly, show enthusiasm, and make eye contact with your interviewer. Don't forget to smile!

Remember that any interview is, first and foremost, your best opportunity to make a positive impression on a potential employer or a referral to employment. Make the most of each interview by being well prepared and ready to answer questions such as these. If possible, secure the full name and accurate pronunciation of your interviewer's name in advance. Bring at least two copies of your current résumé, and have some current information about the company at your command so you can show you have done some research and understand the company and their products or services, as well as the competitive marketplace in which they compete.

Review these questions, and practice your answers aloud at least three times before going on any interview. Do your homework before you step into that office, and your interviews will bring a handsome reward.

The questions in the interview practice session are similar to those that you're likely to be asked if you're actually applying for a job. If you don't practice answering them, odds are that you may say something that you regret.

For instance, if an interviewer asks, "What do you think qualifies you to work at this company?" be ready to answer that using some of your worth points. Do your research on the company in advance. Know something about what they do, and mention what you know about the company and their business in the interview. Before you go on the interview, practice stating your worth points and the information you have dug out about the company. Practice speaking in front of a mirror, and then practice with a colleague who will give you constructive criticism. It makes all of the difference in your delivery. Remember not to speak too quickly, and try to enunciate your words. Ask your rehearsal partner to grade your speed, delivery, and intelligibility. Speech patterns make a difference.

Also, practice both sitting and standing. Be aware of your hands and facial expressions. Overactive hands can be a distraction. However, using your hand or hands to help make a point occasionally can strengthen your communication. Likewise, don't stare at your knees or look at the floor during your interview. You don't have to lock eyes with your interviewer, but make eye contact from time to time, and keep your head up and focused in their direction. Be aware of your legs, and avoid playing with your clothing, shoes, hair, etc. Women, be sure to wear clothing that will not embarrass you if you sit on a couch or deep chair. If you have tattoos on your arms and legs, it might be wise to cover them up for the interview—at least, until you can observe the culture of the workplace. Avoid cologne or smoking right before an interview. Finish your mint or throw out any gum before entering the building. And, it deserves another mention: don't let your mobile phone become a distraction from the human interaction that is at the heart of a successful interview.

You may have an unconscious habit that could become distracting in an interview. Find out in your practice session, and get it under control. Above all, be tidy, organized, professional looking, and prepared for success. We all give off subtle and not-so-subtle cues about how focused and prepared we are in any given situation. Learn how to control yourself and appear poised and confident, even if you have butterflies dancing in your stomach.

In addition to your enthusiasm, experience, and qualifications, which should be evident from your personal demeanor as well as your well-crafted résumé, your interviewer is trying to determine, "Will you work hard, do you know a bit about the business, is there prior job performance that shows you are stable and trustworthy?" If you are going for a job as a manager, versus a technologist or content creator, how you present yourself will be more important. Do you look professional? Do you sound articulate? Are your communication skills displayed to your advantage? Will you be comfortable representing the employer in person and on the phone? Your interviewer may say, "Bill, come to my desk and pick up the phone. We want to ask you a few questions over the phone." Or they may ask you to take an aptitude test to measure your ability to follow directions, do simple math, and assess your command of the written word. One of my students just applied for a job at a leading Hollywood entertainment PR firm, and at the start of her second interview, she was shown into a conference room and asked to draft a short press announcement in ten minutes using pen and paper after being handed a one-paragraph client scenario. Then she was asked to read it aloud to her interview panel. Think ahead, and do your absolute best to be well prepared to show your skills to best advantage.

Here's a list of other considerations that you will want to have thought about before an interview so that you are as prepared as possible as you begin the process of interviewing for a new position.

- **Video and Telephone Interviews.** Increasingly, firms are relying on less expensive ways to conduct early interviews. First, be sure you have access to a reliable telephone and computer that is set up for video conferencing, using Skype, which is free and nearly ubiquitous in business today. Then, be aware that if you are doing a phone or video interview, you'll want to speak at a moderate pace, not so fast that intelligibility suffers. Just as you want to come across as professional and confident in your communication in an in-person interview, you'll want to do the same via phone or video. Be sure that you are in a private room without the possibility of interruptions from family members, pets, or distracting background noise from home appliances. Finally, if you know you will be doing a phone or video interview, it pays to do a test run with a colleague and have them critique your performance. Remember on video interviews, you'll be seen as will your surroundings, so if you have a room filled with posters that may not be appropriate, find a different location and background for the video interview. You want to maintain the same level of professionalism that you'd present in person.

- **Panel Interviews.** While many interviews are done one-on-one, some employers use panels of three or more employees to do interview screening. This can be disconcerting if you have never faced a larger group in a stressful interview situation. The advice offered earlier in this chapter all applies, but with a few additions for panel interviews. If you can, introduce yourself, shake hands, and make eye contact with each panelist at the start of the interview. If that's not practical, look at each one while they are introduced to you and acknowledge them with something like, "Nice to meet you, Miss Jameson." Once the interview gets going, each panelist may ask a question, or one panelist may ask all the questions, while the others observe or ask occasional follow up questions. While you are being asked the question, direct your attention to the person asking the question, then compose yourself and as you give your answer, start with the person who asked the question, but then shift your head and eyes along the panel so that you look towards each panelist over the course of your answer. Basically, you want each panelist to feel that you've given him or her some attention during the process.

- **Applicant Testing.** Hiring is an expensive process, especially if a firm invests in an employee that does not end up being retained. To help reduce the chances of making poor hiring decisions, many firms now engage in various types of testing to try to weed out potentially unsuitable candidates as early in the process as possible. As was mentioned above, one type of testing involves skills and aptitude. Such tests can range from basic math (add up this column of numbers), to taking a telephone message from a hiring manager pretending to be an angry client, from a timed typing test or finding the flawed formula in an Excel budget spreadsheet, to asking you to take a personality type test to determine your likely aptitude for a sales or customer service position. Depending on the firm and industry, you may be asked to submit for a drug test. In some cases, you may also be asked a hypothetical question about a problem or situation at the office to see how you would respond to a dilemma or quandary. All of these tests have been put in place to help determine the best and shortest list of candidates for final consideration, so don't take the tests lightly, if you are asked to engage in any of them.

- **Situational Questions.** Three of the questions in the workshop earlier asked about situations that you had experienced with the expectation that you would reveal more about yourself in the process of asking these somewhat prickly questions. Now that you've grappled with three such questions, here's a more complete explanation of the best way to address such questions.

USING THE S-T-A-R SYSTEM

Many career coaches suggest using a simple mnemonic system to build your answer. It's the S-T-A-R system, which stands for **Situation** ⟶ **Task** ⟶ **Action** ⟶ **Result**. By using a S-T-A-R approach to answering situational questions, you will put yourself in the best light and emphasize that each answer leads to a demonstrable result for your past employer, teacher, organization, or other group that you were working for.

Here's how to practice answering situational questions:

1. Describe the **Situation** that fits the question you have been asked.

2. Briefly state what your **Task** was in relation to the situation.

3. State what **Actions** you took, and finally,

4. What **Results** happened due to your efforts.

For further practice, here's a list of twelve more questions that you can practice with to learn how to perform at your best when asked these types of situational questions. After each question is the skill or competency listed in italics that the employer is looking for evidence of in your response.

SAMPLE SITUATIONAL INTERVIEW QUESTIONS

1. Tell me about a project that you had to organize for work or school? What steps were involved and what was the outcome? (Organizational skills)

2. Tell me about a time when you had to deal with a disgruntled or angry customer or colleague? How did you resolve the situation? (Interpersonal and conflict-resolution skills)

3. Describe a situation in which you misunderstood instruction from a teacher or supervisor. Why did the misunderstanding occur? What steps were taken to resolve the situation? What was the outcome? (Communication skills)

4. Tell me about a time when you considered the pros and cons of a specific situation and decided not to take any action, even though there was pressure on you to do so. (Judgment skills)

5. Describe a situation when you faced multiple deadlines in a short time frame. What caused the situation? How did you handle it? What was the outcome? (Time management skills)

6. Give me an example of a time when you helped solve a problem in a group or team setting. (Problem solving and collaboration)

7. Tell me about a time when you were able to use a newly acquired skill in a workplace setting. What was the skill or knowledge? Describe the situation and outcome. (*Technical skills*)

8. What documents do you create on a regular basis? Do you have someone else proof them for you? What are the typical changes you make before sharing them? (*Written communication, proofreading skills*)

9. Tell me about a situation you faced when something you said or did was misunderstood. What did you do to clarify or resolve the situation? What was the end result? (*Communication and interpersonal skills*)

10. Tell me about a time when you disagreed with a coworker or team member. What was the basis for your difference of opinion? How was the difference worked out? What was the end result of your interaction? (*Interpersonal skills, conflict resolution*)

11. Describe a situation when you were not proud of what you accomplished. What was the challenge or issue you faced? Why do you think your results were not up to par? What did you learn from the situation? (*Self-assessment skills, quality orientation*)

12. Tell me about a time when you had to "go the extra mile" to complete a project. Why were you in that situation? Were there any other ways to complete the project successfully? (*Organization, time management skills*)

Learning to use the S-T-A-R method will help ensure that you can explain how you have been able to learn, grow, and collaborate in the various situations you have found yourself in. A great way to practice communicating your skills and the value of your experience using the S-T-A-R method is to develop your résumé content statements using the same framework!

A final note on the importance of learning how to answer situational and behavioral interview questions: Employers understand that the most reliable predictor of your future achievements and contributions to their firm can be found in your past actions and decisions. So, be ready to go into some detail as you address these types of questions, because your critical thinking, decision making, and actions will be the primary measure that can help to make you a standout candidate for the job to which you most aspire.

> *"Employers understand that the most reliable predictor of your future achievements and contributions to their firm can be found in your past actions and decisions."*

Salary and Benefit Discussions. Generally, these are not initially addressed in the first interview, unless only one interview is expected to occur. Some positions will list the salary in the job posting, but this is becoming increasingly rare today. Normally, if there are a series of interviews and you progress through each round, salary will come up as a natural part of the advancing process. When salary does begin to be a part of the dialog, a simple rule of thumb applies to how to approach such conversations. Make sure that you focus all of your energy and attention on what you can do for the employer throughout each interview and leave any discussion of salary and benefits to the last part of the interview. One way for you to initiate a salary discussion is to ask for the range of pay that is found for the position you may be interviewing for, perhaps near the end of the first interview. That allows the employer to have a little wiggle room, and to explain what criteria (experience, certifications, degrees, knowledge of particular software) will influence any specific salary offer. But, some find it to be pretty presumptuous, and even liken it to proposing marriage on the first date! As such, it is usually best not to discuss salary until you actually have an offer in hand to discuss (and negotiate).

If you've done your research as recommended earlier, you likely already have an idea as to what the pay range will be for the job track you are interviewing on. It's also essential to have a solid grasp on what your actual cost of living is so you know whether or not you can afford to work full time for the salary offered. If it's not enough, you may have to take a second job to make ends meet until you can earn more in your chosen field. Finally, don't be afraid to ask if any medical, dental, optical, pension, or other benefits are included as part of the compensation package once you have an offer. If they are not, you'll have to budget accordingly.

Accepting the Offer. Depending on how long the interview process has been, you may feel elated, excited, and a bit overwhelmed when you actually receive an offer for employment. If there have been multiple interviews and extended conversations, it would be wise to ask that the offer be formalized in an email or document and sent to you for one final review. This also affords you the opportunity to "sleep on it" for a day or two before letting the employer know if you accept their offer. Most employers will not find this off-putting, especially if through the interview process, they've identified you as the best possible candidate from among the field of contenders. Allowing you a brief time period to digest the offer and its ramifications for your personal and professional life is fairly standard operating procedure. You can also take the time to reread everything closely and discuss it with a trusted family member or confidante. Be sure to respond before the time limit you've agreed to, as well. Keep in mind that the time to negotiate any part of offer is *before* you accept the position. And, once you officially accept a position, by ethical standards, you should no longer be actively interviewing elsewhere.

In closing, we can't emphasize enough that when it comes to interviewing, practice makes perfect, so don't shortchange yourself by going into an interview unprepared. The music industry is actually quite small, and if you blow an interview badly, it's hard to come back from that quickly. Always focus and be as prepared as possible. And don't forget that if you are now going out on informational interviews, they may sometimes turn into an informal hiring interview if you make an exceptionally strong impression. In that case, if you've worked through this chapter and its workshop, you'll be well prepared. Good luck!

CHAPTER

18 Auditioning for Your Job: The Role of Internships

The emerging modern music industry is continually changing, and related practical experience has attained "must have" status for any serious job seeker. At the most basic level, anyone without relevant experience and/or internships on their résumé will be hard-pressed to make a case for consideration for a music industry job. An internship offers an effective and needed bridge to your first job in the industry. The right internship position puts you in a working environment where professionals are practicing their craft in your specific field of interest. An internship also allows you to observe and participate meaningfully in the firm's day-to-day business operation. And from the employer's point of view, they offer a glimpse of what you might bring to the workplace if you were offered a paid position.

> "At the most basic level, anyone without relevant experience and/ or internships on their résumé will be hard-pressed to make a case for consideration for a music industry job."

The competition to land music industry internships has increased significantly. Not only are more job seekers realizing that they present one of the most likely paths to employment, but employers are beginning to view their interns as prospective new hires "auditioning" for paid positions. *The Wall Street Journal* recently reported in a June 13, 2013 article, "Interns Take the Lead," that one of the leading entertainment firms in Las Vegas selects ten to fifteen M.B.A. students each summer as interns. Over the next year, the article reported that five of the new hires for the Las Vegas entertainment's management team were former interns that had proven themselves at the firm.

Although we strongly endorse internships, since they provide an unparalleled real-world learning experience, they also may tax your financial health. Many entertainment industry internships are unpaid positions. A few paid internships do exist, and they are the most sought-after. A growing number also require intern candidates to be enrolled in a college course for academic credit. Regardless of whether your internship is unpaid or paid, it can be extremely valuable to your career development if you plan for it properly and set specific goals for what you plan to learn.

To get the most from an internship, expose yourself to as many facets of the company's operations as possible. Avoid no task or activity that can help you grow. If you see the company president is hosting a golf tournament, volunteer to help. If a staff member must stay late to finish a priority project, offer to stay and help. Arrive at work early every day, and stay until all your assignments are completed, keeping a positive attitude the entire time. The more you can rub elbows with both rank and file staff as well as the movers and the shakers, the more benefit you will receive from your internship.

Learning how to set up a recording session, update the firm's online presence, make travel plans for your boss, or work the box office at a concert aren't the only things you want to master. Many benefits accrue for savvy interns who network with the employees they meet. If the junior staff goes out for sushi on Fridays, tag along and listen and learn. Do your best to identify a coach or mentor among the employees, and ask them for advice and guidance.

Another way to maximize the benefits from an internship is to widen your exposure at the company. As an example, if you intern three days a week at a record label, perhaps you could come in one of the other days and observe operations (often called "shadowing") in another department. That way, you will learn more about what's done in, say, the business affairs department, the marketing department, or the promotions department.

The bottom line on internships is that they provide outstanding opportunities to learn and get established in the industry. But there are exceptions: situations where companies may take unfair advantage of so-called "interns" to get free labor, with little or no learning or mentoring offered in the exchange. On occasion, an intern under our supervision was faced with requests for unpaid activities that, frankly, were way above and beyond the call of duty for what amounts to a volunteer position. If this happens to you, compose yourself and bring your concern to your supervisor's attention at a time when he or she is not in the midst of other important tasks. To learn about a firm's business and its operation, you should be exposed to more activities than simply operating a copy machine, making coffee, or washing the boss's car. Be upfront before accepting an internship, and ask for specific information as to what parts of the firm's business and operations you will be exposed to. Explain what areas of the industry you have an interest in and ask for guidance and mentoring in those areas. If it's possible to reach out to past interns via Facebook or LinkedIn research, do so before accepting the internship offer to see how they were treated, and most importantly, how much of an impact the internship has had on their career arc.

If you are enrolled in a college program for internship credit, you have an advantage in that your faculty sponsor should also act as an advocate for you, and usually will contact your workplace supervisor to confirm that your enrollment is predicated on doing meaningful work, albeit at an appropriate level, at their firm. And the faculty sponsor should also emphasize that a key component of any successful academic internship is a workplace supervisor who gives regular feedback to the student on his or her performance.

Don't be too apprehensive about landing an internship. There are thousands of fabulous internships hosted by firms who understand the value of offering an introduction to future industry members via an internship. Remember, many school programs in music business, music products, entertainment law, the recording arts, or other areas of the industry, maintain records of internship opportunities that have been tested by previous students and recommended by faculty. This is an excellent approach to landing the right internship that can be your stepping stone to a greatly expanded professional network and in some cases, even your first job offer.

One studio manager at a world-class Los Angeles music production facility candidly remarked, "The first place we look to fill an opening is our pool of current and past interns. They know our business and what we expect in an employee. More importantly, we have seen them in action and have a good idea as to how quickly they will be able to get up to speed with clients and the rest of our employees. Proving yourself as an intern is the fastest way to be considered for a staff position at our studios." However, not all host firms provide a track from a successful internship to job offers. Some only offer experience and do not hire from the intern pool, so ask about that when you are internship shopping. For students, your school may also offer work-study opportunities that combine a paid position with some type of work experience that can help beef up your transferable skills and talking points for your résumé and interview.

ON THE JOB/YOUR INTERNSHIP

Once you arrive at your internship, a new level of learning begins. Although academic training is important, there's only so much you're going to learn in a classroom environment. When you've got an artist manager calling to find out the latest details about a change in tour routing, or a studio musician breathing down your neck demanding, "Where's the guitar track that I just played?" your motivation to learn quickly is heightened. When you're in a classroom environment, there is a different dynamic. When your boss has instructed you to have the new portion of an artist's website up and functional by week's end so that the band's new video can be previewed there as they launch their national tour, it changes the stakes and your investment in succeeding in a big way.

What will make you, as an intern, valuable and attractive enough to be considered as a potential employee to your future boss? That's the golden question that interns perennially seek to answer.

Figure 18.1 shows some of the key attributes that employers look for when hiring. They also serve as a worthwhile set of skills and attributes that you should try to use during your internships.

MUSIC INDUSTRY EMPLOYER'S WISH LIST

1. **Problem-solving ability** is very important. Bosses generally are bosses because they're the best at dealing with a thousand-and-one problems. So, if you develop problem-solving skills, chances are that you're going to go a long way toward impressing your supervisor. The best way to develop your own problem-solving skills is to take on new challenges, work-study positions, or volunteer opportunities for interesting and exciting roles at school or in your community.

2. **Technical skills** also play a part, too. Today, every new hire must be digitally savvy. Don't overlook the fundamental computer and Internet skills that many baby boomer-aged employers rely on your generation to provide. Do your best to learn basic media production skills in audio and video, and become familiar with the workings of sites such as YouTube, Vimeo, WordPress, UStream, etc. There are many useful tutorials online, nearly all of them free.

3. **The ability to complete assignments responsibly** is a critical skill. Employees who can work effectively in a self-directed manner are a big asset. Part of this skill set is learning how to take direction well and in detail.

4. **Hustle** is required to succeed in this industry. There are not "white-coated operators" standing by at every music industry firm waiting for job assignments. There are just enough people to get projects completed and sometimes not quite enough people to get by, especially in the wake of the consolidation that has occurred in the past decade. So, to succeed, you have to hustle. You will occasionally stay until midnight to complete an important job. It's the nature of the beast. For a great many entertainment industry careers, the hours and schedule are flexible, unlike some other industries. Weekends? Prepare to sacrifice quite a few of them over the course of your career. (If this is sounding bad to you, maybe now is the time to think about alternate fields.)

5. **Perseverance** keeps turning up as another key attribute. Early in my career, a very successful music magazine publisher told me, "Keith, you've got to be in the right place at the right time, and that means being aware of what's going on in all the areas you have an interest, all the time."

What he meant is that if you're serious about a career in the music industry, you have to get plugged in so that you have constant access to the information that relates to your interests. You have to be ready to network every minute of every day, even if you've got a nonmusical day job. You may be pleasantly surprised to discover that someone in the company at which you work has a kid or a nephew or an uncle who works at a label, a booking agency, a social media company, a theme park, or a film studio. Let people know what your aspirations are.

Not to the point of annoyance, but it's good to voice where you are headed in the long run to those you feel close to at your day job. "I enjoy working here, but I'm also writing songs every chance I get and studying how to become a successful songwriter." You may be pleasantly surprised to find out that a distant relative actually turns out to be able to help you make a key career connection.

6. **Integrity** is a key component of your success, not only as an intern, but all the way to the top. When you say you're going to do something, do it. If you say you're going to do something and you realize you can't, don't be afraid to go back and say, "You know, I really can't do that." People will respect you for that far more than if you hide under a blanket and think, "I hope they forgot I said I was going to do that."

Your boss and coworkers are not likely to forget your failure to live up to your promise to perform. The entertainment industry is surprisingly small and most people have good memories. It's okay to regroup and say you can't deliver, or ask for help or more instructions, but it is a huge liability to just blow off an assignment, no matter how trivial it may seem to you. Integrity is an asset that once damaged, proves extremely difficult to repair.

FIG. 18.1. Music Industry Employer's Wish List

FINANCIAL SURVIVAL FOR INTERNS

Once you have identified a prospective internship that appears to provide you with the right learning opportunities, and are in the running to receive an offer for it, the final hurdle appears. The last concern prospective interns have is usually the biggest one: the lack of pay from the employer, even though, as an intern, you must make a firm commitment of time, effort, and energy. If a music firm responds to your inquiries and offers an internship that doesn't pay, you may have to do a little finagling, especially if you have a part- or full-time "day gig" to pay your bills. You may have to ask the boss at your day gig if you could work flexible hours for the term of your internship. That's why it's helpful to let people know a little about your long-term quest to be successful in the music industry. Most people want to see others succeed in the long run.

The worst thing that can happen is that your day job boss will say, "No!" and you'll have to choose to decline the internship or look for a different day gig. Many of our former students have waited tables or worked as baristas, night and weekends, to be able to do an industry internship. In the end, nearly all of them were able to prove themselves and be hired in the industry after paying dues through one or more internships.

The best internship programs are ones in which your role as an intern is managed. This means that when you are interviewing to learn about the opportunity, the employer can lay out, "Here's what our internship offers you and what types of work you will be doing." On the other hand, if your internship description is vague, uncertain, or consists mostly of "clean up and setup, make coffee, stock the bathrooms, wait for assignments as they come up," you might want to look for a little more structured learning environment. Ask a few more questions, because a successful internship is a two-way street—a give-and-take proposition and the best internship host firms understand they will become your teachers for the duration of your time with them.

A good internship program should offer you numerous learning opportunities, which may come in all shapes and sizes. You should have the opportunity to "stretch" your knowledge and skills beyond your current comfort zone. If someone asks you to do something you have never done before, say "Yes," and ask for help or instruction doing it correctly the first time. Pretty soon, you'll be showing another intern how it's done. The most effective internships should include some "a-ha!" moments of revelation where your understanding of the industry takes a leap forward. It's this type of learning that greatly enhances your value in the job market as a music industry professional-in-training.

In the pre-internship discussions, you should be interviewing the intern managers as much as they are interviewing you. "Mr. Music Pro, if I intern at your firm, would there be some learning opportunities for me? What would they include? What skills will I learn that will help me be a better job candidate in the future?" If you get a good answer to that line of inquiry, it's a very positive sign. However, if you don't, or if the manager hems and haws a bit, that's a clear warning sign.

Find out if there will be an opportunity to ask questions of the senior staff at some point. Will you be able to observe staff meetings? Will you have contact with clients (if appropriate)? Will you be filled in on the company's strategic plans and challenges? If they don't have any answer to such questions, you've likely got an internship host that does not understand the learning paradigm required for the best student learning outcomes. If you have to do any errands or traveling, will you be reimbursed for gas? It's smart to ask those kinds of questions up front.

A few internships, usually with the larger companies such as record labels, actually offer minimum wage to interns, as they understand the mutual benefit of offering a paycheck, however small.

Why is that? The intern, even when receiving a small paycheck, is often more committed. And the employer, since they are actually paying, thinks, "It's a resource, we're paying for it," instead of saying, "She's an intern, she sits and reads *Billboard* for four hours and only does fifteen minutes of work, but it has no impact on my bottom line." So, ask questions and as referenced earlier, speak with a current or past intern, and ask them what they learned during their internship.

Another key is to network with your friends and acquaintances. Let your friends who have similar interests know, "I did an internship at such and such company, and they're looking for more people now!" If you're in a school program, network constantly with other students who have completed internships. Your faculty advisor should also be able to tip you off to the firms that in the past have offered the best internship growth opportunities.

It's all right to be picky and seek out a solid internship, but it will take time, research, and perseverance, since the better internship opportunities have the most qualified applicants. Prepare yourself, and remember that you may need to work a part-time job or save up enough money to focus on your internship. Earning will come later in your career. Do not mistake your internship as an earning opportunity. It is a way to enhance your "hire-ability" as soon as you absorb what knowledge you can.

Keep in mind that your internship is a temporary situation, and if it goes well, it is an audition for an industry job. Secondly, in a good internship, there's a balance between learning and earning: completing meaningful work for your intern host firm (earning for them) and your boss, and learning the ins and outs of their business, which will enhance your marketable skill set, including your area-specific industry knowledge (learning for you).

Not all internships lead to your next step on that career ladder. A former student called to say, "Oh-h-h-h, that internship was a nightmare. I had no idea what an entertainment industry public relations firm did. I was maintaining six different databases, stuffing press kits and envelopes, and running a copy machine in a tiny, hot room. I was sorting hundreds of pieces of mail, and one week, I was there until 2 A.M. because there was a movie promotion campaign breaking, and we had to assemble and hand out goodie bags to 10,000 people at an industry event at 7 A.M. the next morning. At the conclusion of my three-month internship, I knew that this end of the business wasn't for me."

Guess what? That was the second most valuable type of internship that person could have had, at that point in her career journey. Why? Because she knew for sure that she was not cut out to work in entertainment public relations.

Remember, the most valuable internship is one that leads to:

- an enhanced marketable skills set, and

- a strengthened and expanded professional network...

...in your number one area of interest. And if you make a strong enough impression, it may even lead to the promise of a job offer at the firm that has seen what you are capable of adding to their team.

 ## WORKSHOP 18. DESCRIBING YOUR IDEAL INTERNSHIP OPPORTUNITY

As you are considering internship options, take this opportunity to make a list of what types of internship might be the best stepping stone for your own career development in your primary area of interest. Next, add to that list the types of jobs, duties, and responsibilities you think you might be engaged in on an ideal internship. Look back at your "Marketable Skill Set," and identify what relevant knowledge or skills that you bring to the table. Make a list on a small notepad, and review it frequently. This is a handy exercise and goes a long way to preparing you for a prospective pre-internship interview. Be sure to be realistic, and remember that the best internships are ones that combine some of the necessary grunt work with the opportunity to observe and learn from the key employees at the internship host firm. Internships have proven to be effective "auditions," as this chapter's title suggested, for literally thousands of aspiring professionals entering the music industry each year. Work hard to land a good one, and you will be on your way to getting onto the path that will take you to a paying gig in the industry!

19 Your Job Search Action Plan: The Three Best Means to Land a Music Industry Job

At last, it's time to map out your specific, personalized Job Search Action Plan building on the skills, knowledge, connections, and industry savvy you've developed.

In this chapter, you'll learn how to maximize your job search by:

- effective use of networking

- identifying and approaching company targets of opportunity

- applying and following up to open position listings

Together, you'll use them to formalize and launch your own Job Search Action Plan at the end of part III.

History has proven that in combination, those actions are the most effective means to landing an industry job. We'll review each method in this chapter. Since you're ready to present yourself in the best possible light, take advantage simultaneously of these three most effective means to identify and land your dream job in the music industry.

1. NETWORKING

Networking was covered extensively in chapter 14. Here are a few more suggestions to use in combination with that chapter's content.

Networking Tips

- *Be courteous and gracious* to everyone, even if they may not be able to help you today. You never know when you may be able to support them, or they you, in the future. Remember, various segments of the music industry are, in fact, small markets where most professionals know one another quite well.

- *Carry your business cards* with you all the time, even at the health spa or at a church picnic.

- If you see someone in your network that doesn't recognize you, take the initiative to go up and *reintroduce yourself.* Never ask, "Do you remember me?" Instead, say hello, and then mention when you met and what you have been up to lately. Be sure to ask them about his or her latest activities and interests, as well.

- *Always return calls and email* within twenty-four hours or the next business day whichever is sooner.

- *Nurture your network.* We recommend contacting one person each week that you haven't seen or chatted with recently. If you can, also try to have coffee monthly with a person you have not seen in six months. This will serve to keep your connections updated and thinking about what your career goals are, while allowing you to be a sounding board for them, the quid pro quo that is the hallmark of the very best networking aces.

2. TARGETS OF OPPORTUNITY

As part of your ongoing research, you should continually identify any target of opportunity, meaning a company that is established, or one that is hot and on the way up in your area of interest.

How do you find them? Hearing about such companies through your network is the best method. You can also scan the magazines and websites covering the industry segments that interest you most. Look for new names and faces, and make a point of keeping a list of such firms and doing in-depth research on them through LinkedIn and other resources.

After identifying target companies, your next step is to dig up all the information you can about that company. Surf the Internet, review magazines and articles, gather clippings, use online directories and even the library to research articles in any business or trade publications, and carefully read any interviews with executives of that firm.

Visit each firm's website regularly so that you know what work they are doing. Become an expert on these target firms so you can speak knowledgably about their products or services. Next, check around your network to see if anyone may have contacts inside your companies of interest. Use LinkedIn to explore your second and third level connections and determine whether a direct connection might be able to make a valuable introduction for you. If so, you are ready to approach that person via your referral. If not, then you're ready to send the company a cold inquiry, one that's well written and demonstrates your worth points, along with your knowledge of their activities and your enthusiasm for the business.

Next, if practical, follow up with a phone call to investigate whether or not you might be able to secure an informational interview and see if any open positions align with your marketable skill set. By being well prepared before you reach out to target firms, you put yourself in a position to make a successful introduction.

Be especially aware of any information that indicates growth or new areas of development for a prospective target of opportunity. Suppose one of your targets is a record label that has been very successful in hip-hop, and now they're branching out into movie soundtracks. Let's say you are a songwriter and have just placed one of your own songs in a locally produced film. You could write a letter to their A&R department, introducing yourself and stating your qualifications, desire, and go-getter attitude. Mention the story in *Billboard* that alerted you to their new soundtrack division. This company may be a good target of opportunity.

Remember, for this kind of approach to bear fruit, you have to include a value statement or worth point that clearly answers the question for the reader, "What can this person do for me today to improve my firm's position in the marketplace?"

Good firms are continuously on the hunt for new talent. Any company that's growing is always looking for new people. They may not be hiring that day, but savvy managers often maintain a résumé/tickler file of people with good skills. So, don't ever be put off when someone says, "We're not hiring now."

Be prepared to answer that statement with, "I've studied your company, I am very interested in what you do, and I would like to ask you to please keep a copy of my résumé on file in the event you need someone with my skills and enthusiasm in the near future." More often than not, they will accept it and may even annotate it to say, "This person has chutzpah."

Remember, resorting to the cold letter approach should be your last option. The most effective way to approach a target of opportunity is through a member of your network who is familiar with the company. If you don't have a personal connection, find out what local, regional, or national trade associations the firm's employees are involved with. This is yet another way to meet and network your way into an informational interview. If you can't gain access by any other means, then complete your research homework on that firm, and initiate a direct approach via cold letter and résumé submission. If you make a strong impression, you may find yourself invited to an informational interview.

3. OPEN JOB LISTINGS

Traditional help-wanted listings in music industry trade magazines have largely become an anachronism as industry employers harness the power of the Internet to advertise open jobs. Others, however, rely on word of mouth or current employees to reach out to their networks of peers to help solicit job applications. Still, it's important to regularly research a range of online industry job posting sites to see what types of jobs and skills are advertised. Every open job listing in your area of interest can help you to confirm which skills are required for the listed position and also what types of positions are most in demand.

The frequency of listings encountered is directly related to the type of job advertised. If you're planning to become a record producer, you are not likely to see any open job listings. For a songwriter, it's liable to be the same story. However, you will find open job listings for administrative assistants, label sales reps, royalty clerks, distribution support staff, marketing and PR assistants, social media managers, and many other positions at the mid and entry level. Refer to the list of music and entertainment online job listing sites in appendix C as a key source of sites to bookmark. Remember, open job listings usually generate a large number of responses. When responding to a listing, be sure to include a brief mention in your cover letter that you are responding to a job listing in a particular website, and use the job ID number if one is listed.

When applying for senior staff positions, a referral, recommendation, or letter of introduction is more common. Employers often promote from within their own company or use their network to identify prospective candidates already working in the business.

Tune up your cover letter, and send your response as soon as you see the listing. This shows you are able to respond in a timely manner. Keep your cover letter as short as you can make it, and as long as it needs to be. If this is a job that you believe offers you a near-perfect fit, a full page is not out of the question. Why? Because you should restate your worth points, key relevant experience, and what makes you a uniquely qualified candidate who aligns closely with the stated position requirements. Paint a word picture that positions you as the best-qualified candidate for that job!

If your cold or cover letter gets too wordy and overly long, there is more potential for you to hit a potential "hot button," which may be a turn-off to the person reviewing it. Remember the one-page-or-less rule when it comes to the length of such letters. Always ask yourself if you can make your points in a shorter letter. The same care that you used to prune down your résumé to a tight, hard-hitting document should be spent on your cover letters. Cover letter editing and fine-tuning are like many of the career skills introduced in this book—acquired skills. The more letters you labor over, the easier it becomes to craft strong, well-written documents that will help your submissions stand out.

Always use short paragraphs, no more than three or four total, each covering a key point you wish to emphasize. Your job is to ensure that the person reviewing your submission thinks, "Oh, he or she has experience in this area, created value here—put this one in the pile of people that we are going to call back." Following these simple guidelines will help your submission make it into the select pile that avoids the dreaded hungry shredder!

In addition to the careful wordsmithing needed, make a good visual presentation, with no typos, or poor grammar. Make it perfect, because first impressions count for a lot.

About a week after your submission, make a follow-up phone call, if you have a number on file for that firm. Keep it short. Ask for "personnel," if the company has a personnel office. If it's a small firm, explain that you are calling to follow up on your résumé submission for an advertised position. Ask to confirm receipt and what your next step might be to keep in touch regarding the opening. Be polite and upbeat, and respect the time of the person with whom you are speaking. The fact that you cared enough to follow up is usually viewed as a plus at small- to mid-sized firms.

For larger firms, it's usually not practical to make a follow-up phone call, so if you have a human resources email address or employment Web contact, follow up approximately two weeks after your submission, simply asking if the firm might share a progress report on the open position number you applied for. Don't be surprised if you learn that no decision has yet been reached, as larger firms sometimes take more time to review and interview than smaller firms. For example, one of our students was recently called for an in-person interview six weeks after applying for a position online.

Some firms, however, have a strict policy of not responding to any inquiry calls relating to open position listings or résumé submissions. Once again, the exposure that music industry open position listings have via the Internet makes any response to follow-ups a perceived waste of resources for many firms. In that case, console yourself with the knowledge that your hard work has resulted in presenting the strongest possible case for your candidacy via your well-crafted cover letter and rock-solid résumé. You can then invest the time you would have spent on following up with firms that don't allow follow-up, getting back to the important work of nurturing your network and identifying your next ripe target of opportunity.

Based on the experiences of our current students, expect that you will have to apply for dozens of open positions before you get your first response. The access that so many job seekers have to online job postings makes it a numbers game, of a sort. In order to generate results, you need to keep the number of your applications going out as high as possible (of course, without applying for any positions for which you are not even remotely qualified). If you do keep at it, you will begin to see results. If you only wait to apply for the one "perfect" job, you are likely to be disappointed, if you don't get a response to that application. Don't forget to regularly update and tweak your LinkedIn profile to be as up to date and professional as possible. Use LinkedIn to also keep an active presence on the music industry groups you have joined. Being a part of the conversations really does elevate your visibility dramatically to many already working in the industry.

Working all of the "big three" simultaneously—networking, targets of opportunity, and open job listings—is key to keeping your job search and career development on the fast track.

FIVE FOLLOW-UP TIPS

Picture a long-distance runner as he runs a marathon. He focuses on all the little things such as maintaining an even gait, proper breathing, knowing the course, how much water to take and when to take it, keeping his toes pointed forward, and so forth. Just as that runner has to remember each of these important details, a music industry job seeker needs to develop and maintain the details of a follow-up system with fierce determination, not casual indifference.

As you develop and expand your network, increase your universe of targets of opportunity, send out applications to open position listings, and begin to secure interviews, you also need to:

1. Attain the monthly goal you have set for expanding your network.

2. Write down your new contacts and add them to your record-keeping system (computer database, 3 x 5 card file, smartphone, etc.)

3. Set a schedule for keeping in contact with various members of your network. Set up a section in your Career Portfolio or computer database to add each instance when you contact individual members of your network.

4. Skim over your entire Career Portfolio once a month, and add to it frequently as you locate and mine new sources of information.

5. Investigate and make contact with companies, explore new or related career options, and get to know the people you discover through research, reading, networking, trade association involvement, etc. That means getting out from behind your computer screen and into your local marketplace, attending events, volunteering, and building relationships in the nonvirtual world.

Don't forget to send important people you encounter a thank-you note whenever appropriate. That really can include anyone who is friendly and supportive of your career journey, be they professional or personal contacts. Performing the five follow-up basics listed previously will help you maintain steady progress toward your next career goal. Making them a part of your daily and weekly routine will hasten the day you are considering a job offer. So, take them to heart, and like the long-distance runner, maintain a steady pace that will lead you to landing a job in your area of interest.

As a closing note on follow-up procedures, a human resources manager from a successful Indie record label reported that more than 50 percent of job applicants who applied for an open position never bothered to follow up. Don't be in that silent majority. Always take the time to follow up each application you submit to see if the position has been filled, unless it is impossible to do so, as noted earlier. If that company is high on your list of targets, keep in touch. The results of your extra efforts may pleasantly surprise you.

WHAT ABOUT YOUR COMPETITION?

Let's review how much competition you are likely to encounter as you employ each of the three job search tactics we have covered in this chapter.

In the case of *networking*, your competition for specific jobs is very low because jobs identified by this method are usually not yet public knowledge. People often learn of jobs through their network well before they are advertised; in many cases, the job is never once openly advertised, so networking is the only means to discover the position.

When you're contacting *targets of opportunity*, the competition will be a little greater, especially if it's a company with fifty or more employees. Such firms are likely to be contacted on a regular basis by savvy job seekers like you. Take heart, the competition is still much lower than open listings. If you've done your target of opportunity research well, you will be armed with a solid perspective on the firm and its mission, its place in the market, and a few relevant questions, thus positioning you to make a strong positive impression when you do make contact.

When you approach a company in response to an *open job* listing, your competition will be the greatest, but you also know that it is likely that the company is actively hiring. One person is often securing a job at the conclusion of that company's search. By following the techniques you have learned from this book, you will have greatly enhanced the chance that it could be you.

Job Search Technique	Level of Competition	Are They Hiring?
Networking	Low	Unknown
Targets of Opportunity	Moderate	Unknown
Open Job Listing	High	Probably

WORKSHOP 19. JOB SEARCH ACTION PLAN

Make a chart with three columns and four rows. If you do this in your word processor, you can save and reuse the forms. Put today's date at the top of the page and the title "Job Search Action Plan." Most recent college graduates will update this sheet once a week, adding to it or starting a new one each week. Keep electronic copies of these sheets saved with the date in the file name "Job Search Action Plan 2-3-15.doc" to keep them separate in your Career Portfolio. At the top of each column, write the three methods of locating a job outlined in this chapter. Then use the three boxes under each heading to fill in three current opportunities to network, three targets of interest, and three jobs you applied for (or plan to apply for). You can, of course, use more than three boxes in each of the categories!

Networking	Targets of Opportunity	Open Listings

CONCLUSION

Putting your own customized Job Search Action Plan to work is the culmination of all the efforts you've made so far to position yourself as someone who is hungry, motivated, well informed, talented, and ready to enter the industry. In part IV, we'll tackle how to keep up your motivation as well as how to help ensure that your career track is a long and continually upward arc as you become more successful in your chosen field.

IV

Putting It All Together:
Your Long-Range Career Success

In part IV, we'll do one last checkup of key points that are important to help you keep on top of your career development game. Then, we'll look into the future and provide some advice on how to keep your career trajectory moving upwards as you build a vision of your future growth in the music industry.

CHAPTER

20 Are You Ready to Hit the Streets?

If you've done your detective work, performed the workshops outlined earlier in this book, developed a rock-solid résumé, and started to build your network of contacts, then you're probably itching to hit the streets and put your new career-building skills to work.

This next section will help you to understand and develop lifelong career habits that will benefit you for your entire professional career.

Keep these four tips in mind:

1. Bring enthusiasm.

2. Communicate the measurable benefits previous employers enjoyed due to your efforts.

3. Follow up religiously.

4. As your career develops, highlight your progressive career growth.

Doing these four things now and throughout your working life in music industry (or wherever your career path might take you).

Enthusiasm is essential to making a favorable impression on your future boss and coworkers. It's hard to convince your future boss that you're the best person to hire if you don't display confidence in yourself. Building confidence requires you to practice communicating effectively with those in the industry.

If you play a musical instrument, you wouldn't perform unprepared. Likewise, if you're going to an interview, whether it's informational or a final interview for the job of your dreams, don't do it without first practicing. Chapter 17 provides a blueprint to develop your basic interviewing skills. Rehearsing your interview will give you confidence. That confidence will translate into enthusiasm and the ability to communicate your skills, attributes, and career goals to those you meet, whether you're at an industry event or an interview. This will make a tremendous difference in the quality of your interview experience. Critique your practice interviews honestly. We all have areas in our interviewing skill sets that can be strengthened with practice and assessment.

What else will help you build your confidence? Start with a good résumé. Regularly practice your interviewing skills. Dig up information on the company with which you have an interview or tour arranged. Be ready with well-prepared and intelligent questions that show you have a basic grasp of the company and their business. Succeeding in your career search requires you to be enthusiastic, knowledgeable, practiced, and confident. The way to accomplish that is *adequate preparation.*

The next key to getting that job is to clearly communicate the **results** of what you've accomplished so far in your working history. Remember, making the best possible presentation on your own behalf in any type of interview requires selling yourself. In sales lingo, that means you need to highlight the "benefits" and not the "features" you offer an employer. Here's an example of the difference between features and benefits.

Say you live in Palm Springs or Orlando. Every car should be equipped with air conditioning, in such hot climates. If I'm a car salesman, and I say to a prospective buyer, "This car has air conditioning. It's really nice," I've merely told a prospective buyer about the A/C *feature.* I'll be much more successful in getting my customer to want that air conditioner if I communicate, "Remember last week when the temperature reached 102 degrees? This nicely air-conditioned car will keep you cool and comfortable, no matter what the weather is like." The comfort that the buyer will experience illustrates the *benefit* they will get if they purchase an auto with A/C.

Think of yourself in terms of the benefits you can create for your prospective employer. Can you make their life easier, more profitable, and more comfortable? If so, how will you communicate this to them? Will they have more free time because of your competency? Fewer worries? Can you increase their bottom line because of what you can do for them, say, using your social media skills? You must communicate the *benefits* that they are likely to enjoy if they hire you.

Practically speaking, there's no better way to accomplish this than by stating your worth points in your résumé, your cover letter, and most importantly, in person during your interview. Skip back to chapter 11, and read your sample worth points aloud. They clearly state the benefits you created in a no-nonsense manner.

Go back to the worth points in the sample chronological résumé in chapter 10. That candidate could use her accomplishments in learning and training coworkers in an inventory scanning system that saved time and created greater efficiency as a perfect way to illustrate the benefits that such organizational skill can bring to an employer. The skills demonstrated by the worth point discussion are completely transferable to any company. If you are using a functional résumé, be sure to emphasize the transferable skills that will benefit your future employer. Now is the time to go back to the worth point chapter, and if you haven't developed a few that you can incorporate into your career package, reinvest the necessary time and energy into finding something you have done in the past that demonstrates your ability to create some type of measurable benefit.

Be careful not to overstate or over-hype your accomplishments. No employer wants an overblown, narcissistic employee. But if you state your worth points and demonstrate how you can contribute to the company, you will have made a favorable impression, one that is likely to land you in the top tier of candidates for the job you seek. To convince them, you must demonstrate that you are the *best person available* for the job at that moment. Worth points are one of the most effective ways to accomplish this task.

Another key action after you've completed an interview is to **follow up** in writing. Re-emphasize the key benefits you believe you can contribute if hired. At some point during your interview, take a moment to ask your interviewer the following question: "Could you identify what are the two or three key attributes it will take for a person to be successful at this job (or in this company)?"

Listen very carefully to the reply, and make a note of what the interviewer says. Then, you can write a follow-up, which will generally fall into two categories. The first and longer document is a thank you letter (or email) that thanks the interviewer for their time and interest, and reiterates your interest in the position and a few key ways you meet or exceed the qualifications the firm is seeking. (You did remember to ask for a business card, so you are sure to use the correct spelling of the interviewer's name and title, didn't you?) Now, you're in a position not only to thank this person for the interview, which demonstrates your professionalism, but you can also briefly restate how your marketable skill set will make you an asset to the company. If you are interviewing for a specific position, you can state that your skills, worth points, enthusiasm, and experience would be an excellent fit with the company, based on what you learned during your interview.

The second type of follow up is a simple, brief thank you note (or email) acknowledging the interviewer and thanking them for the insights they offered you into their firm's business. Even if you don't think you are a strong candidate, at least send a short thank you note the next day.

Should you use snail mail or email for the follow up? It depends on the timing and potential opportunity. For instance, if you were interviewing for a position along with a group of other candidates with a short hiring timeframe, it may be in your best interest to use email to ensure that your message is seen quickly. If you are in the early stages of the recruitment process when there is less urgency, it may be better to send a short, neatly written thank you that will help you to stand out from other candidates as thoughtful and professional. We both appreciate getting a hand-written thank you note from a student or professional partner, and it makes a greater lasting impression than a brief email.

Perhaps the strongest strategy is to combine the follow-up methods by starting with a brief email immediately following the interview or meeting to share your appreciation for the interaction, followed by a handwritten letter or note that reinforces your interest in the company or position and highlights your relevant marketable skill set. It's your responsibility to communicate with your prospective employer why you are the best choice. Employers will rarely read between the lines on your résumé and cover letter. They don't have the time. If you perform well in your interview and then hit them with a follow-up letter that restates your experience, worth points, and your sincere interest, you score a few more points. *Follow-ups* are one more way to make yourself stand out!

As your career develops, it's important to demonstrate your *progressive career growth*—that is, how you have increased your skills, your responsibility, and the value you created for your employers over time.

For instance, if you are climbing the digital music distribution career ladder covered in chapter 5, you probably started off as a data droid, spending hours ingesting content into your company's database. Then, you eventually moved up to production coordinator, then production manager, and finally, advanced over to client relations. That's *progressive career growth*. It shows your progress and represents a very powerful method to sell you to your next boss as someone on the way up. If all you communicate on your résumé is that you "worked at ABC digital music distribution company," you've missed a very important opportunity for differentiation.

Progressive career growth shows a prospective employer that you've evolved. That's one of the career keys your next boss really wants to see. Over time, your résumé will develop from a one-page to a one-and-a-half-page or longer résumé. You should be able to communicate verbally and in writing the way that you have developed and the specific areas where you have created benefits (don't forget those!) on your previous gig. Don't wait until you are looking for your next job to update your résumé! Make a goal of semi-annual résumé reviews to incorporate new experiences and skills. Use as many action verbs and worth points as you are able. Employers are much more likely to hire people who are able to demonstrate that their career is moving ahead.

As you learn to tell the story of your progressive career growth, be sure to sell yourself by showing the solutions you've developed in the past. Once again, we cannot overemphasize the importance of investing the time to develop the worth points that were covered in chapter 11. It's not what you did; it's the impact of your actions for the employer that will get you noticed.

To nearly every prospective employer this is the single, most powerful attribute you can communicate as you search for your next job, whether it's in a year or ten years from now.

MAKE TIME FOR ONE LAST MONEY, GEOGRAPHY, AND GUT CHECK

At this point in your music industry career game plan, we recommend that you conduct one more "reality check." Based on correspondence with some of our former students, there are three important factors that you should double-check about the specific job you have targeted.

- **Salary.** Have you confirmed that there is the potential to earn the kind of salary you need both to survive in the short term and to prosper in the long term? Remember the earning ranges on the three career tracks that were presented earlier? It may take a person a few years or longer to advance to the middle-level management on various tracks. Ask yourself if you are willing to work and sacrifice at the entry-level salaries you have researched to make the climb up the ladder. Verify your salary information once more with working professionals.

- **Geography.** If your family or best friends are all in your hometown, are you ready to move on to one of the major urban centers where the entertainment business is percolating? If you have deep roots in your hometown or perhaps your wife or husband has a solid career there, now is the time to really consider the "G" for geography factor. Are you willing to spread your wings and move? Prepare for new surroundings, new stimuli, and if you are moving to New York, Los Angeles, or Silicon Valley, a significantly higher cost of living. Are you willing to make the move?

Continue to use the Internet to gauge the cost of living in the various cities or regions you are investigating. Since the cost of a similar apartment can vary by a factor of five times from Manhattan to Austin, you need to do the same kind of research on the prospective cost of living that you performed on the various career paths that interested you. (Remember, Craigslist.org provides a quick reference to housing costs in many U.S. cities.) Put those detective and Internet research skills to work. Don't forget possible higher car insurance premiums, parking, and other costs unique to a big city environment, if that's where your career path seems to be headed.

- **Gut Check.** Have you prepared yourself for the rejection involved in working your way into the entertainment business? There are tens of thousands of people seeking employment in the industry, and that competition makes it easy for prospective employers to sometimes treat those who are seeking a job with little or no respect. Unfortunately, it's probable that you will have the door slammed in your face many times in the course of your job search.

Get yourself ready for it. You will experience negativity. To counteract it, make the most of each opportunity when you find a responsive company, interviewer, or mentoring figure—be it a teacher, guest lecturer, or conference panelist.

> "Many signed recording artists make no bones about keeping a day gig until they can earn enough money to maintain a decent, if simple, quality of life as a touring or recording musician. Not doing so would, in the end, be counterproductive to sustaining a long career in the business."

We're not suggesting that you shouldn't "shoot for the stars," because if you don't aim high, you limit your own growth. But be realistic and have a career "Plan B" in place. Many signed recording artists make no bones about keeping a day gig until they can earn enough money to maintain a decent, if simple, quality of life as a touring or recording musician. Not doing so would, in the end, be counterproductive to sustaining a long career in the business.

Even after you have identified your target career path and started investigating companies, it is crucial that you continue to be an information sponge—someone who is hungry for every piece of information on their chosen career path. This is why reading the trade magazines and relevant websites is so critically important. Keeping up with the periodicals and websites that are the "bibles" of your targeted industry will give you a big edge in your job search. Don't get lazy and give up that edge. Save the most important or insightful articles to your Career Portfolio. All of this will help you position yourself as a well-informed job candidate, ask intelligent and relevant questions during interviews, and upon getting hired, be a much more valuable and well informed member of your employer's team.

MAKING YOUR MOVE

When you are armed with your résumé, including as many worth points as possible, when you've done your homework by developing your career road maps, and when you find that your gut, geography, and salary checks all come back positive, then you're ready to make your move by concurrently employing all three of the means detailed in chapter 19 to land your industry dream job.

CHAPTER **21** | # Thriving Throughout Your Music Industry Career

Once you have landed a job working in the music industry, here are some of the keys to sustaining and growing a career that, when combined with your own talent and determination, will help take you to the top of your chosen field.

1. **Find new mentors at your company.** You have become successful, in part, due to the support and advice of mentors and network members. Identify and establish a strong positive relationship with one or more experienced and respected leaders at your firm. They will help guide you and become "stakeholders" in your ongoing growth.

2. **Don't feel/act entitled.** You may have graduated with honors or been student body president. Neither entitles you to any special consideration in the music industry. Realize that you must first and foremost gain the respect and confidence of your coworkers and bosses before you will be given new challenges and the opportunity to advance.

3. **Establish a regular and reliable work routine.** Become the "go-to" problem solver in your work group or department. Make sure you are delivering value to your colleagues every day, and ask for positive and negative feedback on a regular basis. Be early, stay late, and help others be more successful. In doing this regularly, you will become a significant player at each level of your growth.

4. **X + 10 percent.** Make your standard to always give more than what is expected. It will help you stand out in the crowd, and encourage those around you also to give their best.

5. **Don't burn any bridges.** Both inside and outside your firm, conflict is inevitable. Don't make any rash decisions that may have consequences further down the line. Strive to be a collaborator that people admire for your ability to craft win/win solutions. Nobody likes a bully or a passive-aggressive coworker. Never talk trash about a coworker or client, even if those around you with more seniority regularly engage in such negative behavior.

6. **When in doubt, ask an expert.** You won't know the answer to every question or dilemma that arises in your early career. And no one expects you to. That's why it's essential to rely on the advice of respected senior colleagues as you grow your career.

7. **Be a teacher.** All of us are expert at something, and for many joining the workforce today, you are likely a digital native and can assist those senior colleagues with answers to many tech issues that are the bread and butter of today's music world. By sharing your knowledge, you go a long way toward improving your work group and environment.

8. **Lifelong learning.** Commit to it! No matter how strong your knowledge is today, within a few months, there will be some new advance that is shaking up the entertainment world. Budget time to continue to read, study, learn, and grow your skills. Ask if your employer will help cover any costs for online classes or certifications that will improve your job performance. Many will, as it helps improve the firm and its staff—truly one of the greatest assets any firm has.

9. **Give back.** As you climb the career ladder, you may soon find yourself in charge of supervising an intern. Be a great supervisor and help that person to learn, grow and succeed. You should also consider being involved in a trade association and eventually a related charity or nonprofit, not only for the good that you will do, but also to extend your own professional network to other industry leaders.

10. **Work/life balance.** In the early stages of your career, you will likely find yourself consumed by learning, doing, growing, and absorbing literally thousands of bits of information, on the job and as you read, research, and learn. No matter how important your current workload seems, you must set a few boundaries to ensure that you have enough down time to restore your perspective and don't actually lessen your own effectiveness. Whether you jog, play sports, do yoga, or go surfing, find an outlet to help you have a life and interest outside the workplace. You'll be glad you did, and so will your supervisor.

11. *Don't forget why you chose this field.* We all started on our journeys in music due to our love of music and its many positive impacts. Once you are an insider, it's easy to forget the magic that music can bring to many different places, people, and situations. Take time to appreciate how fortunate you are to be a part of our industry, and connect in some way each day to something or someone that helps reaffirm your basic love of music. This will help to sustain you over a long career.

There you have it. That's our advice on how you can continue to thrive throughout a long and prosperous life in music. We are now going to pass the microphone to our "Nine Under Thirty-Five" professionals, each of whom has taken a slightly different path to find their current music industry job. Many are at the early stages of their career, while a few have risen to a mid-level job. Taken as a group, we believe you'll find their stories illuminating and occasionally, inspiring. Like they did for us, you may be wowed by their narratives and how seemingly small events sometimes can lead to a major career opportunity. Enjoy and learn!

V

Interviews: Nine Under Thirty-Five

Meet nine talented and hardworking music and entertainment industry professionals, all under the age of thirty-five, that are forging their path along a variety of avenues in the new music industry. Each has a unique perspective. Some are entrepreneurs, while others are working for companies that are changing the way the industry works. Many are on the first or second rung of the ladder they are climbing in their current area of interest. We hope you'll find their stories and advice as inspiring and illuminating as we have.

Blythe Nelson

Photo by Peter Samuels

Blythe Nelson is an assistant music manager with Guerrilla Management in San Francisco, CA. The company is best known for managing Michael Franti and Spearhead, and for producing "Power to the Peaceful," an annual large scale, free concert and festival in Golden Gate Park that draws an audience of over 80,000 people. Blythe handles preproduction and logistics for the artists, special event productions, merchandise, and creative concepts.

Breanne: Will you share a bit about Guerrilla Management and your role in particular?

Blythe: Guerrilla Management is an artist management company. We bring on musicians to help them in achieving their goals and assist them in creating career strategies and plans. We help them with all parts of the music industry. We're based in San Francisco, California. Right now, we're managing five bands: Michael Franti and Spearhead, Amanda Shaw, Mister Loveless, Ginger and the Ghost, and Playing for Change. We're also an event production company. We've put on the Power to the Peaceful Music and Arts Festival in Golden Gate Park in San Francisco for twelve years, and in 2010, we had over eighty thousand people attend, so it has gotten pretty big. We also helped produced an award winning feature film titled *I Know I'm Not Alone*, which was a documentary on Michael Franti's trip to Iraq, Israel, and Palestine where he played music for the purpose of bringing people together. I am an assistant music manager. My boss is the CEO and founder of Guerilla Management, and I'm her assistant. I also handle all of the office administrative duties and work with all of our bands. I'm the main contact for our Australian band, Ginger and the Ghost.

What are some examples of some of the kinds of things that you do to support the different bands you're managing?

Let's start with Michael Franti and Spearhead. I'm not the main contact, but I do help with budgets for their promotional tours. I create a budget, and we send it off to the record label so that we're reimbursed. Traditionally, they cover all expenses. I also update the tour calendars for all of the band members, so they know what's going on, and when and where they'll be performing. I help with band merch. I fulfill all wholesale orders throughout the office and send those out. Any types of merchandise that needs to go out for promotional purposes or charities, fundraisers, or auctions are things I help to manage as well. With Ginger and the Ghost (a smaller band), I do more. I do everything from booking shows to applying for music festivals for them, to helping with their bio and press kit. I'm creating a PledgeMusic campaign for them right now so that they can raise money for the music video of their upcoming single. I'm their main contact, so I answer any questions they have. I create day sheets for their tours so that they have all the right contacts, times to load in, set times, and all of that. I also update their Facebook events. For the Power to the Peaceful Music Festival, I helped to book the sponsors, the fencing companies, the Porta-Potties, parking, security, and had to participate in all of the meetings with the city to ensure that we were following all of the rules necessary to make sure it was a safe event. On the day of the event, I was there from 5 A.M. to 4 A.M., doing everything from making sure all of the booths were ready to setting up the décor, to getting the backstage green room ready, handing out backstage passes, and assisting with the after parties . . . and a lot of cleaning.

Looking back, when did you know that you wanted to pursue a career in the music industry? When and how did you know that artist management was going to be something that you really wanted to focus on?

I knew I wanted a career in music when I was in the eighth grade. It started when my dad introduced me to music like the Doors, Cat Stevens, Green Day.... I loved how music made me feel, how it could change my mood. When I was going through hard times, music was there to get me through it. I felt like I wanted to bring music to other people for that reason. It helped me get through so much. I knew I always wanted music in my life. I thought I could help people get through the hard times while enjoying myself and working with music.

In high school, I did work hard to get good grades to get into a good college. I thought I'd end up in New York somewhere, but when I was looking at all of the music and business departments at different schools, I really liked what the University of the Pacific had to offer. It had a music business program through the business school. I played guitar and sang in choir, but I didn't feel like I knew enough to audition and study performance, so the fact that I could major in business with a concentration in music management was really appealing.

While I was a student at University of the Pacific, I made sure that I got as much experience as possible. I remember being in my first music business class as a freshman and volunteering to be the coordinator for a working musician symposium. I helped contact the speakers and created the press releases, processed invoices, created a Myspace page, and more. It was my introduction to music business activities. From there, I got involved in the Music Management Club and the collegiate chapter of the American Marketing Association. I was also the VP for the Arts and Entertainment group through student government on campus, and I interned for 209Vibe, a local music review. I was writing artists' interviews and show reviews and helping to put on events. I also helped to put on the Western Regional Music and Entertainment Industry Student Association conference in Pomona. I was pretty busy. When I wasn't doing schoolwork, I was usually doing something music related. I wanted to build up my résumé while I was a student. It's important to take advantage of that student status while you have it! A lot of companies like (or even require) their interns to be students. Take advantage of it when you're in school!

I honestly didn't think I would be in music management. I always liked the event production and event promotion side of the industry. I was looking at booking agencies, event production companies, and venues to work at. That all changed when I attended the Power to the Peaceful festival while I was in college. I loved the whole message behind the event. It's all about peace, love, and loving yourself and everyone around you. Guerrilla Management co-produced the festival. After I left, I did research on the company and loved their mission and message behind their business practices. That's when I realized that I wanted to work for this company, and I began to reach out to them through email. After months of going back and forth in emails, I asked if I could come in for an informational interview, and they accepted. I talked to them about the company and their roles and their artists and the industry in general, and by the time I left, they asked me if I wanted to intern with them. I started that next week. I came in twice a week and worked for free for about a year. I definitely put in a lot of time.

Wow. I assume you were probably working elsewhere as well at the same time in order to pay your bills?

Right.

So, what was it that kept you there? Did you have any kind of promise or expectation that you would eventually be paid or possibly brought on full-time at some point?

For a while, I really had no idea if they would take me on, but this was what I wanted to do. I enjoyed my work, and I was learning so much, there was no part of me that would have even considered leaving that intern position. I was making it work financially, but it was pretty tough, and as it starting coming up on eight or nine months of interning, I realized I needed to think about finding something else if they weren't going to bring me on. That was when my boss started talking to me about taking me on part-time. It wasn't really definite, but it gave me enough hope to keep going. Guerrilla Management is only made up of four people, so it's pretty small, and they don't hire people often. It just so happened that one of the employees wanted to leave and create her own booking agency. When she left, that gave me an in, and I was hired full-time. I got lucky. The timing just worked out. I loved what I did, and I was gaining more and more responsibilities the longer I was there, so that also kept me interested and gave me hope that there would be a future with the company.

Did your education really prepare you for your role, or did you have to learn a lot by just doing it and by figuring it out along the way as an intern?

It was definitely a little bit of both. Coming in and having studied arts and entertainment management helped my overall understanding of everything like royalties, licensing, and other industry-specific information. I think my boss found it refreshing that I already understood the basics of industry processes and structures and jargon.

However, each situation with our artists is so unique that we're always learning new ways of handling these situations. I definitely had a lot of questions and was doing a lot of research during the beginning. It took me a little while to gain the experience to have the confidence to handle larger situations on my own.

Based on your experience and that of those around you, what do you think are some of the key traits, skills, and abilities that lead to success in the industry?

> I am very disciplined in my work. I would get to work early and leave late so that I got my work done, and I did it well and efficiently. I wouldn't ever want anyone to think that I'm taking this position for granted. I do work really hard and I do take it seriously. I still feel very lucky to have this job. I put in the extra hours and I have no problem doing that because it is something that I love.
>
> In my day-to-day work, I make it a priority to stay positive and treat people with respect. I answer the phones in the office, and I make sure that I listen and give everyone a chance to ask their questions and tell their story. I don't want to burn any bridges for myself or the company, so even if I'm talking to someone who has a crazy idea or an unreasonable request or is getting very frustrated with me when I'm telling them that it probably won't happen, I am as nice and patient as possible. I've realized that a lot of other people in the industry that I have worked with don't always do that. I want my professional brand and the reputation of Guerilla Management to be different.

What do you see in your boss or others you admire in the industry that you think is really necessary to be successful in the music industry in particular, beyond a passion for music? What are some of the professional attributes that you think are most important?

> Well, our management team is made up of three women and one man. You don't usually see that within the music industry, and it creates an interesting dynamic. The women I work with are strong, both personally and professionally. I definitely look up to them, and I learn a lot from them. I aspire to be more like them in that they are direct and to the point with people, and have no problem putting their foot down and saying "no."

So, having a strong sense of confidence and decisiveness is important.

> Yes. They're confident, and they portray that to everyone. It gives the artists and other companies that we work with confidence in you that you can get the job done. Again, a strong worth ethic is something that I think is important as well. My boss works 24/7. I don't know how she does it. She is the busiest woman that I have ever met. Just being disciplined and being able to put in the time is definitely important in establishing your career. Also, there's a lot of stress in this profession and a lot of things that come up need to be addressed right away. For example, we might have a band at the airport and someone's seat gets bumped off the flight

and now they can't fly to their show. It's really easy to freak out, but with these things you have to think and react quickly. One thing that I admire about my boss is that, as stressed out as she may be, she's still seems very relaxed. She can laugh it off and take a deep breath and handle a crisis calmly.

So, flexibility and adaptability would be things that are important, especially in artist management when you're dealing with people and events and all of the different areas where you would have the most possibility of unforeseen circumstances.

Exactly. It's also important when dealing with artists that you keep a balance between pressuring them to reach a deadline and giving them space and time to be creative. You have to be understanding of this, and you can't be too harsh on them. Sometimes, pressure is needed, but you need to know how to keep it balanced so that you don't upset them. You just have to be understanding and have thorough interpersonal skills to know how to address situations to make sure that everyone is on the same page.

What would you say are the top challenges for artist managers? Is it dealing with the personalities, or is it the pressure of being the "go to" person for all of the other companies and entities that are dealing with the artist? Is it just the chaotic nature of events in general?

I think dealing with the personalities can be tough, at times, but also being the representative of the artist can be challenging. We're basically the liaison between the artist and all of the other parts of the music industry, like booking, publishing, and all the rest. Having all of their questions and issues coming to us to handle for the artist is difficult. We handle the issues and concerns that we can, but there are obviously things that need to be approved by the artist as well, and addressing those questions and issues with the artist without overwhelming them is a challenge.

The hardest part for me is that I'm constantly juggling twenty different projects and a lot of them last for months and months. Sometimes, I have projects that come to me and need to be done within an hour. I have a long list of to-dos, and I'm learning to be okay about not completing every project right away.

Give us a feel for your typical work schedule, and how you manage to balance your personal life with your professional life.

Luckily, at my company, my boss is very understanding about "nine-to-five" hours. We always put in a hard eight-hour workday, but there are some days where I need to stay late or my boss needs me to stay late. I'm fine with that. It doesn't really affect my personal life too much. It's just a couple of hours here and there. My company actually did reimburse me for a smartphone because I needed to be able to check my emails at all times (beyond the times of the typical workday). I'm constantly checking my emails, because there are times when there are urgent emails that I need to answer right away, even if it's 11 P.M. at night. It can cause a little extra stress at times. There are many perks to this job, one being that I do get to go out to some shows. For instance, I was flown to Red Rocks Amphitheatre in Colorado for the Michael Franti and Spearhead show. It was a huge production. I was there from 8 A.M. to 3 A.M. I created the skirting for the risers and decorations for the amps. I helped pick out the band's outfits and was even painting shirts and jackets for them to wear on stage. I put together most of the props. It was just insane. It was nonstop going from morning till night, dealing with guest lists and passes, but it's so much fun, and it goes by so fast. It's at these shows that I can say to myself, "This is why I do it." It's amazing. The show is so good. For all the work that you do and all the office time I put in, to see the finished project is so satisfying. This is why you do it. This is what makes it worth it.

What are some of the other benefits of working in your particular role in the music industry? Anything else that helps to create that balance for you?

Yeah, I meet a lot of cool people. I've even been able to meet some famous musicians through this job. I try not to get starstruck, but sometimes I can't help but freak out inside. I just met Ben Harper last month. I've loved him forever. I get to go to events and go backstage, and that's kind of cool.

It's funny; a lot of our business meetings take place after work hours, so we'll go to happy hour and meet over drinks. It keeps things pretty relaxed.

Tell me a little bit about where you see your career moving in the future. It sounds like you're really enjoying artist management. Do you want to stay on this path? Is there something else you plan to explore? Do you plan to stay in the San Francisco area or is it, at this point, all up in the air?

It's kind of up in the air for me. I'm still interested in putting on events, so booking interests me. I can see myself going there. I am very happy where I am now, and I don't plan on leaving anytime soon from this company. As for location, right now, I can see myself going anywhere, but a dream of mine has always been to open up my own music venue. It's definitely a long time down the road, but being able to basically pick what bands I want to play at my venue would be awesome. It's my dream, but I want to get more experience in different parts of the industry first before I start my own business.

What career advice would you have for anybody looking to get experience in the music industry?

Students should get involved in as many music-related extracurricular activities as possible, and should *definitely* participate in internships. Take advantage of internships while you're a student because, like I said before, a lot of internships are only available to students. When I was looking for a job, I would find a great internship opportunity with a company I really wanted to work for, but it would only be available for school credit. Don't take that for granted. Also, utilize informational interviews; it's a very important tool. For instance, a lot of people contact Guerilla Management for jobs, and sometimes, it seems like they're a little too demanding, and we're honestly just too busy. Asking for a job or internship is hard, but going in for an informational interview is a better approach and a great way to get your foot in the door. It shows that you have a genuine interest in the company, and you obviously make some great connections that way. Getting to meet someone face-to-face is huge. Also, be persistent, but at the same time, make sure that you're not becoming an annoyance. Don't be too demanding, and try not to show how upset you are when you're not getting the responses that you want. Stay positive! We (Guerrilla Management) can tell when we're getting a good vibe from somebody. We do take that into consideration when we want someone to come in and intern. We had one intern come on who actually did have impressive experience and a great résumé (because she got very involved in activities in school), but what sold us on her was that she was also very humble and grateful for the opportunity. She made that known. Before we even met her, we knew she was a nice person and a hard worker. We liked that.

How do you keep in touch with the contacts that you make and continue to grow your network?

I hand out my business card. Whenever I meet someone, I try to make a point to exchange cards. With my friends who work in the industry, we have Facebook, or we'll email or text each other. I connect with people that I meet at music related events or shows on LinkedIn also, so we can keep in touch. I make an effort to connect with someone soon after I meet them through email, LinkedIn, etc. just to say that it was really nice to talk to them, remind them of the conversation, and tell them I look forward to working/speaking with them in the future. Those small things can make a huge difference in sustaining a relationship.

Candice Choi

Photo by Annie Lee

Candice Choi (age 26) is the owner and director of Musicians in the Making, a community music school in New Jersey. She also teaches piano nearby at the New School of Music Studies.

Keith: Are you teaching full-time or part-time now?

Candice: Full-time, meaning I teach every day of the week. I'm running my own school, and I spent the prior year working as the pedagogy intern at the New School for Music Study. I primarily divide my time between my role there and teaching and managing my own school, Musicians in the Making.

So, you embody the idea of musicians managing a "portfolio career," engaging in two or three pursuits that interrelate. What do you do, and what is your work now? You're a music teacher and more.

I am the director of and owner of Musicians in the Making, a piano studio that offers childhood music classes for children up to seven years old, preparing them to go into piano lessons. What makes us special is that we combine group and private instruction. It is different from the traditional model of a student simply taking a private lesson.

Do you have colleagues? Is it a collaborative environment?

Yes, I have three other teachers that I work with and an office manager. Two of the other teachers are graduate students in piano, and they're highly trained in piano pedagogy. This experience provides them with the same opportunity to grow as an internship.

In addition to heading up your own music school, you are also working at a second school?

Yes, I spent part of my time during the last year, and continuing this year, working at the New School for Music Study in Kingston, NJ. (It's not the similarly named one that's in New York.) It is a renowned center for research in music and keyboard pedagogy. Two prominent pedagogy scholars, Louise Goss and Frances Clark, founded it in 1960. I spend time there observing classes, then teaching classes and continuing to learn under some well-known piano pedagogues.

So, as you are leading your own music school, you are also teaching and learning more about music education at a larger school.

Right. Musicians in the Making was actually modeled on the New School for Music Study.

When you planned to attend college to study music, what kind of plans did you have for your own career?

When I first went to college, I knew I loved music, and I knew I had an interest in teaching. I had the idea that perhaps I wanted to open a music school someday. I think many people didn't really think that would be practical, especially me being Asian, as there is often family pressure to train for a high paying career. I always heard remarks such as, "Why are you going to music school?" or "Are you really going to have a job?" or "Oh, why don't you go study the sciences?" or something like that. I think I was really lucky in the fact that I went in having a direction and knowing where I wanted to go. If I did not have that, my path would have been a lot harder.

How did your academic work prepare you for what you have taken on so far in your career?

A lot of it has really helped, like the more practical classes such as when I took the piano pedagogy class or music business classes as an undergraduate. I thought those were really helpful. But those classes alone would not be enough, if you don't develop your own skills as a performer. So, for me, it was needing to be a really good pianist and also knowing what I'm doing, what I planned to do.

You continued after your bachelor's degree and earned a master's degree.

Yeah, it was more specialized in my undergraduate degree specialty—piano pedagogy and performance. I had a great deal of hands-on experience in my graduate studies. I just made some really good connections, and that is where it all started.

Was there an "a-ha" moment where you thought, "I want to be a music teacher"? It sounds like when you started college, you already had an idea that being involved with teaching music and maybe even involved with managing a music school would be what interested you.

> I think that I have always loved teaching. I have always been fascinated by how kids learn. I had a very influential piano teacher in high school who took me where I needed to be, as a musician, in a short time. As a result, I felt a great deal of inspiration and interest in the field.

What were your first jobs?

> My very first teaching experience was when I was fifteen, and I taught a young child piano. My first real teaching job at an institution was straight out of college. I was doing informal research to look at various community music schools in the San Francisco Bay area. I found this place called Amabile School of Music on the Web. I happened to go home that weekend, and I visited their studio there. I just walked in and asked them if they were looking for teachers. They happened to have an opening, so I kept in touch with the director. I did an interview with them and got the job.

How did the opportunity for your current work at the New School for Music Study come about?

> For one of my graduate piano classes, I had to observe piano teachers from the community. Little did I realize that a highly respected pedagogy center was about seven minutes away from my school. I was recommended to go there and observe some of the group piano classes. After a few weeks of observations, the teacher who I was observing mentioned there were some paid positions opening. He suggested that I apply. A year later, I did and got the job.

> It sounds like part of the story is that they were able to see you as someone who was reliable and responsible. You spent almost a year working under one of the school's teachers learning how their classes worked, while at the same time, they got a sense of who you were and what your capable were.

> Yeah, I asked a lot of questions when I had the opportunity. I think they saw that I was really interested in their program and their teaching methods.

Could you also speak about Musicians in the Making, of which you are now the owner?

> Yes. Musicians in the Making has been under my direction for about a year now. While I was a grad student, someone reached

out to me and recommended me to teach there. At the time, I couldn't do it because I was too busy. However, the school kept my name on file. About a year later, I had been involved in a number of music leadership roles in the community. Due to the earlier recommendation and my visibility in the community, the owner reached out to me. It turned out that I had been recommended to her by a number of different people, such as people I had worked with and people who have seen my fundraising letters. So, my name was just kind of in the community, and it was just through my professional connections. She contacted me, we started talking, and she was really interested. We talked for about five to six months negotiating the deal, with me learning a lot about her business, and she also got to know me and came to believe that I was a good fit for her to hand the business off to. She had the business since 1993, and she was retiring, so her goal was to pass it on to someone that would keep it going strong.

So, by assuming a successful business, it reduced your risk and also gave you a good idea of what you can do to not only take the best of the business that existed but probably add your own ideas to improve it and grow further. Now that you're also managing a business as well as continuing to teach and study teaching, what would you say, in terms of your past experiences, has helped prepare you for what you do today?

Actually, everything was cumulative. Every single experience that I have had in the past has built to where I am. I can choose a few things to pinpoint. One of the internship opportunities that I had in graduate school was to teach group piano classes for children. It lasted a whole year and I worked under an advisor. That provided me all the experience I needed to be able to do well in group teaching right now. My preparation also came from administrative work and leadership skills. I acquired a lot of that when I was a graduate assistant at Westminster Choir College. I was helping to run the piano department with the head of the department. It was an incredibly demanding position that gave me a lot of real-world training. Of course, a lot of the writing and communication skills I actually learned in my undergraduate classes. I didn't have to take too many English courses in college or in graduate school, but a lot of the writing I had learned was through working and taking elective music business classes. Those proved to be very practical and useful.

What do you think are some of the key traits or accomplishments that would help one stand out in the music education field today?

I think not only having an enthusiasm for learning and teaching, but being open to change and open to learning new ideas. Candidates in this field have to be creative and also extremely organized, with a very strong understanding of teaching and how children actually learn.

If you were offering advice to someone who wanted to go into teaching, especially teaching music to children, those attributes that you just mentioned would be important, but what about personality traits or individual characteristics?

You have to be personable and able not only to relate to the student but also the parents. Relating to the parents could even be more important. You have to be a pleasant person while having a strong interest in a child's development, and knowing where they may go in ten years. You must be able to see the long-range goals.

What major challenges do you face in your current roles within the music industry? What kind of changes or things that are happening do you have to work hard at and keep up with?

With teaching, the challenge is making the music relevant. It's making music acceptable and knowing how to relate these concepts to children—whether that is using technology or using something else that they're used to. On the business side, I think the challenge is always selling the products and trying to find new customers. There is a lot of local competition, especially within this area.

Do you have any opinions on music education for adults using the Internet as a learning medium rather than in-person teaching?

I see that there are a lot of YouTube videos and Internet music learning resources. I'm open to the idea, but I always think that it is better to have an actual teacher side-by-side to work with you who has been trained extensively in piano. If it is actually live instruction via the Internet, then I am all for it. I actually had one class that was via Skype. There were pros and cons to it. I think the physical aspect of the teaching, like getting the right touch, needs to be in person. But learning theoretical concepts is definitely possible using the Internet.

How do you use social media in your professional life?

I use a Facebook page for my business to promote what is going on day-to-day with my business, and I also use it for small announcements to attract attention. I also use a personal Facebook page just to promote myself and to let people know what I'm doing personally, in addition to running the school. I've had some inquiries result from that page as well.

How important would you say it is to make new connections and to stay in touch with your colleagues and peers?

It is incredibly important. A lot of my peers are friends and with some of them, we do projects together. For instance, I'll do recitals with them, or we'll brainstorm and talk about teaching problems we're having. I think the difficult part is that piano teaching can be a solitary activity: just the teacher and the students. It's really important to stay connected to the outside world. I have also done a lot of letter writing to stay in touch with people from the past. That has taught me the value of just staying in touch, even if it is just a "Hi, how are you doing?" or something like that.

What would you offer as suggestions from your own perspective or from many of your mentors in how to maintain a healthy work-life balance?

It is so hard, because I think for musicians, music is their life, but it's also considered work. I try not to bring my work home with me. I always try to physically separate the location, and that really helps. But I also always try to have a lot of fun, whether I am working or not, and that helps me maintain a healthy attitude.

What career advice would you share with job seekers today?

Plant your seeds to lay the groundwork for your future. Always prepare for what is next, and always be planting your seeds, hoping that by achieving one goal you can earn this job or this position. Don't just plant seeds so you can put another job on your résumé, but do it because you actually care. With each colleague, customer, or student, always maintain a cordial and professional relationship, and use your best people skills. I think that is so important. Be communicative, and remember that you are really just working with people. Sometimes, we get caught up behind all the technology, but in the end, there are people that want to work with you or don't.

For instance, when I was in graduate school, I had this strong desire to open my own music school. Did I know when I was going to open it? No, not at all. But I strive to find opportunities to get to know a new person or to let someone know about my idea—just planting those seeds around my community. You know, realizing my goal all happened because someone heard about my dream of opening a music school, and then another person that had a music school was trying to retire from their business, and then I was referred to her! That is an example of what I refer to as "seed planting," and it then bearing fruit.

Samantha Juneman

Samantha Juneman is a community manager for Full Service Social Media Agency, Socialtyze. She earned her undergraduate degree in music management and a master's in digital media. She also co-founded and performs with the folk-punk band Sledding with Tigers.

Keith: Please tell me about the company you work for now and your role in that firm?

Samantha: About four months ago, I landed a new gig with a small social media startup in Manhattan Beach, CA. It's called Socialtyze, LLC. We have a really strong community management division, a very strong media planning division, a great analytics team, and a talented app design team. Those four make us a full service social media agency, which is rare today. Most agencies have two of these divisions, but we have all four. We are also developing a powerful data tool "Qu" that delivers amazing data that brands can utilize to understand what their online voice is like and the sentiment of their fans. We provide really strong data you can't find anywhere else. It's such a powerful tool, but challenging to maintain, so right now, the company is trying to balance a steady and profitable social media management practice, while also developing this tool that could potentially change how brands can use social media.

Which of the four teams do you work on?

I'm in the community management division. I manage a team of community managers, and basically, we run the social presence for different brands. One that I'm working on now is The OnLine Network, which is distributed via Hulu. They're launching TV shows online only, and the two shows that they're working on right now are *All My Children* and *One Life to Live.* Their tagline is "It's not daytime. It's any time." So, they're trying to educate a lot of the older folks; they are the biggest group of people watching it. Teaching them how to use Hulu, and how to use iTunes to access the new shows, and it's very interesting.

So, we're leading the soap opera group of people in the world into the digital age for social TV. I work with that team, and we do everything that goes out on Facebook, Twitter, blogs, and any other outlets.

I also facilitate what we do with the App team, making sure that the client is happy and the App team is happy, and then we run media with that. So, it kind of crosses over, but I'm mostly on the community management team.

What career plans did you have when you were going to school, and how did your academic preparation relate to what you thought you would be doing when you left college?

When I first got to college, I wanted to do music performance and music management. My dream was to play in an orchestra for Disney—for movie soundtracks. I realized that probably wasn't going to happen. I was also really into the technology, so I got into recording, and I wanted to work for studios, and work on sound recording and soundtracks. Then, in my sophomore year, I got a really great internship out of the blue with Universal Music. This was what all started it. They had a department called "Net Reach," which is when they had maybe forty interns who were working on all of the real marketing. It was early, early social media for all of their budding artists. We were blogging tour dates online, going into these forums to talk about these artists like we were real fans, and just kind of seeding the conversation to work it from the ground up.

I've always really been into social media, but it had been just a side thing. I was totally into Myspace, really liked Facebook, but only for my own purposes. Then it just clicked, "Oh, this is awesome. I'm really good at social media. I'm really good at computers but I also get to work with music, which is what my true passion is." I think I found a really great connection with that.

Shortly after, I went to study in Liverpool for a semester. I was working with popular music people and seeing what they were doing in the U.K. with social media. There are a lot of bands just getting started, and also a lot of really big bands (the Beatles, just to name one) that were working social media into their marketing structure in the U.K. differently than in the U.S.

So, when I came back from Liverpool, I realized that the social media business was exploding. I needed to learn more, and fast. I was learning a lot of music at school, but the social media thing wasn't something that I could find. I don't think people were really teaching it yet.

So, I grabbed a really cool internship with a composer in Santa Monica, and he was doing kind of half composing and working with artists, and half running with a nonprofit organization that worked with health and music and yoga. They were doing all these really great campaigns and also raising money for music initiatives. It was exciting, but he didn't really know how to use the Internet to promote his projects. To me, it was obvious that it was an essential key to his marketing plan, so I started experimenting with that. I got a taste of community management because I was running all of his social media strategies and pages, and that has been a really cool relationship, and I still consult with him. It's cool because I got to see how much he loved music and what the musicians were doing, and I got to be the middleman between artists and their fans. I facilitated their conversations and helped build an online community.

In my senior year, I was still studying music management and realized that all of my research and my senior projects could focus in on what I was getting interested in—social media strategy, analytics—and what the social media industry was doing with music, and vice versa. I focused my research projects around those areas and realized that I was getting into something that I wasn't done learning about—and that only one semester of college remained. So, I made an executive decision to find a grad program relating to social media, specifically. I could have worked for a little bit and then gone to grad school, but I thought that I might not go back... I didn't think that I would be motivated enough to go back to grad school if I had been out in the working world.

That was a great decision for me, and I finally dove into an industry that I hadn't really been involved with. Before, I was just dabbling in it, but in my grad program, I met lots of great people at Amazon and Microsoft and Starbucks because I was studying up in Seattle. It was such a great hub for great thinking minds that are immersed in the social field. So, now I'm a full-fledged social media manager! I still try my best to work on anything in music when I can. I still play with my band. I still hang out with all my friends who are musicians.

The fact that you decided to explore various career avenues that you were interested in first before you were able to zoom in on social media is a very important story. Was that point when the light bulb went off when you were working for that composer in southern California and you realized, this is actually a job? This could be a job? Was that it?

> Yeah, it did hit me, because he had two interns, and one was doing the kind of studio recording that I had wanted to do when I was a freshman, but I wasn't doing that for him. I was running the social media, marketing, coordinating PR releases, and I realized, "I still get to be in the same place as the other intern but my internship is solid, and this guy's internship is going to end in two months." My supervisor said, "You know you can do the recording stuff too, but what you are doing for me in social media and marketing, I don't know where else I can find somebody to do this." His observation was really very interesting to me and got me thinking, "Why isn't anybody able to do this? Why isn't this so big in the music industry and why are people so behind?" That caught my eye.

How did you land your first paying job in the social media field?

> Technically, my first paying job was with this composer, because after my internship ended and I went back to school, I still did some projects for him and got paid hourly. Then, my first salaried social media job was when I was in grad school in Seattle. About six months into my grad school situation, I had emailed this company I had heard of. They had openings for some jobs, but I really didn't think I was qualified for them. I emailed them just to make a connection and I laid out what my experience was: that I was in a digital media grad program where we were doing some really interesting, experimental work. I made it clear I didn't think I was qualified for the positions, but wondered if they had any other opportunities. I said to them that I had seen the work they were doing and wanted to be a part of that.

> Luckily enough, the person who ended up being my boss later on, wrote back, "You're a really unique person, and we want to utilize your skills. So, we might have a job opening for you, but you have to be patient with me." It took about four months of back and forth phone calls with her to finally land a job there. That was my first community management position. I was a community manager working with their newest client: IHOP (restaurants). I worked on some other clients they had: HTC and Microsoft. That's really where I learned the bulk of my skills. I think I probably learned more from that job than grad school, to be honest.

Yes, but it seemed that your move to Seattle and the work you were doing in your grad program put you in a position to make those important connections, to plug you into a network of people in the social media field, right?

Oh yeah! I mean, it was hand in hand. I brought things to that job that I learned from grad school, and things I learned from that job, I brought back to the classroom.

How did you hear about Socialtyze?

That was a really interesting situation. I had completed grad school in Seattle and was itching to move back to L.A., my hometown. I had gotten my then-current firm to agree that they would transfer me to L.A. because we did have an L.A. office. Then, about a week before I was going to transfer, we lost the client that was located in L.A. Not too many clients left that firm, but it does happen in the agency world. As a result, the transfer was off the table, so I had to scramble to find another job.

I decided to fork over the money for a LinkedIn Prime account, aka their Job Seeker account. It gave me a leg up. You can message hiring managers and see more of who is connected and where. I applied to maybe ten different community manager jobs in L.A. I landed interviews for a bunch of them, but this one, I think fate may have come into play. I had a trip scheduled to Vegas for that same week they wanted to do my interview, and I said, "Well, I'm already going to be down there. I might as well take a few hours to do this interview." So, I went down there for my interview, went through with it, and it actually went really well. The people here had a really great vibe. I left, drove to Vegas, and two hours later, I got an offer. It just worked out so well, and my experience at Spring Creek Group (my previous employer) was a great match to what I would be now doing here at Socialtyze.

What kind of traits or skills or experiences are going to help somebody stand out that wants to be a person working in the digital media space?

Relevant job experience on your résumé obviously is going to help you, but really getting your hands dirty is what will make the difference in that job interview, because a lot of the social media jobs that are out there are very technical. You can say, "Oh, I've done social media for this brand. I've done social media here." But companies are looking for very specific skills.

As an example, we're always hiring community managers, and we want to know what your daily life is like. You have to get your hands dirty, so you maybe don't have an internship, you may just need to try it for your own work. If you have a band, run their Facebook page and their Twitter accounts. Let the fans know what the band is doing. Try things out. Try experimenting. Spend a good amount of time in there using social media, talking to people, seeing what works, seeing what doesn't.

I also think an essential skill is to be analytically savvy. You have to know how to gather and understand data. You can't just go around and try anything and assume that it works—whatever. You have to have some plan in place or some process in place so that you can really see what's working for you based on the numbers. Then, you can assess results and figure out why something didn't work.

I think you just have to go for it, or alternately, you can go to school. You can get a master's in digital media like I did, but you don't have to do that to break into the field. It's all on the Internet. I mean, literally anything you want to learn, you can Google it, and that's what I mean about getting your hands dirty, is you can't wait for things to come to you. You can't sign up for something and expect the knowledge to be funneled down your throat because you're paying tuition.

You really have to get in there and try things. Learn for yourself. A lecture is a way to get information, and it's never a bad thing to go to a lecture and hear what someone has to say, but if you're not trying it out for yourself, you're missing out.

Your examples of success will give you a leg up. If you can really communicate to a hiring manager that you know what they're talking about, you know how to do it, and here's an example of how you did that successfully, that's what's going to land you a job, today.

What do you think are some of the key challenges for people who want to move in the music industry, and what are some of the key challenges facing artists and brands?

There is so much availability for music. Being a small local band is incredibly hard because there are four hundred other ones nearby who also have a Facebook, Bandcamp, and Twitter account. You're competing with them on all these technologies, which are available to anybody. It's all readily accessible.

It's really about the connection of what you do digitally to what you do in the physical space. I feel like you can be all talk on Twitter and tweet out your album every day and follow ten thousand people, but if you're not playing in the local scene and you're not meeting other people who are really important to your career, that disconnect is going to hinder you. If you're a local band or if you're trying to make it into a bigger place, digital marketing is only going to go so far unless you're actually physically out there. Let's say you play at, for example, Plea for Peace Center in Stockton, once a week. Okay, there are ten people at that show, which will probably help you book shows in Modesto or Sacramento or San Francisco. Then, you have to go to those shows, and you have to meet those people out there. Yes, you can tweet them and find them on the Internet, but if they don't have a place to go to find you or to watch you, there is a disconnect there. If you are an artist, you really need to have some kind of physical aspect available to take your digital campaign farther. When you combine social media with live events, then maybe that person who watched your video sees you at a show... then that connection has expanded exponentially. They may recognize you and say, "Oh! I saw that band on Twitter. Those guys are pretty funny. I'm going to talk to them at their merch booth. I may buy an album. I'm going to find out when their next show is."

In your current role at Socialtyze, do you find that some of the time you and your colleagues are sometimes educating your clients?

I've been really fortunate to work in social media environments where literally everyone is just as knowledgeable as I am, which is a really helpful thing. But if you're ever in a position where people you work with don't have the same social media or digital media experience that you have, then yes, you bring that to the table, but you can also learn a lot from everybody else, too. I don't think that because you're in your early twenties and you spend eight hours a day on the Internet that you have this upper hand in knowledge. I think the knowledge is constantly being shared and evolves. You can always learn something from somebody. Keep your mind open, because things are changing so fast.

I can see that happening with agency/client relationships. When brands use social media agencies to run their social presence, there needs to be a crazy amount of trust between one another. Social media is immediate; that's what the beauty is behind it. It's honest, and it's quick.

Lack of trust in an agency/client relationship can really bring social media's effectiveness down, if they're taking two or three days to approve a tweet that needed to go out. Brands can totally benefit from social media education from agencies, and at the same time, agencies can learn from their clients how they do marketing and what their most effective strategy is in various media. A social strategy for one client may not be the same for another. Sometimes, it takes some effort to get on the same page with the client. I think that yes, you are the social media expert of your team, you bring that to the table, but don't shut out all of the other knowledge you can get from everybody else. Being effective really relies on the information you can get from that feedback loop.

Please talk a little bit about your personal brand and how social media played a part in that.

There are platforms available for you to brand yourself. Obviously, you should put the time and effort into them, because if your stuff's not out there, you're not going to get anything. It doesn't matter. If it's there, it's better than not being there— no matter how good it is. I do put a lot of effort into LinkedIn because that's a really great resource to connect with people and see what discussions are happening in your industry, and obviously, that's going to lead to job opportunities, too. I think that if you're confident in creating content, that's a proven way to land your next job.

If you have a blog, your material is out there. It shows that you're a content creator, and you are a social media thinker, and you can publish and analyze what's happening on your pages and be articulate and passionate about what you're interested in. It shows initiative.

Facebook is a really great thing for me, because there's a lot of Facebook groups that are really resourceful. People put a lot of effort into them. So, one I'm a part of is a group of digital media professionals in Seattle. They may not know each other personally, but they know that everybody on there is connected somehow through a friend or a colleague. They post discussions, job opportunities, or questions.

Whatever professional networks you can be a part of, but also contribute to, would be great. That's the cool thing about the Internet is that it doesn't require being present in person to provide help. Also, while I believe that Twitter is a good resource, I actually think that the bulk of the best discussions happen on Facebook and LinkedIn.

Years from now, the platforms are going to change, but I think that the basic idea of that is any place where you can make quality connections with people is where you need to be. Anywhere you can add value to a conversation or even to just sit there, listen, and learn, that is a great resource.

You really have to initiate or be part of a conversation that people care about.

Yeah, definitely. I think that the key phrase with that is "adding value." Whenever you can strengthen whatever part of the conversation you want to be around, it strengthens the setting you're in, so it makes it bigger. Now, you're a part of something bigger. It solidifies your part in it, too.

In the band I play in, Sledding With Tigers, our leader, Dan, does a really great job with always being a part of the conversation; from helping with other bands that may be a part of our folk-punk scene, or our cause, or are our friends. We also share a lot of content from other people. We collaborate with a lot of people. We do split EPs. We play festival shows. We sponsor a lot of nonprofits that maybe our fans are a part of. It's like taking yourself outside of the music that you're creating and realizing what the purpose is and who else is interested in that purpose.

What would you say about how to have some kind of work-life balance? To have a life beyond the workplace?

Yeah, this is something I'm personally struggling with right now, because I am working sixty-five hours a week, because I have a particularly challenging client. Also, I'm new with this company. I think that it's okay to pour your life into what you're working on, as long as it makes you happy. If you feel personally accomplished by spending the majority of your time working on a project that you happen to get paid for, that's great. It's also okay to take a step back to give yourself time to check out for a second because burnout is really easy if you're one of those people who are very particular about pouring in as much to your work as you can.

If you work on something that you love, even if it's something that you love so much that you would do it 24/7, when it's part of your job, it is suddenly not as fun anymore—which is just the nature of the business. With that being said, you also have to realize that it's essential to take a step back. Like, the other day, I had maybe four projects, and I realized that the quality of work I was putting into them was just not what I wanted. I was not comfortable doing it. I just needed an hour to not think about this work. Like go watch *Game of Thrones* or chill in my apartment, or something. You have to give yourself credit. You can push yourself really hard but you also have to realize that you're human. The balance of taking care of yourself is really important because you know, you can't do work if you're broken.

What are one or two key things for a job seeker to do who wants to be working in or around music?

I struggled with that too when I was getting really focused on social media but I was like, "I really like music." I'm also always happier when whatever I am doing involves music. Ninety-five percent of my projects in grad school were music focused, even though I was in the digital media program. I was always able to bring it back to music. When I was in a digital media law class, I studied music sales and licensing. Or if I was in a storytelling class, I made a movie about my social media/music peers in Stockton. I feel like you just have to be really honest with the fact that music is a part of your life and always try to find those connections. If you do that, it will fall into place.

You can find patterns with different industries connected everywhere. It doesn't matter what industry it is. So, you have to be really aware of that and you can't say, "Oh, I'm a lawyer. I'm never going to do music again." Or, "I'm a firefighter. It's not going to be in my life again." You can find those patterns. That's really up to you. I think that you can define the work that you do because that's your life that you're pouring into it. It's your decision.

I don't think because you do a certain job, that music is not related. I think you can find the patterns and work towards connecting the dots.

Music is such a powerful connector. And emotional marketers are always trying to tap into the feelings you can get in a few seconds from a popular song.

David Creel

David Creel is an agent assistant at the Los Angeles offices of William Morris Endeavor, one of the world's leading talent agencies.

Keith: What's a typical day like for you?

David: A typical day starts at 8 A.M. Usually, I'm just checking in and checking my emails. Pretty much my entire job exists through emails and that would be handling a number of different factors relating to all the different shows that we have going on. I am generally working on five or six different tours or various shows happening on various continents, so there is a lot to kind of dig into and address first thing every morning. Once my agent arrives, I work directly for her.

The way an agency is set up is that there are many different agents, and they all have one or two assistants. Each assistant works directly for the agent they are assigned to. I work directly for my boss, and I handle whatever she needs me to handle. I answer her phone, and am the gatekeeper to her office, so everything comes through me.

When you were going to school, what were your career plans? What were you thinking of doing after you graduated from college?

After graduation, I shifted around a little bit. I always wanted to be an artist manager, I would say, and that's been my passion. That's what I did in college. I was managing a band for three years, so that is where I wanted to be, but I knew there were a bunch of different ways to get there eventually.

Is working on the booking side another way to learn more about the talent management business?

Yes, absolutely. Every day, I deal with managers from different artists we book, so I learn about aspects of their job by handling what they need done.

How do you think your academic preparation, both in and out of the classroom, helped prepare you for your professional life?

Within the classroom, I learned to think critically about issues that eventually came up in what I was doing outside of class: working with a band, sometimes doing things wrong, figuring out how to improve; things like that. In my classes, I really got to study the different functions and the different roles of people in the industry and what they're supposed to do. The combination gave me more practical knowledge I could apply in my own projects outside. It gave me more of a breakdown of what the role of a manager is supposed to be so I could apply it and learn by doing outside the classroom.

You're a trumpet player. At what point did you make the decision that you didn't want be a trumpet performer, but you wanted to manage talent? Was there an "a-ha" moment? Or did it dawn on you gradually?

I've been playing trumpet since I was seven, and that's kind of always been my life goal—to play music. But in high school, I realized that I don't really like performing; soloing in particular. I get really nervous. I don't feel like I'm at the point and I don't have the drive to be a soloist. You really have to have that passion to want to put in those 10,000 hours to be great at it. I did realize that passion when I started up a funk group in high school, and I started handling everything. I booked all the gigs, and if we got paid, I distributed the money, and I actually really like that. Then I found out I could go to school to study music management, so I thought, "That seems like a perfect fit.'

How did you land your first job in the music industry?

I did a lot of stuff in college to prepare myself, I would say, but when I got out of school, I found out that it was extremely hard to break in anywhere. I felt like I had a decent network of people who were helping out and looking for me. In the end, I ended up getting a job at William Morris Endeavor without knowing anyone there and no one referred me, or anything like that. I just interviewed, starting with an informational interview. They told me, "We don't have a position, but we would like for you to come check us out." I did that and then that Friday, they called me up and just said, "You start Monday." It was kind of crazy.

What else did you do in college that prepared you to work in the music industry?

In my sophomore year, I got involved with the Arts and Entertainment team on my campus. University of the Pacific is fortunate to have a great team and a great staff surrounding that team. They put on all the campus events, whether it's booking bands in The Lair (the on-campus pub) or putting on a major concert with a headliner. The student team handles every aspect of the event planning, and it's an on-campus job so you get paid to do it. I did that for about three years. During my last year, I ran that team, and it gave me so much experience just doing so many different things, including producing a sold-out concert with the Cataracs and DEV.

I also did a few internships along the way. First, I did two part-time internships during one summer (between my freshman and sophomore year). I worked at the San Jose Jazz Festival, and I was also helping out at A Cappella Records. I was reaching out to artists for them and then for the San Jose Jazz Festival, I was doing everything they can ask an intern to do. All types of things, like running to get stuff and helping prep the stages—everything. I also worked the following summer at Yoshi's Jazz Club where I did a lot of market research. I also did some street-team work for the venue. The following spring semester of my junior year, I worked at Concord Music Group.

What department?

I worked on the A&R side. I proofed several remasters of albums then in production, so I listened to albums for any glitches or flaws, I tracked those, if there were any, and they would go back into production for remastering, if necessary. I also proofread liner notes. That was great. I got to learn a lot about jazz while doing my job. That was a cool job.

How did these experiences prepare you for your job today?

Definitely, how to be a team player. I think that is really essential, especially knowing that that's what I really want to do: to be part of a creative team. That's something that I learned. Being detail-oriented is huge; that is probably the biggest quality that you can have. When people give you a task, they want it to be done right the first time with no mistakes. If you can have that be your number one quality, then that's great. Along with that, being extremely well-organized and just having the passion and drive. Every day, I work between ten to twelve hours, which isn't a normal workday for most people. I get in at eight and I sometimes leave between seven-thirty to eight. So, that's my day.

What would you describe as a few of the traits, achievements, or qualities that would help a person stand out in the workplace today?

> I would definitely say getting started as early as you can. As soon as you know that this is what you want to do, go for it. I know industry blogger Bob Lefsetz said, "Moving up the ladder starts when you're in college now." Everyone I work with at WME has a similar résumé to mine. The guy sitting right next to me, while he was in college, was tour managing for Devotchka and Primus. I was like, "Wow!" Pretty much everyone and all the other assistants had similar types of things in their past, like being on tour and having done a bunch of different types of jobs (or internships) in the industry already before.

Then getting that kind of experience as early as possible is important. Obviously, if you are going to handle talent, you have already mentioned attention to detail and passion for what you're doing. Are there any other skills or personality traits that you can think of for a talent manager?

> I would say, have your ear to the ground to what is popular in music right now, definitely. You can't advise someone if you don't know what's going on, so that's really essential. Also, knowing that it is okay to say no. You shouldn't be a pushover. You need to stand your ground, and that's what artists look for. The group I'm independently managing now even told me that it's good that I do not agree with them all the time. It's important that you develop that relationship with an artist and that they trust you to make good decisions for them or advise them into making good decisions, whether you agree with them or not.

What would you say are some of the major challenges that a talent manager faces today within the music industry?

> Revenue is what I would say is the biggest challenge. There are a lot of smart, talented business people who love music and would be managers if there were a bigger revenue stream there. I think that that also helps because that weeds out the people who aren't entrepreneurs and that can't think of creative ways for the artists to make money, while still advancing their career. I think that's a really great opportunity to jump in there and be creative. You have to work extremely hard. I think you have to work ten times as hard to make a living out of it, but I think that it is an exciting field to pursue.

Do you use social media in your professional life?

> I view my personal social media sites as professional tools. I have a LinkedIn account that is up-to-date, but I don't use it as part of my job at WME. I have a Twitter account, a Facebook account, a LinkedIn account, and my thought is that all of those should be in sync. They should all tell the same information, generally, and give off the same vibe as to what person I want to portray myself as. Whether that is the picture that I put up, or just my bio, or whatever, I try to give the same kind of theme in all of them. It's all about branding yourself; that's what social media is. I try to build a little personal brand, so if I'm going to be searched by a potential employer, they can see the same brand qualities across all platforms.

How important is making connections and staying in touch with them for your career?

> I think that is the most vital aspect of the music industry. I was very fortunate to get my job at WME without knowing people specifically, but I don't expect that to happen moving forward. The artists that I consult with currently outside of work, I landed because other people recommended me. I keep in touch with a large alumni base from my school. I even keep in touch with people in high school who have turned out to help me out in my professional growth as well—really, just anyone and everyone that you can talk to. You should be trying to build a good relationship with people you meet, first just as a person and, when appropriate, as a professional. You never know who that person is going to be that will help you out and give you that key to help open the next door.

Are you at the point of your career development where you don't have to consciously nudge yourself to say, "Okay, I have to get in touch with some people for my network?" Has it become second nature yet?

> I would say that it is about 50/50. I have a decent network of close friends that are also in the industry that I have no problem hitting up, you know? Like what's the job market like over here? Do you want to be a part of this project? There are also people in my extended network that I do have to motivate myself to contact because I don't know them as well, but there could be an opportunity there. So, you have to put yourself out there. The worst that you're going to get is "No."

How do you maintain a healthy work-life balance?

I would say that my past year has not been a healthy work-life balance, but it's tough because once you get started, it's all about being better than the next person and being more involved than the next person. If it's truly what you want to do, if being in the industry and working with music is your passion, then working hard actually makes it a little bit easier, because that is part of you being healthy as a person, as well as doing what you love.

I would say, definitely take time at the end of the day for yourself. You can't always be networking. You can't always be trying to move ahead. You have to go play basketball or something. Go to the gym. Go see a movie. Go do something completely outside of the music industry. Don't always be bringing it up in conversation, because people will then think that you're just a robot— an industry robot. It's important not only to build connections professionally, but personally, because sometimes a professional connection will result because of a personal relationship.

What recommendation would you give to an industry job seeker today?

Be patient. It took me three and a half months to get a job, and that was quick by the current economy's standards. I was on the computer every day, calling people every day, revamping my résumé, rewriting my cover letters. Be patient, but be persistent. Don't be afraid to call someone ten times, which I have done, and I said "I'm going to call this person one more time," and that was the time they picked up the phone. It's always going toward your goal, a little bit at a time, and pushing a little bit more than what you're used to.

Lauren Kasper

Photo by Jordan Braun

Lauren Kasper is director of label business development at Beats Music, one of the leading digital music subscription services. She works in San Francisco's SOMA (South of Market) area, which is home to a number of leading digital music companies.

Keith: What career plans did you have when you were going to college and how did your academic preparation relate to what you believed you would be doing after school?

Lauren: Well, when I started at University of the Pacific, I wasn't quite sure what I would end up doing, but I knew that I would want to, in some way, work in independent music. I knew I would like to relate to artists and deal with the business end of what it is to create music—helping artists who are making music with the business side of things.

What happened in college that ended up being helpful?

Learning how deal structures worked and understanding how agreements underlie everything that happens in the music industry—that was all on the course work side. Outside of that, I think it was the experiences of internships, meeting people from the industry, and learning how to make those network connections outside of school that actually helped me land my job. But also, understanding that every situation that you're put in is a potential for a future job possibility. So, I was always trying to make a good impression and always doing things for free, trying to grow my experience—so that when I'm placed in a situation, I can rely on those past experiences. For instance, helping a friend put out a record or volunteering to help do a band's social network marketing.

Was there an "a-ha" moment when you said, "Yeah, I really want to work with the indie artists and work on the music business side of things?"

My path started before I got to Pacific. I realized that I really wanted to have a certain lifestyle, which was to collect records, hang out with people who were making music, and find a job that could be meaningful to me. If I had to have a nine-to-five job, let it be about music all day. I really love independent music, people who run labels, collecting records, and I sort of just fit in with this lifestyle and crowd well. I knew that this is what I wanted to do every day, and I could do it for ten years or fifteen years.

How did you actually secure your first opportunity in the industry?

My first real music business role was at IODA (one of the pioneering digital distribution platforms started in 2003). I learned of that internship opportunity from my instructor. I had a phone interview, and they accepted me. My first taste in the music industry was digital distribution. It has been probably the key experience that allowed me to do what I'm currently doing.

At MOG [the predecessor to what is now Beats Music], I started out as a catalog manager. During my interview at MOG, I was told by my hiring manager that I was the most qualified applicant for the job because I understood how music is distributed to a DSP (Digital Service Provider) and MOG was on the other side of that.

What did you do immediately after finishing college?

I graduated from Pacific, and I worked as a new media intern at Fearless Records. That was a crucial and important experience because it gave me a holistic view of what happens on the record label side in order to create and sell the recordings that are the start of the distribution chain. It also gave me a taste of marketing and how labels actually work. That was a small company, and there wasn't a lot of opportunity for a paid position there. So, while I looked for a paying position, I did try to maintain contact and work for them as much as possible.

Then I found an ad on Craigslist for a company called MOG, which I was familiar with from its incarnation as a social network. It had morphed into a subscription streaming service during the interim. So, I interviewed for a catalog manager position, and my background in digital distribution, and specifically in content acquisition and digital distribution at IODA, was very helpful—knowing what content we would be missing, what is important, who are the labels, and who are the key players involved and how we received our music was key. I had a good background for my work at MOG from IODA. From there, our company grew, and so I took on more responsibilities, and eventually, we were purchased by Beats Electronics. I have stayed on at Beats Music.

Looking at the music industry today, what would you say are some of the traits or achievements that might help someone stand out when they are applying for jobs?

I think there are a lot of transferrable skills that I would recommend to anybody looking for any kind of work that also apply to the music industry. One of those is to strive to be somebody that people want to work with. Be friendly, be helpful, be available to them; there is no job that is too small for you. If it meant that I had to clean toilets at MOG, then I would have done it. Once you have that job, "emulate your betters," is what I would suggest. Learn from people who are above you. I always looked up to my supervisors or managers for how to act in certain situations, how to speak about something, and when not to speak! Try to make their jobs easier in every way possible. That is how you learn to be them.

From your perspective, what are some of the benefits of working in the music industry?

Well, in my role specifically, I get to interface and hang out with people who are creating music. You get to go to shows and concerts, and that's considered "working." You get to go to conferences and hang out with people in a party-like atmosphere, and that is always fun. Not only that: every day you come into work and you can have the reward of experience and knowing you are working in music, and it is not selling widgets.

Obviously, the music industry in the last fifteen years has been reinventing itself in a whole new way. What would you say are some of the major challenges that you and your firm face in how the music industry is evolving?

Well, I think that the digital music world is very exciting because it is the forefront of how music will be consumed in the future. I think that a lot of the challenges for us are that the technology is ever evolving. It is a high demand career field, and so we are always looking for data guys and software engineers. Unlike perhaps pressing records, in digital music, you have to be able to understand the technology and explain it to— at least in my role— people who are not always technologically savvy or early adopters. There is a little bit of customer education that has to happen, and that is also a marketing challenge.

In order for a subscription music service to really take hold, they have to reach a certain scale for it to be profitable to content providers and record labels. I think the largest problem we face is just getting to scale and getting past the point where people, artists, record labels, and everyone feels comfortable with this new technology and it becomes sort of old hat. That's our challenge.

It's a big one, but I believe we're making progress.

Yeah, I think that we will get there. I mean, I have been using streaming services for the last six years. I know the value of it. I think that as people start using it, they will feel like they're opened up to a world of opportunity, and it will really enrich their lives with music in a way that has not been possible before.

How do you use social media in your own professional life?

I definitely make sure that I have an up-to-date LinkedIn profile. I am using it as I meet people and collect business cards. I have a Facebook page, and I do use it for work. I accept professional friends as a part of Facebook. I see that as sort of blurring the lines between work and personal life a little bit. In music, you meet a new colleague or somebody at a label, you develop more of a friendship… it's different. It's not like I'm a person from Microsoft, and we must be very business professional. Music is casual, and you want to share and talk about things that interest both of you, like shows and bands. In a lot of ways, you have to be a bit of a social butterfly in the music industry. You need to be able to make friends with people. Having a Facebook profile that is genuine to you is important. I only post social media things that I would want my mom to see. In that way, you maintain professionalism in both places, but you can be more fun and casual on Facebook.

How important would you say it is to keep making new connections and staying in touch with your colleagues and peers, both at other companies like yours and just all over the music business?

I would say that it's relatively important. As I have met people out at conferences—for instance, SXSW—I started either by following them on Facebook or their Instagram account, and so, it kind of keeps us connected there. Even if you're just mildly interacting with them, it's a way to just remember who they are and what they do. When an opportunity arises, say if I'm going to New York, it helps me get in touch with those people. I can say, "Hey! I don't have anything to do on Monday night. Do you want to have dinner? Are there any good shows happening? Let's get together." It's a good way to remind yourself of who you know in certain places.

Any suggestions on how to strive and maintain some kind of a work-life balance?

> Okay, this is real talk. When you're young and you don't have a family, you should be working your butt off. You should be available online during the weekdays as late as you need to be, checking your emails and answering whatever is important and needs a response. Of course, take time for yourself. I take a day off here and there, and I go visit family. If I am going to a show, I don't worry about the work emails, but I try to come in early. I try to stay late. I try to be as involved as necessary. Then, you sort of bank that work ethic early in your career, so when you're going to have kids or you get married and now you really need to have the work-life balance, then you can sit back on your laurels a bit and get that time you need to take your kids to the doctor or go on a family vacation. That is really how I see it.

What career advice do you have for those planning to pursue jobs in the industry today?

> I would say take anything that you can get—even an unpaid internship that is two days a week—get every experience. You'll never know what it is that thing or person that you will meet doing that role, that is going to provide you with an opportunity later. If you are genuine and committed to everything that you're doing, and trying to do it the best that you can, people will see. People will see that in you, and they will want to help you. I found that to be very true. If you are very positive and a good person to work with, if you work hard, try your best and admit when you need help, people will help you. You'll find that for those people, in the act of helping you, it will form this tie that will be a bond you'll have throughout your career, and that is how you develop long-lasting relationships.

Dan Radin

Dan Radin is Director of Audio Products at SteelSeries, a leading manufacturer of video gaming headsets and game play peripheral devices. Dan also serves as a management consultant with music loop soundware startup, the Loop Loft.

Keith: Let's talk about your path in music, which has taken quite a few twists and turns.

Dan: Sure. I've spent the last eight or nine years in the MI (music instrument/product) industry. I originally started my college education as a music education major. I went to Rutgers University, and I pursued the music education bachelor's degree, got to the student teaching part, and realized, "Nope, I can't do this for the next fifty years."

I was struggling to figure out what I wanted to do. I love music. I loved teaching people music. I still love teaching private drum lessons, but the classroom was just not the right fit for me. As I was working on that degree, I was also working at a local Sam Ash Music store. At the time, I was very good at it, but I still wanted to finish my degree. I continued to work there and found that Berklee College of Music had a music business bachelor's with a specific music products track within it. Music products had always been something I had been passionate about, and my success in retail selling them had only confirmed that. So, that music products focus was what attracted me to Berklee. I transferred my general education units and basically just did the music business program there. I finished in about a year and a half, and then landed the NAMM scholarship (the President's Innovation Award) to attend the convention, and that's how you and I met.

The music products track also had an internship, and that led me to connecting with the Zildjian company, which was south of Boston, and that's what really got my career started. It kind of ignited my passion for music products. All along, I knew that one of the things I was passionate about in music was the gear. It was the opportunity to make the musician's experience different or better or seeing them work through better equipment, better gear, better instruments. So, I did the internship at Zildjian. That got my foot in the door to the industry.

The other thing that happened at the same time was that, as part of the NAMM scholarship, I did some mock interviews with CEOs of companies. I was paired up with the CEO of Sennheiser U.S., which I didn't realize was in the backyard of where I grew up in southeastern Connecticut. That mock interview became a real interview a few weeks later and led to my first full-time industry job. I worked for Sennheiser for three and a half years. Started off as a jack-of-all-trades in marketing, and then moved into their product management group, where I gained my first corporate experience and my first product management experience with third-party brands Sennheiser distributed, and then also on Sennheiser-owned brands like Neumann premium studio microphones and Klein + Hummel (now Neumann) studio monitors.

Eventually, my wife (a fellow Berklee music business alumnus) and I wanted to move to Los Angeles because she wanted to go back to school to focus on entertainment law. We felt like L.A. was the place to go for her education. There wasn't an opportunity for me to continue at Sennheiser from L.A.

So, I contacted one of my colleagues from my Zildjian internship, who had moved on to work in the L.A. office of a company called Numark, which is now called inMusic. InMusic is a group of companies owned by an entrepreneur, Jack O'Donnell. He owns Numark, Akai Professional, Alesis, Alto Professional, MixMeister, ION Audio, and now M-Audio and the AIR Software group. I called my friend when we were looking to relocate to L.A. just to say, "Hey, I know you're out there. Let's reconnect. Let's talk about neighborhoods, places to live, your experiences."

"Your network is what saves you; it's what helps you get your foot in the door. Personal recommendations have driven a lot of my success. Connections with real people—their recommendations— are what matter."

Networking is a recurring theme in this interview, and I think this is the point I want to get across for your readers: what has made my career really successful has been networking. Your network is what saves you; it's what helps you get your foot in the door. Personal recommendations have driven a lot of my success. Connections with real people—their recommendations—are what matter.

I agree with you completely.

Right. So, anyway, that casual contact turned into an interview at Numark in L.A. where I was offered a position. They brought me into their engineering office to be the marketing copywriter, basically to translate engineer speak and product specification to "user speak." I was tasked to create the info customers would use for decision-making on a purchase or getting interested in a product. So, that was a great job. I was responsible for writing all the customer-facing copy, for all of the brands, everything from spec sheets to the copy that goes on the box, to advertisements to websites. It really made me a better communicator, both verbally and in written form. It also taught me to be able to quickly research and understand different types of customers, different segments, especially in segments and industries I didn't have any direct experience with. I had started at Zildjian as a drummer. I then moved to Sennheiser and learned the recording and live sound markets. Now, I was talking to hip-hop producers and DJs and even everyday consumers with the ION Audio brand. I had to learn the motivations that drive decision making for each of those different types of customers and speak in authentic language with them.

I would strongly recommend that if you have the opportunity to do any type of professional writing, to do it. It really strengthens your professional skill set. In time, the L.A. office closed, and I was able to negotiate to stay on, working remotely, which was great. I was finishing my master's degree, I explained that to them, and they were cool with that. So, I continued to do the same job for a couple of months and also found out that the former Alesis product manager was moving on to another company and interviewed with management for that job. It was a different type of product management job than what I had done at Sennheiser, where I had worked for the U.S. distribution subsidiary of the parent company in Germany. At Alesis, I was working for the parent company itself, and I was involved in everything from researching the market to specifying the products to working with design and engineering and marketing to actually launching products from start to finish. That was a really amazing learning experience for me because that was the first time where I was actually influencing the products' development, as opposed to providing the marketing.

So, you were more the back end, in your earlier product management role.

Right, now at Alesis, I was involved in the back end, the front end, and in-between; it was everything. That was the first time where I really felt like I was doing something that I was built for. I was taking all my experience in sales and marketing to this point, and also my passion for products, and blending the two. It was a great fit.

At the same time, I was going to school part-time for my M.B.A. When I got to the last semester of the M.B.A., I realized I had a certain number of courses left to go and that I needed to go closer to full-time or add an extra semester. So, the last semester, I took more courses and decided to work part-time. That's what led me to the Loop Loft, which has been an interesting consulting gig. It's a small company in a brand new category: audio loop content. Music (MIDI) loops are a fairly established segment, but audio loops are a new thing—an alternative to renting a studio and hiring musicians. You're actually buying content that sounds like real people playing, because it is actual recorded artist performances. They each have what makes that artist sound unique, and the Loop Loft purchasers can use them sort of like Legos to build their tracks. They are different from using MIDI loops or a sequencer where things are very generic and sterile and don't have that human feel. So, the Loop Loft's product was interesting, too, and it looked like it could be a new model for the future.

Yeah, the players that have developed that expertise have spent years doing it.

…and have unique personalities and character when they're playing. That makes them, as unique individuals, attractive for producers to hire. You know, you hire Steve Gadd to play on your record because he sounds just like—Steve Gadd. You don't hire him because he sounds like a drum sequencer. And conversely, you may hire someone like J.R. Robinson or Questlove, because they *do* sound a little bit like a drum machine, but they still have their own musical personalities, too. So, regardless of the instrument, giving producers and artists access to human performances with their own unique sound and character and personality is really what the Loop Loft is about.

As I was finishing school and consulting with the Loop Loft, I was contacted by a recruiter—actually through LinkedIn— on behalf of a company called SteelSeries, which is a Danish company that manufactures video gaming peripherals, gaming controllers, mice, keyboards, controllers, and headsets for video gamers. SteelSeries was looking for an audio product manager— somebody to primarily handle their headsets.

I had also been doing some big picture thinking about the market sector I had been in so far, music products, especially regarding its future profitability. I asked myself what are the drivers, what will result in new customer acquisitions? Realistically, I tried to predict how much opportunity is there long-term in this industry? What I saw was that in my view, there were a number of factors that were likely to cause a downturn in the music products industry. I reviewed a NAMM study that said that since 2000, the number of active musicians had declined by more than 20 percent. And what's driving that is that our free time has been chopped up into so many different places, and I think that gaming is one of the places that is stealing from the MI industry. Of course, the Internet, TV, and other things too, but gaming is sort of a parallel industry to MI because MI is moving in a much more consumer direction, too, as more companies make devices to integrate iPads, iPhones, etc. into music making.

Meanwhile, you traditionally had people playing video games on a PC or a console, and they were the "gamers." But today, what's evolving, is that the console is migrating toward becoming a hub for various types of home entertainment. Microsoft's Xbox One is an entertainment console. Sony's PlayStation 4 is very similar. These devices are now something that you could play games on, stream Netflix and Hulu on, and you can also get the NFL package on. They're really battling for the share of the consumer's living room in addition to a share of the gaming market.

Additionally, we all walk around with computers in our pockets now. Living here in New York, I see more than half of the people on the subways are playing some type of game on their handheld computer. When I talk to people who don't live in New York, they say that their kids are all playing games in the backseat of the car on an iPad. So, the fact that we are all walking around with these incredible handheld computers means that SteelSeries has an opportunity as a gaming company to really dramatically grow the market from what was a niche—the hardcore gamer— to a share of the much larger consumer electronics market. For me as an audio person, this is a really great challenge. To help take this company that has lots of credibility in the hardcore gaming market—you'll see our products at every competitive gaming tournament—and help the average person discover great sound. It is a really interesting opportunity because they come from this high end. There's a lot of great technology, and a substantial software development team, so a headset can be much more than a couple of drivers and a headband. They could have more technology built into them too, and that's an exciting opportunity. That brings us up to today; I started at SteelSeries this week.

So, as the home entertainment hubs proliferate, there's an opportunity to have your SteelSeries products move to a wider audience among all consumers.

Absolutely. But what I hope the reader will take away from that whole story about my deciding to look beyond MI, is that they should look at how music or how audio can introduce them to the wider business world but not necessarily limit themselves to the music industry, as it has been for the last fifty years, which is struggling to exist in a profitable matter. Don't limit yourself by thinking, "If I'm not working in a music company, I can't do things that I'm passionate about." My career illustrates how I'm applying my passion for sound, a passion for audio, and a passion for music to a growing industry. That's really what I want to get across. You have to be willing to change. You have to be willing to be flexible and not get comfortable. I think that if you get very comfortable, you're likely to have a very short career. Change is constant. For me, it's essential that I do something I'm passionate about so that I can really affect substantial change in an organization or industry. To do something that impacts peoples' lives through sound, audio, or music. That's why this position intrigued me. It's a growing industry that will draw on me to use my passion for sound.

At Berklee, most of the students in the music business program, when you asked them what they wanted to do after they finished, said, "work for a record company, manage a studio, manage bands." Those jobs haven't been growing for quite some time now. So, I think for people to want that as their primary income driver, they're setting themselves up to wait tables for a very long time, unfortunately. You can still do that stuff. You can still do that stuff as passion projects on the side, but you're setting yourself up for a very limited probability of success by saying, "This is the *only* thing I'm willing to do. This is the *only* thing that will make me happy."

I think, as you said, you really have to peel it back and see what part of music makes you happy, and then find new and innovative ways to apply that in today's world.

What do you think likely attracted the recruiter that pitched you for your current job, and what were you able to convey in the interviews that made them comfortable knowing that they were getting the right person for this role?

It was a combination of having done serious product development work beginning to end. The fact that I have introduced and have grown new categories of products and the fact that I had deep experience working with a cross-functional team of engineers, designers, developers, marketers... being that Swiss Army knife is what you have to be as an effective product manager. You have to find a way to get all those various team members excited and interested, and you must speak each of their languages fluently.

Right! Be that intermediary who makes sure that they are all communicating adequately while you are also keeping an eye on the big picture.

As far as what might have cued them that I was likely the right candidate? I think my passion for sound and technology came across. I'm sure my education didn't hurt, but it also wasn't required. I tried to share my own philosophy, which is to always look at every job I've held, even at the entry level, as being a general manager or partner. So, no matter what you're doing, whether it's working at Starbucks or running the show, if you think of yourself as the founder of the company, or think of yourself as the general manager of a division of General Motors, I think that's a very attractive mindset for today's employers. Whether you're actually going to start your own company or not, thinking of yourself as an entrepreneur or as an *intrapreneur* (an entrepreneurially minded employee inside someone else's firm) is incredibly valuable to companies, because most firms' management has become very flat.

They want you to run your own ship, be accountable, and be innovative. Managers increasingly want to give you a general plan and watch you run with it. Today's manager prefers to tell you, "Hey, you're about to run into a brick wall," rather than dictate, "Run in this direction at this speed, for this time, and stop after taking exactly twenty-five steps, no more, no less."

Individuals have to take responsibility for their own continuing education. You can't count on your employer to support you or help pay for it. I didn't get any assistance with my graduate education. I know some firms don't really encourage it because they think it may raise their payroll costs. So, I think you as an individual need to own the decision that "I'm going to go back and get more education to make myself look more attractive to the overall job market." That may not necessarily encourage or influence advancements at your current employer, so you have to be willing to take a little risk on top of the fact that there will be some costs involved. Whether you're going for a one-day training course, or an advanced degree, you may invest time and money and not end up with a raise. You have to trust those added skills, the education, those experiences, and your expanded network will help you in the bigger picture.

What excites you about moving into an area where the market potential is billions of consumers?

This is something I've always wanted throughout my career, and I've always been strategic in taking positions at music companies that touch consumer electronics—that's what I've always wanted to do. As Jimmy Iovine said when he launched Beats with Dr. Dre, "Headphones are the new speakers." That's why I feel like this new move is a great fit for me.

How do you use social media in your professional life?

> "Those are the things that are really good on LinkedIn—specific, measurable accomplishments; I think if you're looking into social media to further your career, you need to have some of that hard data in there."

I keep my LinkedIn profile up-to-date and as detailed as possible. I feel that the more specific you can be about your skills, the better. Have a really well-written bio; I think that's also very important. I don't think you should define yourself by your job title on LinkedIn because we're not in the days where you have a twenty-five or thirty year career at one firm anymore. You need to have a headline that describes you—the professional, the individual, and not be defined by the job that you hold today.

When LinkedIn launched, people used it as "I'm just going to put my résumé there." I think there are pieces of that that would be good. I think the way that people think about résumés is often a list of the things they've done and places they've been. But the really effective résumés are a list of accomplishments, for instance that you "grew sales by 70 percent in two years... introduced 22 new products in the market in the first 6 months, and so on." Those are the things that are really good on LinkedIn—specific, measurable accomplishments. I think if you're looking into social media to further your career, you need to have some of that hard data in there, but that's not always easy to develop as a rookie.

Yeah, for the new college grad, it's a bit harder.

Yes, if you've only had an internship, it's very difficult to say that I've done this and this and this, but I think that if you start from that point, put some numbers on it, put some metrics to it, employers will see that you get what they really care about... tell them what you actually *achieved*, not what position you held.

> *"I think that it's
> very important
> to very carefully
> weigh every word
> that you post
> publicly and really
> understand the
> implications that
> you are broad-
> casting. There is
> no delete key on
> the Internet. Once
> it's out there, it's
> there forever."*

On the other hand, I think that I've been very careful to limit the crossover of my professional life in personal social media. That's not necessarily the most cutting edge way to get a job. I know people use Twitter and Facebook to try to get jobs. Maybe if you're looking for a job as a social media professional, that would be appropriate. I think the further you get into your career as an executive, that could be to your detriment, because employers look for someone who can control the message.

I think that there are many executives who are successful in the way that they use social media, but I think that it's very important to very carefully weigh every word that you post publicly and really understand the implications that you are broadcasting. There is no delete key on the Internet. Once it's out there, it's there forever. You cannot take it away even if you delete that tweet or that Facebook post.

How do you keep in touch with your network? Do you set aside time every day? Every week?

Every job I've ever gotten up until SteelSeries was because of a personal connection, a network point, or a recommendation from someone in my network. This job that I'm moving to was initiated due to LinkedIn, and became possible when the recruiter had a conversation with me and I was able to convey the feeling that I would be a good fit.

Second half of the question? The answer is that it's hard. I'm not as good at this as I'd like to be. I try to keep in touch with people through social media, through occasional phone calls, but it's hard, especially if you've moved around as much as I have. I don't have a system for keeping in touch. You just keep up with people, remember to give them a call, or shoot them an email. I know that people move around much more, so I don't have a great answer to that question. I don't know the actual data, but my guess is that the average person coming out of school today probably will have fifteen jobs over their entire career. So, I think that's definitely something I wish I had better framework for maintaining.

Do you spend any time thinking about how to maintain a work-life balance?

I think that this is really important, and this is something that we've kind of hit in different variants throughout this talk. You have to be very clear as an individual as to what is important to you. For me, work is one of those things. Maintaining a relationship with my family, my wife, is another one of those things. Fitness, doing something physical most days a week is something up there with me. Not only is it a stress reliever, but also it is accomplishment oriented. So, if work's not going well, I can do something good in the gym. Playing music is another one of those. This might be difficult for somebody very junior in their career, but for me, ten years into my career, I always made it very clear the way I function, and that these are things that are almost equally important to me as my work.

I will not be an optimal employee for your company if I don't have time to get to the gym, eat well, see my wife, call my parents, and occasionally play the drums. These are things that will keep me well-balanced. These are things that help me manage stress. These are things that will keep me well-rounded as a human being, because you depend on me to be a creative professional for your organization.

It is of the utmost importance that I don't become a robot that does nothing but work. I think you have to push back a little bit to carve out some personal time. Yes, you have other interests; yes, you're going to pursue them and no, you're not going to be available 24/7. It's fine to answer emails at night, but for me, I need to set boundaries.

One of the things that I have done in the past and will probably continue to do in this job, is turn email accounts on and off. In the iPhone, you go into settings. Just turn it off at night and for the weekend. That doesn't mean that I don't check my email once in a while. It doesn't mean that you can't check in occasionally and answer emails that are urgent, but if you're working all the time, all you're going to do is burn yourself out, stress yourself out. Working more doesn't necessarily translate to working better, working more efficiently, more effectively.

I think you have to limit your hours of exposure to work because—particularly for music people, for creative types—you need to be able to recharge. You need to be able to see things that are not directly related to your work. One of the books that I've recently read, Steven Johnson's *Where Good Ideas Come From*, is a great read about how most good ideas are basically remixed ideas from other places, other industries, other technologies applied to different settings. If you are a well-rounded person, you're not just seeing life through the world you inhabit at work from 7 A.M. to 7 P.M. If you aren't getting outside stimuli, you only see things from the inside perspective. You might get an idea from the baseball game you went to. You might get an idea going to see a show that you went to. You might get an idea at an art museum. It's very important to have outside influences that are not directly attached to the industry in which you are working in.

Let's say you happen to be sitting at a restaurant and overhear someone saying "I hope to be working in the music industry. I just graduated from college," and you've got fifteen or thirty seconds to give them just one piece of advice, what would be your focus point to share with them?

Put points on the board. It's all about accomplishments. Regardless of what you're doing, you need to put points on the board, because that's what leads you to more fulfillment, more control, and the ability to say, "This is what I want to do and I'm going to go do it." People that don't accomplish things don't get to say those things.

So, if you're a product manager, launch new products—lots of them. If you're a copywriter, write a lot of really effective copy. If you're a record producer, produce a lot of really good records. The more productive you are, high quality productive, not just throwing crap out there, the more you'll eventually get to be the captain of your own ship. And that's what we all want. Being the captain of your own ship is much more valuable than making an extra ten thousand dollars a year. Control of your career, your lifestyle, is so much more fulfilling than being able to say, "I made eighty or ninety thousand dollars." It also speaks to that work-life balance question. So, point toward the work that will allow you some additional control over your life and career.

Photo by Bernard "Barney" Lee

Elisa Asato

Elisa Asato is the assistant to the president of Indie label Rostrum Records, home to Wiz Khalifa, Mac Miller, and a growing roster of artists. Rostrum also provides artist management services. The company is located in Pittsburgh, PA.

Breanne: Could you please tell us about the company you work for now, and your role?

Elisa: Rostrum Records is an independent record label and management company. Our current roster includes Wiz Khalifa, Mac Miller, Vali, Donora, Boaz, TeamMate, and Leon Thomas III (from the hit show *Victorious*). My boss, Benjy Grinberg, founded our company in 2003, and in less than a decade, it has grown to be one of the most successful independent music companies in the industry.

As the assistant to the president, I am responsible for keeping Benjy organized and am basically an extension of him and a buffer to the world outside of the company. What that really means is that I book travel, manage his schedule, keep him up-to-date with all of the artists' schedules and activities, and prioritize emails and reminders for him. Besides that, I also act as an office manager for the Pittsburgh office ensuring the day-to-day activities in the office run smoothly. When it comes to my role outside of the office, I help out with whatever is needed. For example, if I'm at one of our artist's concerts, I will help to make sure all the guestlist/important people get in and are situated, and will make sure our artist is okay. Besides hospitality-type duties, I also will help out with tasks such as (most recently) setting up Mac Miller's album listening party in New York and his release party in Los Angeles. Since we are a small company, my role isn't defined to a certain amount of bullet points. I help whenever it is needed for whoever needs it.

What career plans, if any, did you have when you were going to school? How did your academic preparation relate to your intended professional pursuits?

When I attended college, I wanted to move to L.A. and become a personal manager. I decided I wanted to be a personal manager after reading Donald Passman's book, *All You Need to Know About the Music Business*, for my Intro to Music Business class (which I still have and am actually rereading as I type this). After reading that book and finding out that personal managers are the main team players/made the most money, I figured that's a profession I should probably pursue, since being an entertainment lawyer hit the snooze button for me. It was because of this desire that I decided to apply for the student government Arts and Entertainment (A&E) team my freshman, spring semester as well as specialize in studying Arts and Entertainment in the Eberhardt School of Business. (I actually ended up graduating with a specialization in both Arts and Entertainment and Marketing.) I believe the knowledge I gained from both my studies and my experience with A&E really helped to prepare me for what I was trying to pursue.

Instead of just learning about contracts in the classroom, I was also preparing and negotiating them while working for A&E. It was this combination that helped to further spark my interest in pursuing a career in the entertainment industry—specifically music. With A&E, I had the opportunity not only to help run all the entertainment on campus, but also participate and work behind stage as part of the production crew at NACA West (National Association for Campus Activities). It was here that I really started to appreciate live concert production and the work that goes into putting on a show. From there, my love for the industry was solidified when I volunteered at the Academy of Country Music Awards as a Westwood One Radio Remote Talent Escort. I learned of this opportunity through a fellow sorority sister of mine who had volunteered before, and she encouraged me to apply. As an escort, you are assigned an artist (whether it be a single, couple, or group) and have to keep them on schedule as they interview with major market radio stations from across the country. This experience was stressful, exhausting, and frustrating, but also invigorating. Even though I was on my feet for almost seven hours running around the ballroom trying to set up interviews in the most time-efficient, route-friendly manner, seeing artists up close and getting to work with them was a rewarding, but a little surreal experience. At one point, I was in the middle of a group that included Rascal Flatts speaking with my artist, JaneDear Girls, while right across from me was Taylor Swift, and directly to my left was Jewel. It was because of this initial experience that I volunteered again the following year for the GRAMMYs.

How did you land your first job in the industry? How did you land your current job?

I met my boss, Benjy Grinberg, when I was volunteering as a Westwood One Radio Remote Talent Escort at the GRAMMYs. I was assigned Wiz Khalifa, which was exciting since his song "Black and Yellow" was beginning to really take off. His height was a bit intimidating at first (he's 6'4"), but he was so kind to me that I became focused 100 percent on helping him complete his interviews as efficiently as possible. Among Wiz's entourage was Will Dzombak, his day-to-day/road manager; Brannon Scales, who works with Atlantic Records; and Benjy Grinberg, his personal manager—now, my boss. At the end of the day, as Wiz was rushing to leave, Benjy handed me his card and told me to contact him. That night, I wrote an email to him reminding him who I was and sincerely telling him how great it was to work with them.

From there, I stayed in contact with him by emailing Benjy every three weeks or so depending on his response time. Even after I graduated and moved back home to Hawaii, I kept in touch as I began to apply for other jobs. In the back of my mind, I secretly hoped that he would hire me, and I was applying to other jobs as backups. It was around the end of August that I started planning to move to Los Angeles. I didn't have a job offer, nor did I have a clue what I would do once I got there, but I knew I just had to be around entertainment, and something would happen. I actually ended up living temporarily with a relative in San Jose, CA, as I tried to figure out my next move. In late September, Benjy contacted me, asking if I could meet him in L.A. to interview. Elated, I nursed my aging 1991 Honda Accord to L.A. I met with Benjy at the Sunset Tower Hotel in West Hollywood. It was pretty informal as far as interviews go—more a "getting to know each other" meeting. It was not until mid October that he invited me for the final in-person interview in Pittsburgh, PA. He flew me out, and I stayed there for about a week just helping out around the office. We went to a Mac Miller show in Cleveland (my first show of his), and he offered me my job at the end of that week over dinner at Fat Head's Saloon. From there, I had less than a month to pack up, find a place, buy a car, and move to Pittsburgh.

What kinds of traits or achievements help one stand out in the workplace? What particular traits or skills are especially valued in candidates interested in your specific area of the music industry?

Let's start with the traits. You need to be hard working, detail-oriented, enthusiastic, and willing to be accountable for your actions. You also need to have a thick skin so you can take criticism and stay focused. Own up to your own mistakes, while learning from them. Don't take anything personally; it's just business. Keeping an open mind and remaining flexible are also important.

As far as skills, you have to be able to write well and at a professional tone and level. You also have to work at maintaining the various communication channels in and out of the office every day to ensure everyone that needs important information has it. There is no such thing as "normal office hours." You have to be able to make a change to your schedule on a moment's notice—pack and leave the next day when needed. Work literally becomes your life.

What major challenges do you face in your current role within the music industry? What are some of the benefits of working in the music biz?

The major challenge I personally face in the music industry is figuring out my next step. Some people seem to know exactly what they want to do and the steps they need to take to get there, but I'm still figuring out what path is best for me. Coming into the industry, I had an idea of what I wanted to pursue, but now that I have been in it for two years, my interests have evolved.

There are many other positions that interest me, such as becoming a tour manager or publicist. My interest in tour management came from being on tour with Wiz, Mac, and Boaz for the *Under the Influence of Music Tour* last summer, which also featured Kendrick Lamar, ScHoolboy Q, and some members from Taylor Gang. I loved waking up in a new city and would take a run every morning around the venue and sometimes out to the streets to explore a bit. The family atmosphere that develops while you're on tour is great, and I enjoyed learning and observing the effort that goes behind producing a successful tour (production, sales, hospitality, etc.).

Looking at possibly becoming involved in music publicity has also become more interesting to me because of my Wango Tango (an L.A. day-long music festival that features a wide range of A-level talent) experience last year. I was in charge of our artist, Vali, that day. I took her on the carpet, to the gifting suite, and basically helped promote her to everyone in the industry that was there. It was a great experience that really intrigued me, being one of the people that has a hand in creating and fostering the image for an artist.

Besides still finding the right niche for me personally, another challenge is the amount of competition you find at all levels in the industry. It can be intense, and no matter how talented you are, there will always be someone else gunning for your job. Mistakes aren't overlooked, and everyone is replaceable. Still, you can't focus solely on that, and since landing my job, I have met a lot of fun, hardworking, inspiring people that make me want to work harder. Their creativity is contagious. And those people are also willing to support me and help me continue to grow, so that's a big positive.

Do you use social media in your professional life? How?

Yes, I do. I signed up for Twitter because one of my work colleagues was using it a lot, but it has proven to be a great way for me to keep up with current industry news. I connect with people on Twitter or Instagram, which helps to build more relationships.

How important is staying in touch with your peers? How do you do this effectively?

It is very important to stay in touch with your peers, because you never know if you'll need to use them or their contacts in the future. Networking is key, especially in this industry, and maintaining and fostering those relationships will benefit you in the end. No one knows what the future brings, so it's best to keep the odds in your favor and not burn any bridges.

Any suggestions for how to maintain a healthy work-life balance?

My main suggestion for maintaining a healthy work-life balance is to be proactive when it comes to meeting new friends and joining new clubs/organizations. Trust me, I work a ton, and I moved to Pittsburgh only knowing my boss and a coworker. I decided that I would put myself out there and joined an indoor co-ed soccer league, which has nothing to do with work. I've also asked my associates to introduce me to their friends, which is how I met a lot of my current friends in Pittsburgh. Once I was able to forge a friendship with one person, they introduced me to others, and from there my circle of friends kept expanding.

It is unhealthy to let work engulf your whole life, because in the end, you'll be unhappy and unsatisfied. Creating some type of life outside of work, even if it is as small as playing soccer on Thursday nights, will help you keep your sanity.

What career advice would you share with music industry job seekers today?

> As we say in Hawaii, "Go for broke." What this means is put everything you have into your pursuit, because you don't want to look back and wonder, "What if?" I kept an open mind once I was hired and saw this experience as a new adventure. Pittsburgh was the last place I thought I would live, but I figured, "What the hell, why not?" Yes, I was lucky enough to land my job, but it was my choice to stretch outside my comfort zone and move to a completely unknown city. It is taking these types of risks that you need to do at the start of your career when you're young.
>
> Also, remember that failure is a natural part of life, and it is how you handle yourself afterwards that tests your true character. Learning from your failures will help you grow as an individual. As cliché as it may sound, when one door closes, another one opens. Don't focus on that closed door, but rather, take advantage of the new door that may have been cracked open for you. Lastly, don't stay unhappy in a job you despise because it is the "right" place to be. Find what you're really passionate about and pursue it.

Photo by Kelly Shaw

Ken Shackelford

Ken Shackelford is quality assurance technician at INgrooves, a digital media distribution and technology company in San Francisco, CA that provides services for hundreds of independent labels and thousands of artists, working with over 600 digital and physical retail partners around the globe.

Breanne: Please start by sharing a little about INgrooves and your role there.

Ken: INgrooves is a media distributor and functions as the "middle man" between labels and online retailers which we call digital service providers, DSPs. Examples of DSPs we have partnerships with are iTunes, Spotify, Amazon, etc. We aggregate music, video, mobile, and eBook media on behalf of our label/publishing partners, collect and pay out royalties, our music content, video content, or other new content. We facilitate the upload of this content to online retailers. We sign our content, independent label content, and we also sign major label content. Our clients receive customized sales, marketing, synch licensing, and administrative support designed to maximize exposure. My specific role in the company is actually in quality assurance software testing.

This wasn't my original role at this company. When I first joined, I was recruited into the distribution department which is basically the front line of handling the content, using our software platform to deliver the content and tapping a strong relationship with our online partners like iTunes, Spotify, Rhapsody, and so on. After doing that for a number of years, I ended up managing that department, but felt I needed to take on a more challenging role. I moved on to my current position, where I am responsible for software testing. I'm now handling the back end of our software platform to make sure that things run smoothly for everyone using the production environment of the platform. I also have a pretty close relationship with our business development team, which signs partnerships with new retailers, working closely with the new retailers to engage them in our platform, and eventually passing them on to our distribution departments and automated delivery system.

Your role seems to be highly technical.

You could say that. I didn't study much computer science during college, so I'm not actually programming or anything, but it is definitely more technical than I ever thought it would be.

When you were in school and going through business classes and music management coursework, what was it that you were planning on getting into or working towards? What was your dream job in the music industry at that point?

Well, before I actually got into the school and in the department, I always wanted to do some sort of an A&R role before I really even knew what that meant. I think most of my classmates pictured that, maybe because they knew that term and didn't really know anything else. We all just wanted to be in the industry somehow, and that seemed like the most intriguing path. By the time I graduated, I thought about all the different aspects of industry, and I thought I wanted to go into management. I actually moved down to Los Angeles right after school and got an internship at a boutique music management company. The firm used to manage Janet Jackson and the Backstreet Boys way back in the day, but by that time, they had just a few smaller artists. I worked there for a while as an intern until a fellow college alum mentioned there was an opening at a digital music distribution company called INgrooves. As I learned more about the company, I became convinced that I wanted to be in the digital side of things. I actually wrote my senior thesis on how I thought music subscription revenues would overtake à la carte digital sales; that the Spotifys of the world would have a bigger market share than the iTunes. While this is not quite the case just yet, online streaming and subscription models have proven they can make a serious dent in the digital pie chart. Eventually, I got this job offer with INgrooves, and it was right up my alley. I expressed a bit of doubt to the alum stressing I didn't have much experience in computer science, only a strong passion for the music industry. He said, "You know, I'm kind of in the same boat as you. I never thought I would work for a company like this, especially for this department. Trust me. It's a great time. It's a great job." The rest is history.

What do you think it was about your skills and abilities that gave your alumni connections the confidence to recruit you?

Well, to be completely honest, my contact at the company was my friend in college. We were in the same fraternity. That automatically helped a lot because we really knew each other. He knew I was a good guy. We took the same classes, spent time together socially, and shared a lot of the same values. He knew I could do the job. I'll admit, I was a little skeptical at first, but he gave me a rundown of all the things I should know before the interview. By the time I got to the interview, I had done my research and my homework and was prepared. I think that was a huge advantage for getting into the company.

So, building relationships and keeping an open mind are important?

Absolutely. We've had a number of student groups come by to visit the company, and I've only had maybe less than ten emails back with interest saying "I'm really interested in INgrooves. I'm not exactly sure where I would fit in, but I would love to find out and get more information." That's a pretty small percentage, considering how many people actually come through. It's quite possible that they just weren't interested in this space within the industry. But, just the simplest email from those that were, immediately made me want to help them out. That's all it took.

In other words, just taking initiative in the first place and being proactive about making those connections is going to be really important.

Of course. I think it sinks in with some people and maybe not others but as I said earlier, there is a very probable chance that some people don't want to work in the digital space. They may want to work in management or touring or physical distribution, but we have management here—we have label reps who are basically managers of content. There are new careers in the digital space that definitely weren't taught when I was in school because it was just starting off as an industry. It's changed a lot.

If you had to hire someone to do your job, what skills and qualities and abilities would you look for?

Well, a foundation of knowledge in computers and networking would be important. You don't need a doctorate in IT or anything like that, but general knowledge and experience are necessary. A very high sense of, and attention to, detail is needed. Since we're talking about software testing, we need communication to be as specific as possible. And, of course, you need a pretty deep-rooted interest in the music industry. That's the driving motivation in the people in my department and this whole company.

Sometimes, I joke that I don't always feel like I work in the music industry, but then we'll have a team meeting where we'll be talking about all of the albums that we are already working with and all the new albums that we're signing, and that kind of brings it all back.

What are some of the challenges of working in digital music?

The fact that the industry is still kind of figuring itself out. I would say that one of the biggest challenges right now for any of the aggregators, including our competitors, is really ensuring all of the content that we're delivering is actually up and correct at all the stores. There is so much visibility given to just iTunes, Amazon, Google Music, and Spotify, but there are so many other partners, and we are distributing over a thousand titles every week. In addition to that, we're doing a lot of change requests for things like copyright changes, release date changes, or artist name changes. We're also doing takedowns, and it's just all of these new processes that weren't so easily available when sales were strictly physical. If you just sent out two million CDs to all of these box stores, you couldn't just tell them all to pull them suddenly because track 2 has a typo on it. You would either just have to live with it or spend a ton of money to fix it. Now, it can be fixed, so it's an expectation. There is so much demand by labels or artists for that kind of attention.

Prioritizing things like that can be challenging, especially when you start considering how much content an aggregator has. One other thing I should mention in terms of challenges relating to my department is that there are bugs that affect delivery and affect all other processes in the company. Everyone is just trying to make someone else happy. If there is a bug that is preventing the next major album from going out correctly, there is just a lot of rushing. We call it a fire drill. We always have a fire drill around some new, really important album, and those kinds of fire drills hit our department immediately. When it happens, we're basically in our seats until things are fixed.

What is a typical workday like for you?

I'm a little bit all over the map. When I first joined this department, I was in a support role where, if there were things that were needed day to day in reports or bulk changes (say, we needed a thousand albums to be changed from a $4.99 price point to a $6.99 price point), I would handle those projects in the database. I was in a support role for a long time, which helped me learn a lot about the platform, the software, and the code. I recently transitioned out of that, and I'm solely in QA testing, but I'm still available for a lot of the fires that do come up. For example, today there was an album that absolutely needed to go on iTunes. It was failing, and it wasn't clear why, so we needed to investigate and get that working as soon as possible. Things like that come up every day. We are always working on one project or another, and sometimes put that on hold and help out real time problems. Then we would go back to what we're working on.

Do you find that you're able to keep (mostly) standard hours?

That's what we strive for. Through the four plus years that I have been here, there have been periods of time where we need all hands on deck and on-call over the weekends. Then there are times when it's slow and we can work a normal nine-to-five and be fine with that. It kind of just depends on what we have in our project schedule, who the clients are that we're actually building up these projects for, and the urgency of the timelines. A lot of stress goes into finishing major projects, and when they wrap up, we can take a deep breath and move on to something else.

What are some of the cool benefits and the great things about working for a company like yours?

First and foremost, I'm staring out the window right now at Alcatraz and Pier 39, so it's not a bad view. We have a Ping-Pong table. We're a tech company with a really relaxed dress code. When concerts come through, we can usually get free tickets. We have artists come through the office and perform for our events. Everyone feels very motivated to work for this company. Everyone knows how to have a good time after work, but can still get right back into it the next day.

Can you talk a little bit about maintaining connections with your peers and your professional network?

Well, it's pretty easy with a few of them, because we work right next to each other and with each other in the same company. Beyond that, I have a few contacts that don't actually work in the digital music space but work for other companies like Yahoo! and Google. Basically, it's pretty easy to just send them a one-liner every so often to see how they're doing. Email and Skype make it really easy.

Do you utilize LinkedIn?

I think that it's a very beneficial site. I've been using it for about four years now. I have been seeing so many more alumni and friends outside of the digital music industry, and people that I may not even know ask for connection requests. I probably get fifteen to twenty a week. It seems like everyone has been starting to use it in the past few years. I think that it's easy to use, and as important as your résumé. I have seen success stories from many other people.

If you were looking for another job in the music industry today, are there certain websites or social media tools that you would use?

> That's a good question. I would use LinkedIn. But, I have had success, not looking for jobs but just going straight to the companies I'm interested in. I've built relationships with a number of the retailers we work with, and it seems everyone really wants to help each other out. If I wanted to go work for another company and if I had a contact over there, I would probably just shoot them an email saying, "I'm interested in your company. Can you just keep me in mind if you have something open?" Digitalmusicnews.com is a resource specific to our industry that we use all the time—our job postings are always in there. It's a great place to find current jobs and contacts.

Job seekers today tend to depend a lot on the Web or social media tools, sometimes to the detriment of building actual, productive relationships. Would you say your network of actual relationships is still paramount?

> It's incredibly important. You don't want to burn bridges, and that's the bottom line.

What other career advice would you have for anyone looking to get into the music industry?

> Well, anyone who wants to be in the industry should have an overwhelming enthusiasm for it, wherever they end up, knowing that they're contributing to something that they love to do is paramount. They should love to listen to music and experience live shows. I'd like to say that everyone here is first and foremost a music fan. You can see that immediately when you're interviewing someone. If you have passion, you're not going to be complacent in whatever role you get into. Obviously, for whatever role you eventually want to get into, there's plenty of information online to help in preparing for a possible interview—use it! The last thing you want to do is be caught off guard by a common question. An informational interview or just a quick chat with someone who is doing what you want to do puts you so far ahead of someone who is just reading a chapter in a textbook prior to an interview.

What is your top reason for working at INgrooves and the top reason why you love the digital music industry?

> I would say the top reason why I work in the digital music industry is because I had a gut feeling early on that digital was eventually going to completely take over the market. I knew it was a growing industry and not a dying industry. The reason I work at INgrooves is that when I first got there, it was still a relatively small company. We would have bi-weekly meetings back when there were maybe thirty people in the office. Our CEO would give these great speeches (which he still does today). We just had one today, actually. It's basically an update, a snapshot of where our company is and where we plan to go. It was just always so motivating, and we always felt like we were really a part of something bigger. Each time we would have a new meeting, there would be something more exciting to talk about, like signing our deal with Universal or inking our partnership with Fontana Distribution. The meetings continue to make us feel like we are part of something special, and that feeling is enough to keep me here.

What's next? What is the next position that you might aspire to or the next big music trend to look for?

> I'm working to broaden my technical skills while still keeping my foot in the music industry. I never want to become a fully-fledged "tech person." I wouldn't want to move to another company outside of the music industry or into a role just doing software QA. I've thought about eventually working in more of an operations role where I could combine and apply both my technical skills and also my interest in management. That may or may not exist within this company, but new music services and new labels are coming up every day, and so are new roles and positions.

Photo by Anna Jones/PR Photos

Emma Peterson

*Emma Peterson is CEO and founder of Tikly, which touts itself
as a fan, artist, and promoter-friendly ticketing service; an
alternative to the behemoth Ticketmaster. Since she founded the
firm in 2011, Tikly has grown to have more than 750 clients in
forty states and four countries, including the U.S.*

Keith: Please tell us a little bit about your company.

Emma: I am the founder/CEO of the artist-focused ticketing
platform called Tikly (www.Tikly.co). I launched the business in
April of 2011, so we've been around for almost four years, and
we're having an absolute blast running the company! We provide
an online ticketing platform that empowers touring musicians,
venue owners, and event organizers to sell tickets to their fans or
their supporters or their registrants or however they categorize
themselves. It's a happier, easier, cheaper, more aesthetically
pleasing option, as far as ticketing pages go. It's based on the
idea that the ticketing industry itself, and the practices employed
there, are quite outdated. We wanted to build a ticketing
platform tailored to the people who put on the show, whether
a single musician or small music venue owner or the concert
promoter that is investing the time, effort, and energy into
putting on a show or providing live events to their community.
We want to make sure that we are doing right by them and that
they feel comfortable using our service because it allows them
to actually offer advance tickets to their audience that truly
are cheaper, as opposed to the more expensive other options for
online advance sales.

I think that's something that's always riled hardcore fans—that the ticketing transaction doesn't add much to the value, from the consumer's point of view.

No, it doesn't, and after I spent some time on the road, tour managing a band called the Nadas, I recognized that not only was dealing with the ticketing industry a negative experience for the ticket buyer, it certainly wasn't helping the ticket seller either—except for the occasional venue that you might find that has a nice set up with X, Y, or Z ticketing company where they make a little extra off the top. Our attitude was that there are so many people out there that are trying to do good work and provide such an important piece of culture in their community, and they're a part of who aren't well served. Musicians need to get money in their hands so they can put gas in the tank and get to the next city. Venue owners need to be able to open their doors and know that they're going to make money and put on a show that will be worthwhile. Otherwise, they're better off not having a show on a Wednesday night. Our attitude is that it's all about empowering people, whether that be the ticket seller or the ticket buyer, to feel comfortable selling and buying in advance.

When you were in school, did you think that you would have a career related to the music or entertainment industry? And did any coursework or preparation while you were a student help you to think about getting into the music world?

I got a communications degree from the University of Northern Iowa. I knew that I wanted to be involved with live events in some capacity, but what I focused most of my time in college on was actually just attending events and also participating on the University of Northern Iowa's speech team and doing a lot of traveling and getting in front of people as a type of performer, myself. I didn't really take any music-focused coursework. But I did intern with two different companies. One was Phantom EFX, a video game company—so that was in the entertainment industry. Then I interned for Authentic Records based in Des Moines, Iowa, an Indie record label here in town.

At the end of both of those internships, I was offered a job at both companies. I accepted both and so what I ended up doing was graduating from college a year early. During what should have been my senior year of college, I spent two days working for a video game company, two days working for Authentic Records, and then Friday and Saturday and Sunday, I was touring across the nation with the Nadas, the flagship band for the label. That's what really got me exposed to the world of being a touring musician and seeing firsthand the trials and tribulations that everyone goes through regarding the ticketing industry.

It wasn't just the Nadas' perspective, because we were performing nearly every weekend in a new city with a different band, so I really got to understand the woes, the good and the bad, of the ticketing industry from all perspectives of everyone involved across the board. No one was truly singing the praises of any ticketing companies at all. There was perpetually a thorn in their side. I didn't exactly think that I would run my own business or even necessarily find myself involved with the ticketing industry, but I was just constantly exposed to real problems and it was actually harming my passion that I mentioned earlier for live events, that live culture. I love the challenge of getting people out and attending shows and communicating with one another.

Some time after that year on the road, I got to the point of saying, "Well, you know, I can't find a good solution, so perhaps I should go build it." I asked my friend Ben Milne who started a company called Dwolla, Inc. I had gone to Ben and asked if we could use Dwolla to at least lower service fees for our fans. He said, "Of course," and we worked through that. But I kept coming up with other ideas, like maybe we should be able to also sell merchandise alongside our advance tickets to further incentivize our fans to buy in advance. Quite frankly, he basically dared me to start my own company, and I thought he was a fool at first because I thought, "No, that's just something *you* do." Sure enough, it took off and now we have about seven hundred clients and we're live in forty states and four countries including the U.S.

What kinds of additional skills, traits, or achievements would you think would help someone stand out today for a career in the music or entertainment industry?

I think there are a couple of key characteristics. I'm going to talk about characteristics and then we can talk actual skills. Characteristics can go a really long way, and a person's integrity and passion make up roughly three-fourths of the battle to stand out. That's the kind of attitude and key characteristics about a person, a brand, or about a company that makes people really gravitate towards them. To know that you're working with somebody who you can truly trust and rely on, it goes such a long way, because there's the possibility of a lot of shady dealings in the business. I firmly believe that much of the success of Tikly thus far has been because people appreciate that we do really pride ourselves on the level of integrity that we pour into our business. We're truly available to be worked with on the behalf of our clients as well as anyone who may want to partner with us. We're all ears so that's been a key ingredient in our success.

But, integrity and passion are just so important.

As far as skills go, it's just such an online world right now and that's the best way to scale your experiences, as a music business. Growing a brand is probably the most desperately sought-after skill that I can think of. That can take many forms, such as finding somebody, whether it's a person who can step in as a tour manager, or in some groups, they've gotten pretty far with a band member building their brand. One of the musicians that they share the stage with, who can step up and really say, "We want to be career musicians." If that's what your group wants, then we have to treat our band (or it could be a venue) as a legitimate brand. And learn to see our fans as a community of individuals that we have a relationship with where, and for whom, we are relevant. Also learning to spot where the trends are going, how people are releasing their music today, and what is relevant versus not. It changes between genres and types of artists and locations around the world. All these things are pretty fluid, but at the end of the day, you get the farthest as a career musician or manager by being able to grow a community in such a way that you know that when you put on a new album or release a new single, or you have a big show coming up and you need the support of your fans, that people are going to show up. If you can get one thousand people to buy your album, then you're really on to something. So, in my mind, that's the most sought-after skill. That's why people love using systems and platforms like Pledge Music and Tikly, because they're both tools to help build a brand. Using the technology effectively basically helps to hone the skill set.

What are some of the major challenges you see going forward, in terms of how to keep Tikly evolving?

As an online company, we don't have some of the same challenges a traditional brick-and-mortar firm faces. I can live in Des Moines, Iowa and have a company that is selling tickets across forty states. That's the good. The challenge that I am currently facing is making sure that we have enough account managers and account executives, as well as a pool of capable interns, to work with the range of customers that choose to work with us, whether it's a fan club or a 1500-seat venue. We also pride ourselves on being able to provide good customer service and maintaining our integrity. For all the artists that we might be bringing on in the very near future, we want to make sure that they feel that there is somebody perpetually there for them if they have a question, any time of day.

Growth is a bit of a trick because we haven't taken on any outside investments yet. We are a self-funded company that affords itself, but there's a lag time in the music ticketing industry where you sign on a new client, no matter how big or small, and then their tickets don't go on sale for perhaps a few months. Deciding when and how many people I need to add is a bit of a juggling act. Is it account executives to land new clients, or operations people to work with existing accounts?

What are some of the benefits of working in the music or entertainment industry for you or your team?

It's a whole lot of fun. I'm twenty-five and at a position in my life where, unless I'm enjoying my work, I might as well do something different. Working in the industry that I am in is perpetually rewarding and worthwhile. Tonight, for example, I'm going to head up to Minneapolis to be a guest of one of our clients, the band called the Mastersons, Chris and Eleanor Masterson, and they perform tonight with Steve Earle. My team members and I are driving to Minneapolis and are going to check out Steve Earle and John Hiatt. Not every job can provide that sort of a perk. Not only do we get to do what we love, but we're paid in both salary because we have to afford the rent, and also life experiences. You just don't get that working in a cubicle nine to five. There's some degree of fun, uniqueness, and adventure that comes along with the music industry that perhaps you wouldn't get if you were working at, I don't know, maybe an insurance company.

How do you use social media in your professional life?

Just to grow my network. I truly believe that a majority of my success as an individual—I mean both of my internships that turned into jobs—were secured through social media. It evolved through Twitter where I just reached out to them and asked for more information. More than anything, it's staying in touch, staying interested and available. There's not a lot of appreciation that goes very far for people who are unavailable—people you just can't get a hold of. We try to make ourselves, as a company, very accessible to all of our clients and prospective clients, as well as to the people who would buy their tickets to make sure that they're having a good experience. The same thing goes for me as a person. If an opportunity comes up to speak at a conference or to do an interview, no matter how big or small, that's an opportunity there that we take seriously. If we can make it work, we do our best to be visible and accessible.

How important is it to stay in touch with your colleagues and peers?

One of our largest marketing strategies has been attending conferences like South by Southwest, Folk Alliance International, CMJ in New York, and the list goes on and on. We attend those, and we make it a point (because we are mostly focused on the touring musicians' experience, as a ticket seller) to throw showcases and parties at all these different conferences. We provide a positive experience that people can remember after they leave that conference. It's hard to communicate just how valuable attending industry conferences end up being, as well as just being a total blast. Given that, for those of us who do live in the same area, we go out for coffee or beers whenever we can. Beyond that, it's getting in the habit of sending relevant emails, not being abusive of people's time, while making sure that people understand that you truly are there for them if they need anything—no matter whether you're able to provide a service, an ear, or even just sharing ideas back and forth with any colleagues, or even some of our clients. We're better off for it.

I'm perpetually connected to just about anyone. With some of our larger partners, we stay in touch through Skype or Instant Messenger when we want to have that immediate connection to one another because we're kind of in this together. Beyond that, it can get to that part about integrity where people see your face, talk to you, and they can count on hearing back from you in a timely matter. That just solidifies your integrity, and grows the perception and expectation that you're somebody that can be relied upon.

It all comes back to those relationships and the trust that you build.

Yes, because so much of our industry is a handshake industry, in a lot of ways. It always has been and continues to be, although for the ticketing industry itself, there are quite a few competitors who are less interested in a handshake and integrity, and more interested in getting a client to sign on the dotted line. There are plusses and minuses to either, I'm sure. At the end of the day, if you can be top of mind to somebody who might run across a great opportunity, you want to know that you put forward the best impression and understanding of who you are and what your business does that you absolutely could have done. That way, they truly do feel comfortable referring someone and saying, "Hey, you should check out this business." That's how we have won a lot of our larger clients, through our partner channels where it felt completely natural for our partners to say to their own clients, "We're so excited to work with you, and we think you should check out this other company (Tikly) we also partner with, and here's why."

As the founder of a startup learning to scale it up as you grow, how do you try to maintain a healthy work-life balance?

It's pretty difficult. Truth of the matter is, I'm a really big believer in just being honest about when things are awesome and when they're not. I mean, not that you need to write a blog post about everything, but you have to be able to surround yourself with people, whether that be family members or coworkers or colleagues or drinking buddies, with whom you can just be honest about things. When they ask how things are, you don't just automatically say that they're good and hope that they just stop asking questions, right? That's just not how you grow. That's how you get bogged down and things start to eat you away.

I've found that that has been the biggest benefit for me is surrounding myself with good people and also understanding when I don't know something, not to be so proud to think that I can just figure it out—instead of just asking other people for their opinion, for their advice, and to share their experiences. You're just far better served by it. And then they feel more comfortable coming to you for advice further down the road.

As far as a work-life balance goes, you've got to get sleep. I remember the first year of Tikly, I was probably more like those startup stories where you don't do a lot of sleeping. You do a lot of working, thinking, and reading. It was really fun for the first four months to be that excited about something, but then it gets a little bit harder and you start to get burnt out—not that you become disinterested in your product or your company, by any means, but your body just can't maintain that unless you're one of the lucky or even crazy few who, as far as anyone can tell, just doesn't need sleep. I've come to learn how to do a better job of making sure that I consider the company and myself. If you're going to stay up nonstop for a few weeks, it's eventually going to stop you—you're going to get sick. In my opinion, you're going to be worse off.

I also like going to gigs that we didn't sell the tickets for. It's fine to just enjoy yourself and not to have to worry about, "If I go to this gig, am I going to have to sit there and talk to the owner the whole night?" While we love our clients, there's some degree of space that you need to have.

What piece of advice would you share with a music industry job seeker today?

Your integrity is by far the most important thing in this industry right now. Working in the ticketing industry and learning its history have taught me that, while there have been some really great people that came before us, there have also been a lot of really dishonest people. The ticketing industry itself has been fraught with a lot of negativity and tricks. For example, a ticket listed as fifteen dollars ends up costing thirty dollars. If you have that integrity piece, as long as you know that you are doing your best to be as honest and as positive as you possibly can be, people will gravitate toward you because that is what everyone is desperately searching for in our music industry overall right now: To work with good, reliable people and great talent. That's how we won our largest client, so I don't know if there is any other better advice that I can offer.

Appendices

Appendix A: Authors' Career Paths

Both Breanne and I have included a narrative of our individual career paths, because we believe that very few careers in the music industry follow a predictable, straight-line path. We hope you find our two quite different stories useful as a reminder always to listen for the sounds of doors opening with new opportunities for you.

Photo by Dale Pickett Photography

Keith Hatschek

In 1965, as a teenager, I came to California from North Carolina. I grabbed onto the first thing that interested me in my new environment: music.

My family arrived in the Golden State just before school adjourned for the summer. It was just kismet that people up the street had a band. The boy who had been playing bass moved away, and there was no one to fill in. After the guys checked me out for a few days, they said, "Well, if he has a skateboard, he can't be too weird." They came to my house and said, "Look, anyone can play the bass, it's only got four strings. Why don't you come on over here, and we'll try to show you how to play it."

As a teenager, I had scored—social interaction! It helped that I grew up listening to music. My parents listened to the radio and records, and my dad played the piano when he was young.

So, I started to play the bass, and of course the cool thing was that when we practiced, girls stood outside of the garage. Right away, I knew there was definitely an opportunity here for something beyond just blisters on my teenage fingers.

I took to playing music. I loved it. The two things I liked the most were the interaction with other musicians and the mathematical nature of music. If you've ever arranged or composed music, you may have felt there's a very close relationship between mathematics and music, in terms of how the elements fit together—a symmetry.

I loved music. I loved sound. I continued playing in bands. By the time I was in eleventh grade, we were getting paid $300 a night to play at dances. It was big money in the 1960s. Wow, $300. My share seemed like gas money for the rest of my life!

From there, I went to college at the University of California, Riverside, and for one year, I was in the music program and I was doing great. The chair of the music department, "Doctor Don," encouraged every student with an interest in music to pursue his or her musical dreams. Doctor Don used to play in Paul Whiteman's orchestra during the heyday of the big bands.

His belief was, as long as people are listening to music and their toes are tapping, then they're learning. So, I was playing in a jazz ensemble, learning how to write four-part harmony and studying theory. However, I wanted to be close to my friends, so I transferred to the University of California campus at Berkeley, with enough credits to be a junior. I immediately flunked out of every aptitude test you take to make sure that you are really a junior in the music program.

When I went to do my interview, my instrument was the jazz guitar, leading the teacher to ask, where was my "real" guitar? I said, "Well, this is a real guitar, it has six strings—there's my music, and here is my audition tape."

He replied, "I'm sorry, you'll have to go down to the basement at the student union where the pep band plays, and that's not for credit. You will have to start over as a freshman with a recognized instrument."

So ended my collegiate music performance education. I switched gears and earned a degree in history, just to basically escape college with a degree. And I kept playing in rock bands. I had a band in the Bay Area in the 1970s. We eventually secured a development deal with Capitol Records. Unfortunately, we learned that the songs we had recorded for Capitol didn't attract the attention of radio programmers. Our record deal was over a few months after it had happened. That introduced me painfully to the harsh reality of the record business. In the 1970s, if your song wasn't on the radio, you (and your record label) didn't make any money.

I was playing on a jingle session one night in San Mateo, California, at a now defunct studio. The engineer fell asleep at the mixing board during a take. We were done playing, and we said, "Play it back." Musicians are in one room, the studio, and the engineer is in another room, the control room. We couldn't see the engineer. We were standing up, and we finally went in the control room and the engineer was dead asleep on the mixing board.

That experience changed my perspective. I went home and thought, "If that guy can have a job running a recording studio and he falls asleep on the job, I can do better." Famous last words!

After this experience, I visited two legendary studios, Wally Heider's and the Automatt, in San Francisco. I said I want to work in the studio and the managers all said, "Don't do it. Don't do it. Do anything but that."

Undeterred, I thought, "I'll show you guys. I'll build my own recording studio." I was in my twenties—and I knew I could conquer the world. So, I built a studio in 1979 in San Carlos, California. Bayshore Studios was born as a rehearsal room for bands, and acquired a TASCAM 3340 4-track, then evolved to an 8-track recorder. I picked up two partners along the way. We bought some more gear, and some more gear, and yes, a bit more gear.

After a few years I got married, and my wife and I started a family. One day I came to the realization that, "Wow, I am working twenty hours a day, seven days a week, and I have a family. Hmm, what am I going to do?"

I decided to close my business and go to work for another studio. A tough decision to make, but in hindsight, it was absolutely the best thing to do. I had done my own apprenticeship to learn the basics of recording and business. Next, I had a successful twelve-year run at a studio called the Music Annex, which was one of the largest and most successful audio production companies in the San Francisco region. I started as a tape copy room person and engineer for my previous clients.

After a year and a half at the Music Annex, I was answering the phones while the regular phone traffic manager was out to lunch. While I subbed on the phone, there were more sessions booked. The owner of the studio thought, "Hmm, maybe there's an opportunity here. Every time Hatschek is on the phone, our bookings increase. So, if I put him on the phone all day, think how much time we could book!"

He made me an offer. "I'm paying you this much as an engineer, and you're not working all the time. (Beginning engineers seldom are in session all day.) I'll pay you a bit more to work in studio management, selling studio time and coming up with ideas so that we can hustle some more business." And I said, "Okay, I'll try it."

I still did a few sessions with bands I really liked and for projects I was well suited for. I got more involved in planning and studio management. Business increased. Music Annex opened two new divisions to develop a market for audio post-production in 1984 and for cassette and the then-new compact disc duplication in 1986. Business increased some more. The company was profitable, and my earnings rode the crest of the company's growth. I got promoted. I got promoted again. By now, not engineering sessions didn't faze me because I was stimulated and challenged by helping to grow a successful multimillion-dollar studio business. And I was able to afford to purchase a home for my family.

One of the prime products was the duplication of audiocassettes with music and spoken-word programming. It was a great business. The company did very well through the 1980s and early 1990s, and then pretty soon people started saying, "Yeah, I think I'll just put my record out on a CD. I don't need a cassette."

I went to the owner and suggested that we should consider the sale of that division of the company. That was the division I spent most of my time managing. The owners agreed, and after about a year, we located a buyer. And once the sale was formalized, it hit me, "Wow, the company is selling this division! It's really happening. All those people are going to report to another person, not to me anymore."

It became clear then, in 1995, that I needed to find something else to do. That's when I came up with the idea of starting my own consulting practice. And pretty quickly, it grew into a full-service, music technology marketing and public relations agency. We specialized in working for companies in broadcasting, recording technology, and the media industries. We helped our clients tell their story through press relations, advertisements, direct-mail campaigns, videos, and all types of marketing programs to increase their profile and sales.

Although I had begun teaching part-time at San Francisco State University in their successful Music and Recording Industry program in 1994, I hadn't contemplated teaching full-time until I began speaking at various colleges and universities in support of this book's first edition, in 2001. Shortly thereafter, I was visiting with a friend and colleague who had graduated from the University of the Pacific's Music Management program, and he mentioned that the program's founder had retired and the search was underway for a new program director. The idea took root, and the next day, I called him for a referral to Pacific. After a series of interviews, I accepted the position and wound down my agency business, so that by 2002, I spent the majority of my time teaching some of tomorrow's music industry leaders what I have learned in thirty-five-plus years in the music business.

Far from slowing down, joining the robe and gown set in higher education has simply allowed me new areas for growth. In addition to refining my classroom teaching and curricular design skills, I've enjoyed being a mentor to junior faculty and have also developed into a researcher looking at the life and work of the jazz pianist and humanitarian, Dave Brubeck. I've been invited to present my interdisciplinary research on him around the world, and found enough lessons in the intersection of jazz performance, civil rights, Cold War diplomacy, and music business practices during Brubeck's career to be endlessly engaging. I've also made many new friends that are also jazz researchers along the way and interviewed dozens of fascinating people who were touched by Brubeck's life or music. A book on Brubeck is now underway. When the day comes that I want to step away from full-time teaching, I plan to teach occasional enrichment classes for adults on popular culture, music, recording history, and topics that still fascinate me today and tomorrow.

I've come a long way since sitting in that garage in 1965 learning how to play the three-note bass line to "Gloria." I have developed a broad range of skills: first as a musician, then as a recording engineer, then as a studio manager. Making the jump to the business side of the recording studio game was a break that soon showed me how much I could grow in that area. Then I pursued a tighter focus on marketing, promotion, and advertising for a range of clients around the world, before shifting to higher education. Every move has built on the skills developed in the previous jobs. That's why devoting one's self 110 percent to whatever you are doing right now is so important to your long-term career growth. As my friend, John Wittman, from Yamaha Artist Relations, advises students, "Play one note at a time, and play it really well."

I believe my own career is typical of many careers in the entertainment industry. Most people come to it with a set of skills and perceptions of what they see themselves doing, but the fact is that at the end of many successful careers, people have jumped tracks a number of times to take advantage of new opportunities. You find a lot of the people in the A&R departments of labels that were once members of bands. You find a leading entertainment attorney or personal manager who once worked in a music store. You find label presidents that started out as gofers at a booking agency. You'll meet personal managers that started as theater ushers, and many company presidents or music business teachers who, on occasion, still strum their guitar or blow their horn to stay connected to their core passion: music.

Breanne Beseda

I thought it was important to share my career path because, like many of you reading this, I thought I knew for certain that I was meant to work in the music industry. But, life and choice and opportunity and change shaped my career path differently than I expected. I don't work directly in the music industry today, but I am proud to be working with students, faculty, alumni, and employers who are shaping and growing the music industry (and many others). And, I know for certain that I have landed where I am meant to be.

When I was four years old, my parents bought a used upright piano from a local music store. Though I had to sit on a thick phonebook in order to reach the keys, I would sit there for hours, captivated by the sounds I was able to create with my tiny fingers. I immediately started taking weekly lessons, and even at that young age was able to begin learning basic theory and technique. It was a game. It was fun! More importantly, it was the beginning of my love for making music.

Flash-forward through childhood, where I played the piano every chance I got for school talent shows, regional recitals, national merit competitions, church services, and virtually every family event. I began writing music and trying out other instruments, including my own voice. My dad played the guitar and my mom would sing along, and it wasn't uncommon to find our living room full of scattered sheet music, microphones, cords, and cases. As a teenager, I continued to study and write music. I continued to perform, and I even began to teach. I began to really, truly appreciate how music made me feel. It helped me to deal with hard times, celebrate great times, and work through my feelings about all of the times in between.

When it came time to apply for college, I started to investigate music schools and majors. I discovered that a few schools offered programs in music management or music business, and quickly became convinced that I had found the perfect college major—one that would allow me to incorporate my passion for music with a business education that would allow me to qualify for "real" jobs (and ease my parents' apprehension). I applied to every school in the nation that offered a music management program (at that time there were only about a dozen) and ultimately chose to attend University of the Pacific. After successfully completing an audition, I was admitted to the Conservatory of Music as a music management major with the option to also study piano performance and/or composition. During orientation and my first week of classes, it became painfully apparent that I had made a mistake. After some honest soul-searching, I knew that I did not have a future as a professional performer. As much as I loved music, I thought it would be better to switch to a business major with a concentration in music management. This allowed me to focus the core of my studies in business—accounting, finance, law, operations, management, marketing, and strategy—while still incorporating the music industry and music management classes as electives. I pictured and prepared for a career as a record label executive or major tour manager, where I imagined I'd put my business education to work "behind the scenes" to help artists share music with the world. But at the same time, something unexpected was happening. As I took more and more business classes, I found myself drawn to marketing. Much like music, I found that marketing was a cool combination of strategy, creativity, and communication. Like music, it's ultimately about creating connection. And as my interest in marketing grew, my concern about the sacrifices necessary to build a career in the music industry also emerged.

I completed my degree in just three years and was only twenty years old when I walked across the stage in my cap and gown. I was leaving college with a great education, but very little relevant experience. I had been offered an entry-level position at a small jazz record label in San Francisco, but the salary offer would have required a second job just to pay rent. At the time, it seemed that the only other real option for a job in the music industry meant moving to Los Angeles, something I was not prepared to do. This dose of reality forced me to reconsider my options and open my mind to opportunities beyond the music industry. I decided to apply to graduate school to continue to explore marketing as a possible path.

One year later, I was walking across the graduation stage again, this time with the designation of M.B.A. and a full year of experience as a marketing intern with a telecommunications company headquartered nearby. I accepted a full-time position with the company and began my career in marketing communications, and eventually transitioned to strategic marketing. Over three years with the company, I had the opportunity to learn and grow, and was trusted to help lead some pretty fantastic projects. I expanded my experience and skills and grew my professional network with incredible mentors and lifelong friends. I loved the people I was working with, and I loved the marketing function, but I wasn't passionate about the product. Not at all. I needed a change.

Almost as soon as I got serious about looking for something new, an opening on a job site caught my eye: Marketing Manager, University of the Pacific, Eberhardt School of Business. It seemed perfect! It would be a small jump in pay, title, and responsibility, but more importantly, my "products" would be programs I was proud to promote, people who inspired me, and a place I considered a home.

I served as the marketing manager for the business school for two and a half years. At the same time, I also developed and managed my own event coordination business. I was very busy, and very happy. Right when it seemed that things were falling into place and going well professionally, a family situation required me to move out of the area. I was able to land a position as director of marketing and operations with a small design firm, but the experience was not a good one for a number of reasons, and yet another urgent family situation compelled me to return to the area a short time later. I was on the job hunt again, just six months after leaving the job I loved at Pacific.

I was at a low point, both personally and professionally, when out of the blue I received a phone call from a friend and former coworker at Pacific. She told me that she was able to secure funding for an assistant director to partner with her in the area of career development for business students, and she wanted me to apply. I was hesitant at first—not only would it be a drop in pay from my last position, I really didn't have any direct experience or expertise in career management. Then it hit me—it would really be a marketing role! I'd be teaching students how to brand and sell themselves to potential employers, and using marketing strategies to communicate with companies about why they should recruit at Pacific. I would get to be in the classroom teaching and out in the field learning about business needs. My job would be about creating connections. I would get to return to working with my Pacific family, and would have the opportunity to make a real impact in the lives of students. I couldn't pass it up.

That was seven years ago, and I'm still at Pacific. Countless résumés, classes, interviews, events, and guidance meetings later, I still love helping students to develop, launch, and manage their careers. I love helping alumni and employers to connect with bright students, and I love building connections with colleagues who challenge and inspire me. I continually learn through teaching, and I love that I get to be a positive and influential force in the success of the people and programs I work with every day. Although my role in the music industry is an indirect one, I love that I get to help launch many music industry careers. I still get to make an impact (and live vicariously!) through my music management students, alumni, and colleagues.

Music will always play an important role in my life. I've continued to play and perform for family and friends, and occasional special events. These days, most of my musical performances include a used upright piano in my own living room with my two-year-old son (who, at this point, seems more interested in being a drummer). As we play and sing together, I'm reminded that my most important audience is sitting in my lap. Music is powerful. It's emotional and it's influential. It creates connections. And for some, it may even create a career.

Appendix B: Selected Resources

A Note about Pricing References

Subscription rates and terms are fluid in this arena, so while the fees quoted here were accurate at the time this edition went to press, they may not reflect current charges at the time you will be researching these sites.

CAREER AND INDUSTRY RESEARCH TOOLS

Books and Directories

A library that has a reference or business reference department is a perfect place to spend some time during your career research. The reference books listed below may be found at most public and school libraries. Reference librarians are also a wonderful resource to assist you in locating information about companies that you may be researching. If you ask for assistance in researching a specific company or career path, you will be surprised at the resources that the librarian will be able to help you locate and use. Remember, the human brain really is the most powerful computer.

Directory of Corporate Affiliations. New Providence, NJ: LexisNexis, 2013. An essential guide to who owns whom in corporate America, especially helpful in the current era of entertainment company consolidation. There are three different directories available: Public companies, private companies, and international companies. Online and printed editions available.

Hoover's Handbook of American Business. Charlotte, NC: Mergent Publishing, 2013. A two-volume directory of U.S. corporations. Provides basic data on company size, locations, types of business activities. Quick company snapshots may be found at Hoover's Online for many publicly held companies; however, the printed directories have much more information available than the free portion of the Hoover's website.

Hoover's Handbook of Private Companies. Charlotte, NC: Mergent Publishing, 2013. Useful for researching privately owned companies.

The Indie Bible. New York City, NY: Music Sales Corp., 2013. Available as an eBook for $40, this is basically a directory for aspiring artists that wish to build an audience and industry connections. It features an extensive section on radio stations that will play new music, Indie labels looking for new talent, and music blogs, magazines, journals, and Web reviewers that will accept submissions of independent music.

Musical America: International Directory of the Performing Arts. East Windsor, NJ: Commonwealth Business Media, 2013. A reference work that lists information for jazz and classical artists, agents, promoters, arts organizations, and much more useful data. Their website is full of resources, articles, breaking news, and more.

National Directory of Arts Internships, 11th Ed. Barton, Christensen, and Dean, co-editors, Los Angeles: National Network for Artist Placement, 2008. A comprehensive guide to locating internships in the performing arts fields, updated occasionally.

Opera America: Career Guide for Singers, 6th Ed. New York, NY: Opera America, 2003. A comprehensive guide for vocalists considering careers in the world of opera. Please note that there is now an "Artist Tool Box" available on the Opera America website with a number of very useful self-help exercises, worksheets, and articles for aspiring singers.

Plunkett's Entertainment and Media Almanac. Houston, TX: Plunkett Media, 2011. In-depth profiles of 400 of the leading companies in the music, media, and entertainment industries. Excellent and up-to-date set of articles describing the latest trends, as well as a host of industry statistics that highlight which market segments are expanding most quickly. Highly recommended.

Ward's Business Directories, 52nd Ed. Farmington Hill, MI: Thomson Gale Publishing, 2009. Similar to the *Hoover's Directories* but also provides data on the firm's market share. A special volume in the set allows for geographic-based search.

GENERAL INTERNET RESOURCES

The following Internet databases and search tools may be accessed at most public and college libraries. They are all subscription-based services, but provide an extensive array of articles that may be searched to investigate companies and careers. Search engines such as Google, Bing, and Yahoo! can be helpful, but they often do not include full-text articles from many leading magazines, newspapers, and business journals. Accessing in-depth articles such as these may be done via these resources. Remember, if the company you are researching offers stock to the public, it will have detailed reports publicly available online in the form of its quarterly (10-Q) and annual (10-K) reports.

Factiva. Formerly the Dow Jones information service, Factiva is a comprehensive search tool that provides access to a nearly limitless range of contemporary news articles and reports from all of the major sources of information. It might be helpful to ask a reference librarian to assist you in your first few searches to learn how to best access the information it can locate.

Lexis/Nexis. Another search service that provides a rich library of contemporary news and business data. Publicly held companies will have their annual reports available here, as well as often posted on the firm's own website.

Academic Search Premiere and *Business Source Premiere.* These two databases are available at many public and school libraries and aggregate many useful resources for investigating specific companies, trends in the music industry, and leading personalities in the business.

Billboard. www.billboard.com/biz. This is the homepage for *Billboard* magazine's online business magazine, *Billboard Biz.* It's full of breaking news of the music industry and a good means to keep up with business developments in the U.S. and abroad. Billboard.com, the online edition of the weekly print magazine, has slightly different content slanted more toward artists, releases, charts, and consumers, so both sites are worth bookmarking. The free versions offer plenty of information to keep you up to date, although you have to navigate through quite a few pop-up ads on the Billboard.com site.

Google Finance. This is a free site that has a fairly easy-to-navigate set of linked pages to give you a glimpse at a company's performance, current news, and other related companies. For a company like Apple Computer, there is a rich repository of links, news, and data, whereas for a smaller public company such as Guitar Center, there is only a short summary of the business (pulled from Hoover's Directory) and useful links to breaking recent news stories that include the company. Other music industry firms such as Winmark (Music Go Round), Steinway, and Yamaha have a bit more information available.

Job-Related Websites

RileyGuide.com. Although it is not a job search engine, this site provides a tremendous range of useful advice and tips on everything from job interviewing to salary negotiations. There is a large database of easily accessible information labeled with the heading "Networking and Support Groups" as well as tips on how to get involved in local and national networking organizations. It has a handy A to Z listing of career fields and industries including Acting and Entertainment, which has some useful links. The site is free to use.

Vault.com. This site has free and pay portions to its site. The Vault's "Gold Membership" ($19.95 per month or $120/year) provides access to ratings and reviews of select employers, detailed salary information, and unfiltered opinions from employees and interns about the what a firm's culture and work environment are actually like. Within the free section, there are articles, how-to tips, excellent information on internships, and especially helpful company snapshots for some of the larger entertainment firms. Check to see if your school or college may have a "Gold Member" subscription to this service that you can use to access the full range of information.

ArtistsHouseMusic.com. This site was developed by industry veteran and music business educator, John Snyder and features hundreds of interviews with industry professionals from all areas of the business. There are also some very informative articles and other career related resources that many industry job seekers have found most beneficial. Although the site is free, a nonprofit has been set up to help support its continued growth through donations, so consider supporting this valuable resource if you find it useful.

Berklee College of Music: Career Development Center and *Industry Job Designations.* Visit Berklee College of Music's Career Development Center online to view a number of free online resources that any music industry career seeker should check out (www.berklee.edu/cdc/explore-career-resources). The *Music Industry Salary Guide* is a tremendous resource, and there are links to other helpful career planning documents. Their Careers in Music page has a very comprehensive directory of dozens of music-related jobs (www.berklee.edu/careers-music-0).

University of Hartford: www.library.hartford.edu/allen/allen_musicresources.asp. University of Hartford's Allen Library has this useful free site that allows you to do subject specific searches for resources, book titles, and websites. Click on the lower drop-down menu, which reveals a list of subject areas, and click on "Management." You'll see a list of helpful resources.

The Musician's Atlas: musiciansatlas.com. Originally an annual directory that most DIY bands carried in the glove box of their vans while touring, now it's morphed into an online music management resource that provides instant access to club bookers, agents, radio, music stores, music supervisors, and many other necessary bits of information a DIY artist needs to have available to grow their career. You can also build email lists, send email blasts, pitch your music to industry players, etc., using the platform provided. Basic version is $20 month; Pro version is $40 monthly.

Careersinmusic.com. This site features a helpful directory of many different jobs in the music industry and includes general salary range and descriptions of the roles and responsibilities of such positions. In addition to salary range information, the site provides what education/training may be required, and suggestions on how to get started with the specified job. The site's founders are also now developing curriculum in specialized areas of the industry such as how to write music for apps, and how to produce and sell original music to production libraries or television and commercials.

Job Directories and Search Engines

We'll start with some of the larger search engines and work our way down to industry-specific job listing boards. Unless otherwise noted, these directories are free to use, although a few offer a free version and a more powerful paid membership version.

Monster.com. One of the largest and most comprehensive job listing sites, Monster.com allows a tremendous amount of customization through its various search and sort options. For instance, it allows you to refine your searches by zip code and location (especially helpful with respect to New York City and Los Angeles, where the proximity between your job site and your home may be crucial to your quality of life). By allowing you to narrow your search criteria such as: date the job listing was last updated, job location, job category, whether a job is posted by an employer directly or by a staffing firm, and by numbers of years experience required, you will be better able to zero in on the jobs that are best suited for you. For someone just starting out in the industry, you can also quickly eliminate mid- and senior-level jobs from any search focusing on the most likely jobs for which you qualify.

CareerBuilder.com. The second of the large, general-purpose job search engines, it has many of the same features of the previous site, along with an easy way to sort jobs that are defined by the helpful listing firm as "entry level." You can also limit your searches to listings that include select keywords or industry terms to see what comes up. For those planning to relocate to a major entertainment center, you can geographically limit your searches to those regions and quickly assess the level of hiring and internship activity in each market. A recent search in the L.A. market resulted in more than thirty positions open in a variety of areas including record companies, television stations, film companies, and more.

Craigslist.org. This site has one great advantage over many of the other sites: each version of Craig's List is localized for a specific market. In addition to a variety of job listings searchable by category, on the same site you have information on housing and other categories that may be useful to research, especially if you are planning to relocate for your job. A recent search in the San Francisco Bay Area under the categories Art/Media/Design and TV/Film/Video turned up a few jobs for a variety of established and startup gaming, social media, and video production and distribution companies. Another way to search is to use the Jobs header, then type in a key word such as "music" or "video game" and see what results are generated. You might also check under the "Gigs" section at the bottom of the page, as a recent look here for San Francisco and New York turned up a number of film and label internship opportunities.

Entertainmentcareers.net. A well-organized site that offers many categories to view job and internship listings. A recent search under the "Music" category brought up sixty jobs, all of which were in the greater L.A. or NYC metro regions. It also has regional jobs banks for Chicago, NYC, and Northern California. One of the best sources to look for an internship listing, a recent look revealed 779 internships posted here. While the postings can be viewed free of charge, there is a membership option ($25 for 90 days, $70/year) that provides early access to job listings (before they go public), customizable email and job posting alerts, as well as storing your résumé and cover letters for immediate use in applying for listed positions.

VarietyMediaCareers.com. Part of the *Variety* magazine family, this portion of their website is a good resource for looking at various types of entertainment industry job descriptions. The majority of positions listed are for two of the industry centers, L.A. and NYC. The site focuses more on broadcasting, marketing, and cable TV-related positions, but a number of music-related jobs were listed when the site was reviewed recently. Among the 1,455 listings, there were 173 in music, 356 in television, 272 in online, and 316 in broadcast categories. It has a very useful job alert feature that can be set up to provide daily or weekly notifications when positions are posted that fit your predetermined criteria. You can also post your résumé into an anonymous bank that can be searched by employers, which may lead to greater exposure for job seekers.

Music-jobs.com. This site offers U.S., as well as U.K., Brazilian, and Italian versions, potentially of interest for those considering an international career or internship. You can view posted jobs on the site for free, but if you are actively pursuing a music industry job, it might be wise to consider the $10 monthly membership. As a member, you can see the name of each employer that is posting a job, upload your résumé to the site, where the reportedly more than 1,000 employers who use it for hiring view it. It also has gig and message boards to share information with other job seekers. A current look revealed more than 300 music industry jobs and 40 internships posted. A handy feature is that members will be sent a weekly summary of which firms have looked at their résumé. A recent nice upgrade is a "region" search function, which currently showed New York City, Brooklyn, San Francisco, L.A., and Chicago, as well as the ability to sort job listings by state.

Artjob.com. This site specializes in listing jobs, internships, fellowships, and other opportunities in the arts field. It covers a wide range of fields spanning visual arts, performing arts, commercial art and design firms, film, public arts agencies, academic arts departments, galleries, conferences, commissions, nonprofit organizations engaged in the arts and cultural policy, and more. You can do a search by job titles, for instance, "Operations" or "Marketing," and see the position title, first few words of the job description, and the location for the more than 1,400 listings currently posted at the time of writing, but to get the details on any open position, you must join the site: $25 for ninety days, $40 for six months, or $75 for a full year.

MusicalChairs.info. This is a free site that features both performance and administrative and management jobs in the classical music field. The information is updated frequently, and at the time of writing, showed postings for fifteen arts administration positions in North America and seventeen for the European region. One of the handiest features of the site is a worldwide directory of symphony and opera companies with links to the organization's website, office contacts, and even a list of the players. For someone building a list of arts presenters to solicit employment from, this is a real time saver. Currently, it lists 437 companies in the U.S. and 41 in Canada.

Showbizjobs.com. Another very well-organized site, it also allows sorts by region, job category, salary range, full-time vs. part-time or contract positions, and more. The basic search services are free; however, for $35 you can purchase a six-month SBJ Pro membership, which allows you to register and post your résumé and job interests. The many testimonials by registered members who landed industry jobs indicates that, for those who don't or can't make the time to search daily for new job listings, this might be a good strategy. As a member, you can apply for jobs with two clicks and utilize the Show Runner feature, which is an automated notification when new jobs are posted in your categories of interest. The site boasts that more than 700 industry recruiters use it regularly. A few other helpful features of this site are that you can view short company profiles, and also search by industry and how recently the job has been listed. This is especially handy as you can set the search feature to only show jobs listed in the most recent twenty-four hours or week, for example.

Mymusicjob.com. This site also has a wide range of both U.S. and international job postings, and offers search criteria including country, region, job category, and full-time vs. part-time, internship, summer job, etc. The site has been going through a number of redesigns at the time of writing, so check in to see what it currently offers. It also seems to list a significant number of music jobs in the Middle East.

4entertainmentjobs.com. This is a site that has many similar features to those listed above, plus options to build a portfolio for recruiters to view including résumé, cover letter, and references. Currently, the site showed 5,221 job and internship listings and claimed more than 3,000 employers used the site. The site has a seven-day trial membership option for $9.95 and charges $29.95 per month for its services.

Musicianspage.com. This site actually specializes in finding performance opportunities—yes, gigs—for musicians. It has a simple search feature that enables gig seekers to categorize their searches via instrument, genres, and skill level. Also useful is the front page, which features a constantly updated "Latest Music Jobs or Projects" section that allows performers to quickly locate jobs and gigs. Upon a recent viewing, there appeared to be a number of opportunities for commercial gigs in the Middle East and a number performing on cruise ships. There is also an entire portion of the site that allows musicians to post their music, receive feedback, and share sheet music. Using the site requires registration, and like other sites noted here, it also has various levels of membership that allow more features to be activated.

Other Books and Reference Sources

Aczon, Michael A. *The Musician's Legal Companion, 2nd Ed.* Stamford, CT: Cengage Learning, 2013.

Avalon, Moses. *Confessions of a Record Producer, 4th Ed.* San Francisco: Backbeat Books, 2009.

Brabec, Todd and Jeff. *Music, Money and Success: The Insider's Guide to Making Money in the Music Industry, 7th Ed.* New York, NY: Schirmer Trade Books, 2011.

Crouch, Tanja. *100 Careers in the Music Industry, 2nd Ed.* Hauppauge, NY: Barron's Educational Books, 2008.

Dannen, Frederic. *Hit Men.* New York, NY: Vintage Books, 1991.

Field, Shelly. *Career Opportunities in the Music Industry, 6th Ed.* New York: Checkmark Books, 2008.

Feist, Jonathan. *Project Management for Musicians: Recordings, Concerts, Tours, Studios, and More.* Boston: Berklee Press, 2013.

Gordon, Steve. *The Future of the Music Business: How to Succeed with the New Digital Technologies, 3rd Ed*. Milwaukee: Hal Leonard Books, 2011.

Grierson, Don. *It All Begins with the Music: Developing Successful Artists for the New Music Business*. Independence, KY: Cengage Learning, 2009.

Half, Robert. *How to Get a Better Job in This Crazy World*. New York: Signet, 1995.

Hatschek, Keith. *The Golden Moment: Recording Secrets of the Pros*. San Francisco, Backbeat Books, 2006.

Kimpel, Dan. *Networking Strategies for the New Music*. Los Angeles, CA: Alfred Publishing, 2011.

Kusek, Dave and Leonhard, Gerd. *The Future of Music: A Manifesto for the Digital Age*. Boston, MA. Berklee Press, 2005.

Passman, Don. *All You Need to Know About the Music Business, 8th Ed*. New York: Free Press, 2012.

Payne, Richard A. *How to Get a Better Job Quicker*. New York: New American Library, 1982.

Stim, Richard. *Music Law: Running Your Band's Business, 7th Ed*. Berkeley, CA: Nolo Press, Berkeley, CA, 2012.

Stone, Chris. *Audio Recording for Profit*. Woburn, Mass.: Focal Press, 2000.

Industry Biographies

Branson, Richard. *Losing My Virginity*. New York: Crown Business, 2011.

Burton, Gary. *Learning to Listen: The Jazz Journey of Gary Burton*. Boston: Berklee Press, 2012.

Copeland, Ian. *Wild Thing: Memoirs of Ian Copeland*. New York: Simon and Schuster, 1995.

Cornyn, Stan. *Exploding: The Highs, Hits, Hype, Heroes and Hustlers of the Warner Music Group*. New York: It Books, 2002.

Dickerson, James. *Women on Top*. New York: Watson-Guptill Publishers, 1998.

Finkelstein, Bernie. *True North: A Life Inside the Music Business*. Toronto, Ontario: McClelleand and Stewart, 2012.

Holzman, Jac and Gavan Daws. *Follow the Music*. Santa Monica: First Media Books, 2000.

Jones, Quincy. *Q: The Autobiography of Quincy Jones*. New York, Harlem Moon, 2002.

King, Tom. *The Operator: David Geffen Builds the New Hollywood*. New York: Random House, 2000.

Kooper, Al. *Backstage Passes and Backstabbing Bastards*, updated edition. Milwaukee: Hal Leonard Books, 2008.

Martin, Sir George and Jeremy Hornsby. *All You Need Is Ears*. New York: St. Martin's Press, 1995.

Olsen, Eric, Paul Verna, and Carlo Wolff. *The Encyclopedia of Record Producers*. New York: Watson-Guptill Publishers, 1999.

Ramone, Phil with Charles Granata. *Making Records: The Scenes Behind the Music*. New York: Hyperion, 2007.

Slichter, Jacob. *So You Wanna Be a Rock and Roll Star*. New York: Broadway Books, 2004.

Small, Mark and A. Taylor. *Masters of Music: Conversations with Music Masters*. Boston: Berklee Press, 1999.

Swedien, Bruce. *Make Mine Music*. Milwaukee: MIA Press/ Hal Leonard, 2004.

Thompson, Ahmir "Questlove." *Mo' Metta Blues: The World According to Questlove*. New York: Grand Central Books, 2013.

HARD-TO-FIND BOOKS

If you are searching for a book that is out of print, try www.alibris.com, www.abebooks.com, or the used listings on Amazon.com. These websites have useful search engines to help you locate out-of-print and hard-to-find books. At the time of writing, every one of the out-of-print works referenced in this book was available on one or more of these sites.

Periodicals

Much of their content is available online.

Billboard	Hits Daily Double
DigitalMusicNews.com	Pollstar
Mix	Music Connection
Pro Sound News	Tape Op
Electronic Musician	Rolling Stone
Keyboard	Pitchfork Media
Recording	Sound-on-Sound (UK)
Musico Pro (Spanish language)	Spin
	Hollywood Reporter
Hypebot.com	Variety

Appendix C:
Music Industry Trade Associations

All of the information in this section was confirmed for accuracy at the time of writing. Please search by organization name if any of the contact information changes after publication.

UNITED STATES

Academy of Country Music
5500 Balboa Boulevard
Encino, CA 91316
818-788-8000
www.acmcountry.com

American Association of Independent Music (A2IM)
132 Delancey Street, 2nd Floor
New York, NY 10002
646-692-4877
a2im.org

American Music Therapy Association (AMTA)
8455 Colesville Rd., Suite 1000
Silver Spring, MD 20910
301-589-3300
www.musictherapy.org

American Choral Directors Association (ACDA)
545 Couch Drive
Oklahoma City, OK 73102
405-232-8161
www.acda.org

American Composers Alliance
802 W. 190th Street Suite 1B
New York, NY 10040
212-925-0458
www.composers.com

American Federation of Musicians (AFM)
1501 Broadway, Suite 600
New York, NY 10036
212-869-1330
www.afm.org

American Guild of Music
PO BOX 599
Warren, MI 48090
(248) 336-9388
www.americanguild.org

American Society of Composers, Authors and Publishers
(ASCAP)
2 Music Square
Nashville, TN 37203
615-742-5000
www.ascap.com

American Society of Music Arrangers and Composers (ASMAC)
5903 Noble Avenue
Van Nuys, CA 91411
818-994-4661
www.asmac.org

Audio Engineering Society (AES)
60 East 42nd Street
New York, NY, 10165
212-661-8528
www.aes.org

Broadcast Music, Inc. (BMI)
320 West 57th Street
New York, NY 1009
212-586-2000
www.bmi.com

Center for Computer Research in Music and Acoustics (CCRMA)
Stanford University Department of Music
Stanford CA, 94305-8180
650-723-4971
ccrma.stanford.edu

Chamber Music America
Mailing Address:
UPS Box 458
243 Fifth Avenue
New York, NY 10016

    Office Location
    99 Madison Avenue, 5th Floor
    New York, NY 10016
    Between 29th and 30th Street
    212-242-2022
    www.chamber-music.org

Consumer Electronics Association (CEA)
1919 S. Eads Street
Arlington, VA 22202
703-907-7600
www.ce.org

Country Music™ Association (CMA)
CMA Headquarters
One Music Circle South
Nashville, TN 37203
615-244-2840
www.cmaworld.com

College Music Society
312 East Pine Street
Missoula, MT 59802
406-721-9616
www.music.org

Creative Commons (alternative to traditional copyright)
444 Castro Street
Mountain View, CA 94041
650-294-4732
www.creativecommons.org

Gospel Music Association (GMA)
4012 Granny White Pike
Nashville, TN 37204-3924
615-242-0303
www.gospelmusic.org

Guild of Music Supervisors
P.O. Box 642200
Los Angeles, CA 90064
www.guildofmusicsupervisors.com
www.facebook.com/guildofmusicsupervisors
info@guildofmusicsupervisors.com

Harry Fox Agency
℅ National Music Publishers' Association
711 Third Avenue, 8th floor,
New York, NY 1007
212-370-5330
www.harryfox.com

International Association of Venue Managers (IAVM)
635 Fritz Drive, Suite 100
Coppell, TX 75019
972-906-7441
www.iavm.org

International Computer Music Association
1819 Polk Street, Suite 330
San Francisco, CA 94109
www.computermusic.org

League of American Orchestras
33 West 60th Street
New York NY 10023
212-262–5161
www.americanorchestras.org

Music Business Association (aka Music Biz, formerly NARM)
1 Eves Drive, Suite 138
Marlton, NJ 08053
856-596-2221
www.musicbiz.org

Music Publishers Association
243 5th Avenue, Suite 236
New York, NY 10016
212-327-4044
www.mpa.org

Nashville Songwriters Association Intl. (NSAI)
1710 Roy Acuff Place
Nashville, TN 37203
615-256–3354
nashvillesongwriters.com

National Academy of Recording Arts and Sciences (NARAS)
3402 Pico Boulevard
Santa Monica, CA 90405
310-392-3777
www.grammy.org/recording-academy

National Association for Campus Activities (NACA)
13 Harbison Way
Columbia, SC 29212-3401
803-732-6222
www.naca.org

National Association of Broadcast Employees and Technicians
(NABET)
501 3rd Street NW, #880
Washington, DC 20001
202-434-1254
www.nabetcwa.org

National Association for Music Education (NAfME, formerly
MENC)
1806 Robert Fulton Drive
Reston, VA 20191
703-860-4000
www.nafme.org

National Association of Music Merchants (aka NAMM)
5790 Armada Drive
Carlsbad, CA 92008
760-438-8001
www.namm.com

National Association of Broadcasters (NAB)
1771 N Street NW
Washington, DC 20036
202-429-5300
www.nab.org

National Association of Schools of Music (NASM)
11250 Roger Bacon Drive, Suite 21
Reston, VA 20190 – 5248
703-437-0700
nasm.arts-accredit.org

National Systems Contractors Association (NSCA)
3950 River Ridge Drive NE
Cedar Rapids, IA 52402
800-446-6722
www.nsca.org

National Association of Record Industry Professionals (NARIP)
P.O. Box 2446
Los Angeles, CA 91610-2446
818-769-7007
www.narip.com

New Music USA
90 John Street, #312
New York, NY 10038
212-645-6949
www.newmusicusa.org

OPERA America
330 Seventh Avenue
New York, NY 10001
212-796-8620
www.operaamerica.org

Percussive Arts Society (PAS)
110 W. Washington Street, Suite A
Indianapolis, IN 46204
317-974-4488
www.pas.org

Public Relations Society of America (PRSA)
33 Maiden Lane, 11th Fl.
New York, NY 10038-5150
212-460-1400
www.prsa.org

Recording Industry Association of America (RIAA)
1025 F ST N.W./ 10th Floor
Washington, D.C. 20004
202-775-0101
www.riaa.com

Retail Print Music Dealers Association (RPMDA)
14070 Proton Rd. Suite 100, LB 9
Dallas, TX 75244
972-818-1333
printmusic.org

Screen Actors Guild: American Federation of Television and
Radio Artists (SAG-AFTRA)
5757 Wilshire Blvd, 7th Floor
Los Angeles, CA 90036-3600
Switchboard: 323-954-1600
Toll-Free: 855-SAG-AFTRA/855-724-2387

New York Office:
1900 Broadway, 5th Floor
New York, NY 10023
(Between 63rd and 64th Streets)
212-944-1030
www.sagaftra.org

SESAC, Inc.
55 Music Square East
Nashville, TN 37203
615-320-0055

152 West 57th Street, 57th Floor
New York, NY 10019
212-586-3450

6100 Wilshire Blvd, Suite 700
Los Angeles, CA 90048
323-937-3722
Fax: 323-937-3733

981 Joseph E. Lowery Blvd NW, Suite 102
Atlanta, GA 30318
404-897-1330

1221 Brickell Avenue
Miami, FL 33131
305-534-7500

International:
67 Upper Berkeley Street
London W1H 7QX
England
Tel: 0207 616 9284
www.sesac.com

Society of Professional Audio Recording Services (SPARS)
9 Music Square S., Suite 222
Nashville, TN 37203
800-771-7727
www.spars.com

Songwriters Guild of America
5120 Virginia Way, Suite C22
Brentwood, TN 37027
615-742-9945
www.songwritersguild.com

SoundExchange
733 10th Street. NW, 10th Floor
Washington, D.C. 20001
202-640-5858
www.soundexchange.com

West Coast Songwriters
1724 Laurel Street, Suite 120
San Carlos, CA 94070
650-654-3966
www.westcoastsongwriters.org

CANADA

Special thanks to our colleague Steve Sherman of Red Deer
College, Alberta, for assistance in compiling this data.

Association of Canadian Choral Communities (ACCC)
A-1422 Bayview Avenue
Toronto, ON M4G 3A7
CANADA
Phone: 416-7519-1165
Cell: 226-500-3131
accc@choralcanada.org

Canadian Academy of Recording Arts and Sciences (CARAS)
 and 2013 JUNO Awards (CARAS)
345 Adelaide Street West, 2nd Floor
Toronto, ON M5V 1R5
CANADA
416-485-3135
Fax: 416-485-4978
Toll-Free (in Canada): 1-888-440-5866
info@carasonline.ca

Canadian Band Association (CBA)
Executive Director and Canadian Winds Manager: Ken
204-663-1226, Fax: 204-663-1226
15 Pinecrest Bay
Winnipeg, MB R2G 1W2
CANADA
www.canadianband.org

Canadian Independent Music Association (CIMA)
30 St. Patrick Street, 2nd Floor
Toronto, ON M5T 3A3
CANADA
416-485-3152 ext. 232
www.cirpa.ca

Canadian Music Centre | Centre de Musique Canadienne (CMC)
CMC National Office
20 St. Joseph Street
Toronto, ON M4Y 1J9
CANADA
416-961-6601
info@musiccentre.ca

Canadian Music Educators' Association (CMEA)
16 Royaleigh Avenue
Etobicoke, ON M9P 2J5
CANADA
416-244-3745
cmea.ca

Canadian Music Publishers Association (CMPA)
320–56 Wellesley Street West
Toronto, ON M5S 2S3
CANADA
416-926-7952
www.musicpublisher.ca

Canadian Musical Reproduction Rights Agency Ltd. (CMRRA)
320-56 Wellesley Street W.
Toronto, ON M5S 2S3
CANADA
416-926-1966
www.cmrra.ca

Foundation Assisting Canadian Talent on Records (FACTOR)
247 Spadina Avenue, 3rd Floor
Toronto, ON M5T 3A8
CANADA
Local: 416-696-2215
Toll Free: 1-877-696-2215
info@factor.ca

Society of Composers, Authors and Music Publishers of Canada
(SOCAN)
41 Valleybrook Drive
Toronto, ON M3B 2S6
CANADA
416-445-8700 • 1-800-55-SOCAN (76226)

> Quebec:
> 600 de Maisonneuve Blvd. W., Suite 500
> Montreal, QC H3A 3J2
> CANADA

> East:
> 45 Alderney Drive,
> Suite 802, Queen Square
> Dartmouth, NS B2Y 2N6
> CANADA

> West:
> 504-1166 Alberni Street
> Vancouver, BC V6E 3Z3
> www.socan.ca
> CANADA

Music Creator and Publisher Members:
1-866-307-6226
members@socan.ca

Songwriters Association of Canada (SAC)
41 Valleybrook Drive
Toronto, ON M3B 2S6
CANADA
Phone: 416-961-1588
1-866-456-7664 • Fax: 416-961-2040
www.songwriters.ca

INTERNATIONAL

Association of Independent Music (AIM)
AIM, Lamb House, Church Street, Chiswick, London, W4 2PD,
England
+44 (0)20-8994-5599
www.musicindie.com

Music China Trade Show (Asian Music Products Trade Show)
Co-sponsored by China Music Industry Association (CMIA) &
Musikmesse Frankfurt (Shanghai Division)
www.chinaexhibition.com

Musikmesse (EU Music Products trade organization)
Messe Frankfurt GmbH
Ludwig-Erhard-Anlage 1
60327 Frankfurt a. M.
+49 69 75 75-194 12
musik.messefrankfurt.com

Index